From the twentieth-century Indian philosopher and poet Aurobindo:

The Vision and the Boon, 1949

How long shall our spirits battle with the Night

And bear defeat and the brute yoke of Death,

We who are vessels of a deathless Force

and builders of the godhood of the race?

In the vague light of [our] half-conscious mind,

Where in the greyness is thy coming's ray?

Where is the thunder of thy victory's wings?

Only we hear the feet of passing gods.

All we have done is ever still to do. . . .

The new-born ages perish like the old. . . .

Baffled and beaten back we labour still;

Annulled, frustrated, spent, we still survive.

In anguish we labour that from us may rise

A larger-seeing [hu]man with nobler heart,

The executor of the divine attempt

Equipped to wear the earthly body of God . . .

. . . .

The unfolding Image showed the things to come.

A giant dance of Shiva tore the past,

There was a thunder as of worlds that fall;

Earth was o'errun with fire and the roar of Death

Clamouring to slay a world his hunger had made;

Alarm and rumour shook the armoured Night.

I saw the Omnipotent's flaming pioneers

Over the heavenly verge which turns toward life

Come crowding down the amber stairs of birth;

Forerunners of a divine multitude

Out of the paths of the morning star they came

Into the little room of mortal life.

I saw them cross the twilight of an age,

The sun-eyed children of a marvelous dawn, . . .

The labourers in the quarries of the gods,

The messengers of the Incommunicable,

Carrying the magic word, the mystic fire,

Carrying the Dionysian cup of joy,

Approaching eyes of a diviner [hu]man,

Lips chanting an unknown anthem of the soul.

High priests of wisdom, sweetness, might and bliss,

Discoverers of beauty's sunlit ways

And swimmers of Love's laughing fiery floods,

Their tread one day shall change the suffering earth

And justify the light on Nature's face.

F. JAY DEACON

Magnificent Journey

Religion as Lock on the Past,
or Engine of Evolution

Middletown, Rhode Island

2011, 2014 Groundwave Publishing

Published in the United States by Groundwave Publishing
4 Johnson Terrace, Middletown, Rhode Island 02842-5510

groundwavepublishing.com

Cover image: from photo by F. Jay Deacon

ISBN 978-0-9838297-2-0

Library of Congress Control Number: 2011934527

Spirituality
Current Affairs
Human Ecology—Religious Aspects
Same-sex marriage—Religious Aspects
Religion and Science

Author's website: jaydeacon.net

PERMISSIONS ACKNOWLEDGEMENTS

Poem by Hafiz on p. 61 from the Penguin publication, *The Gift, Poems by Hafiz*, copyright 1999 Daniel Ladinsky and used with his permission.

Excerpt from Aurobindo, "The Vision and the Boon" and "Man a Transitional Being" from *The Essential Aurobindo* edited with Introduction and Afterword by Robert McDermott copyright © 1987, 2001 by Lindisfarne Books and reprinted with their kind permission.

Excerpt from James N. Gardner, *Biocosm: A New Scientific Theory of Evolution: Intelligent Life is the Architect of the Universe* reprinted by kind permission of the author.

Leader (Editorial) from *The Guardian*, Sept 12 2001, copyright © 2001 Guardian News & Media Ltd and reprinted with permission.

Excerpts by Geoffrey Lean, James Lovelock from *The Independent* and *The Independent on Sunday* copyright © 2005, 2006 by Independent Digital News and Media Limited (IDNM) and Independent Print Limited (IPL) and reproduced with permission.

Excerpts from J. Krishnamurti from *On God*, HarperCollins 1992, copyright © 1991 Krishnamurti Foundation of America and used by permission.

Excerpt f rom Ilya Prigogine and Isabelle Stengers, *Order Out of Chaos: Man's New Dialogue With Nature*, Bantam, 1984, used by kind permission of Isabelle Stengers and Maryna Prigogine.

Excerpts from Brian Swimme, *The Universe is a Green Dragon*, copyright © 1985 Inner Traditions–Bear & Company (www.InnerTraditions.com), reprinted by kind permission.

Excerpts from Annie Dillard, *Holy the Firm*, pp. 43-44 and 65-58, copyright © 1977 by Annie Dillard, reprinted by permission of HarperCollins Publishers.

From *Markings* by Dag Hammarskjöld, translated by W.H. Auden & Leif Sjoberg, translation copyright © 1964, copyright renewed 1992 by Alfred A. Knopf, a division of Random House, Inc., and Faber & Faber Ltd. Used by permission of Alfred A. Knopf, a division of Random House, Inc.

Excerpts from *Beginnings Without End* by Sam Keen, copyright © 1975

Excerpt from Garry Wills, *Certain Trumpets*, reprinted with permission of Simon & Schuster. Copyright © 1994 Literary Research, Inc.

CONTENTS

INTRODUCTION

HOW IS IT THAT, somewhere in this thin round life-friendly shell of water and land suspended between the incandescent core of this very hospitable planet and the upper atmosphere surrounding it, a little black dog and I snuggled yesterday on the sofa and wondered. Or rather *I* wondered and he napped. So alike, and different. He, aware of the moment (or his dreams of whatever black labs dream about); I, aware of myself in the moment, and conjuring past and future, and contemplating all this, and something Beyond all this.

Contemplating explosions of stars—casting out the essential stuff of which I and Thunder are made. Trying to grasp how it all could once have appeared out of a nothingness that was inconceivably full of potentiality, where neither time nor space meant anything at all (who needed them?)

In moments, some majestic silent music washes through me and, to borrow Emerson's words, "I have enjoyed a perfect exhilaration. I am glad to the brink of fear." Those moments count for a lot because, faced with the daily impress of the culture in which my life is imbedded, taken in by the ego's rigged perspective, I need the felt counterweight of that far wider, deeper perspective. And whether I *feel* it or not, it's the perspective from which I see, and mean too live. That consciousness drives my sense of the possible and decides the choices I make.

What is this Life that I live, and what is this Life that the planet lives, and its warming star and the expanses of Universe I cannot see in its daylight?

I sit here, more than halfway through the days I have been given, contemplating this, in an old house whose former occupants are now gone. They will have contemplated these things, in their way, and attributed to a god the greater powers and intelligence that did this. That is the way it has been: whatever was greater, or wiser, or stronger—that, or him, or her, they called God. What has come to be was the work of gods, or of demons.

I contemplate. What this little dog cannot, need not, do. It isn't just an exercise in wonderment or conjecture, because from this contemplation come days of living, roads taken and not taken, a ranking of worth and the relative weight of things. Moral imagination is the ability to see, beyond the immediate horizon, the consequences of what I value and do and refuse to do.

I contemplate, too, what undergirds, forms, enlivens all this. Sometimes I have thought that this dog is a mystic, knowing well the ground and source of Being, but I am projecting. No, it's another capacity of those who own the name human. This higher consciousness of the greater Kosmos* is a careful and quiet listening. The old god-stuff is easier, I know. You substitute the old Beliefs and wrap them in a bit of ritual because you know there is more than meets the eye, but it is a substitute still. It may comfort or reassure for awhile. It does not awaken in us what is wisest or most alive. It cannot engage the most profound human capacities for knowing and for evolutionary consciousness.

This is a bit like the way we understand ourselves. We have a store of easy, learned answers to the question of who we are. They come from the earliest days of our lives, in relation to a mother whose life at first seemed the same life as ours, and who eventually became a part of a world outside ourselves, alternately gratifying and disappointing us. Who we are is any of the many players in this past drama. Who we are is a collection of people and causes and postures we have come to identify with. Who we are is a set of defenses against the things that

---

* *With a K.* Emerson referred to *Kosmos:* The Greek spelling reflects Emerson's sense of a Pythagorian term meaning the whole of Being at every dimension, not merely the material starry heavens implied by "cosmos." He joins Whitman and others, including the contemporary philosopher Ken Wilber, in both spelling and meaning. Says Wilber, "We might say the Kosmos includes the physiosphere, or cosmos; the biosphere, or life; the noosphere, or mind, all of which are radiant manifestations of pure Emptiness, and are not other to that Emptiness" (From interview, "The Kosmos According to Ken Wilber," in *Shambhala Sun*, September 1996).

threaten the ramparts of our being.

Or rather, who we suppose ourselves to be. These, too, are substitutes.

They are substitutes for something we recognize as ourselves in a deeper sense. But where is that authentic self? We sense its absence. We do what we can to fill the vital space. And so we face the world—*ahem*, here we are, let me introduce myself. Regrettably, what we have to present is false: that construction called *ego*.

THERE IS, BENEATH AND beyond this pretense, this counterfeit, that shrouds, impersonates, and imprisons it—there is something else, something more essential and vital and real, and there are moments when it is palpably real. Sometimes we simply become more conscious, the clouds roll away. Sometimes it's that impulse—an urgent drive toward the highest possibility, an impulse to make something of that possibility manifest, to create, unfold, *evolve*.

You know you are not something separate from this Universe of Life. The Upanishads anciently insisted, *Thou art That!* What was the impulse that, before anything was—not space, not time, not a material universe—erupted into being? What intelligence, what energy was it? Were you there?

Thirteen point eight billion years ago, they tell us, all this unbounded potentiality burst into manifestation. *Bang.* And through the long aeons of this magnificent journey since, it has slowly advanced into its greatest achievement (that we know of), *human consciousness.* The Universe aware of itself. And whatever I am, it flows through that long passage, from that infinite ocean of creative potential. I *was* there.

That realm before anything was, from which all came and will come, hasn't gone away. Spiritual traditions announce the fact of access to that realm, the realm where you were never yet hurt, never yet defeated, never frightened; the realm before you ever won or lost, ever were disappointed or exulted, before ever you breathed the toxins of flattery or humiliation. You can go there: before you crossed the threshold from infinite unmanifest potentiality and turned down the corridor of struggle into the din of time and space and experience to try, to want, to hope and do and feel. The greatest spiritual traditions invite you there, to that place before your first hope was truncated and made small, before walls falsified the horizon, before you could not see the Goal and began to choose between substitutes.

Emerson announced that access: *the doors of the temple stand open, night and day, before every man.* And he said: *We lie open on one side to the deeps of spiritual nature, to the attributes of God.*

From *this* place—might we go forth to renew the world, create the world that will be?

I CONTEMPLATE BECAUSE THERE IS a true and a real to contemplate. Somewhere buried under the efforts of the past to name it, there it is. Our search may give us clues to what we are looking for.

Somewhere, under all this surface and defense, there is something that might flow freely, spontaneously, and authentically as if from Beyond, flow in your very being and personhood. You can be a force of nature. The fulfillment of your potential as a human being is possible.

This is the part of me, of you, that is meant to look, with recognition, into the heart of Being. If, in a timeless moment, all this once exploded from a void, we too are manifestations of that Unmanifest, as some ancient mystics called it.

There is an intelligent design. How does the grass know to grow? But the intelligent design is not that of the God that former ages talked about and dared not question. "Intelligent Design" today is a subterfuge to hold open the presumptive place for that God who sent Joshua into Jericho to exterminate the heathen—men and women and children and animals—who already lived there. It isn't that of the God of the presumptive authority of this or that scripture or holy book who declared that I, a gay man, ought not to be. The old answers are no longer good enough. They never were. The poet Rilke said we must live the *questions.* We must live them, and contemplate deeply whether or not they are even the right questions.

If we consult our humanity and our evolving human consciousness, we'll leave the religion of a primitive murderous deity—in the past. Yet such religious views sometimes seem to drive both American global policy and terrorist fanatics.

There is a greater crisis, of course. A thunderous chorus of scientists tell us we are destroying this spectacular habitat Earth. We do it because we have lost the moral imagination that can comprehend where our greed is taking us. We do it because we haven't found our way to our essential divine-human selfhood beyond our greed, whose creative powers might yet reveal a higher possibility.

We are a strange amalgam of god and dust. (More on this is Chapter 8.) We reach for something that we might be, must be, but are not yet. We do this even while some not entirely conscious forces within us greedily undermine that possibility. Our religions are accustomed to account for this by looking backward, positing a golden past, an original perfection from which we have fallen. The fables are everywhere of a perfect past, but there was no perfect past. If there is a paradise it lies in a future that is ours to create. We have never been to that paradise, even if something of us apprehends it, belongs to it, and always reaches for it. We are works in progress. There is more that we shall be.

Yet we are deluded and in need of spiritual awakening. This is not altogether a new concept: poets and visionaries have always spoken of these things. But now the consequences of our blundering way are palpable. (Not incidentally, we also know a great deal more about the historical development of our religious traditions: and we have learned that, whatever we may have been taught, whatever we may read in the ancient texts, it ain't necessarily so.)

It is time for a new quality of consciousness.

Many have come to speak of the urgency of such a revolution of consciousness (call them *Evolutionaries*). There was the nineteenth-century Transcendentalist visionary Emerson and those whose minds and hearts he opened. There was the great twentieth-century Indian mystic-poet-philosopher-liberation leader Aurobindo. There was the Jesuit priest-paleontologist Pierre Teilhard de Chardin (whose luminous writings were embargoed until after his death by the Roman Catholic church). Now there's Ken Wilber, a contemporary American spiritual

spiritual philosopher. There's a far-flung community of people inspired by Wilber's sometime collaborator Andrew Cohen who, before he managed to antagonize too many of his students with his demanding regime as a guru to a worldwide community of students, articulated a powerful perspective he called "evolutionary enlightenment."[1] He guided them beyond the static conception of enlightenment that has dominated much spiritual thinking. Among this new generation of thinkers, teachers, and spiritual adventurers is Cohen's former magazine editor Carter Phipps, who offers a history of evolutionary spirituality in his *Evolutionaries: Unlocking the Spiritual and Cultural Potential of Science's Greatest Idea.*[2] All of these honor Emerson and trace the emergence of their vision through him. A growing host of others is rising.

Wilber has led the way in the project of integrating ancient religious traditions, insights of developmental psychological thinkers, philosophy, and work from a multitude of other disciplines, guided by his own groundbreaking insights. There are many others.

At the core of everything that is, and made conscious in the human presence, is an authentic evolutionary impulse. Now, the further movement of evolving consciousness and culture is in our hands.

Wilber's contribution, "Integral" spirituality and philosophy, offers a schema of developmental *levels* of the evolution of consciousness suggested by numerous previous thinkers beginning with Jean Gebser in his very dense 1949 classic *The Ever-Present Origin.* He identifies the first as *archaic* consciousness, the first that could be called human and no longer the realm of the great apes. The stages rise through *magical-animistic,* to *mythic-conventional,* to *rational-scientific,* to *pluralistic,* to *integral,* and beyond. (More on this in Chapter 1.) Human consciousness and culture advance through these, as does each individual life, until stopping, perhaps getting stuck, somewhere. Each stage includes the previous, while simultaneously transcending it. Wilber has compared, too, *lines* of development: for instance, *spiritual, cognitive, ego, value, moral, social,* any one of which can rise through the evolutionary stages. And he shows how different *states* of consciousness are available to just

---

1 For more on this evolutionary perspective, see Andrew Cohen, *Evolutionary Enlightenment: A New Path to Spiritual Awakening.* New York: SelectBooks, 2011.
2 New York: Harper Perennial, 2012.

about anyone, but these state-experiences will be interpreted according to the developmental *stage* an individual has attained.

Some of these concepts have lent clarity to my own understanding, and they are here. If you're familiar with them, you'll recognize them. If you're not, this book will be no less accessible to you. And it must be said that the emerging truth and vision is unfolding from a swelling throng of people in our time.

THE WORLD WILL BE AS WE make it: the power is in our hands, if, ecologically, it isn't already too late. Recent American national leadership could recite the old religious phrases and invoke God and morality, but it was morally bankrupt and devoid of vision, religious or otherwise. New leaders have risen in America, most of them notably lacking in courage. Our leaders have seemed lost.

We cannot postpone our awakening. The moment presents us with tasks that require not less than everything.

The little black dog nestled against me: we share the Life of this Universe, a kinship. He seems a miracle to me, which only throws into perspective the miracle of humanity. He has no awareness of this urgent task, and bears no culpability if we fail. Maybe you have a child, who might grow into such an awareness, and who will know if we, in our time, failed or succeeded; may grow to take up his or her own tasks.

It was the founding figure of American Unitarianism, William Ellery Channing, who said

> There are seasons in human affairs, of inward and outward revolution, when new depths seem to be broken up in the soul, when new wants are unfolded in multitudes, and a new and undefined good is thirsted for. These are periods when the principles of experience need to be modified, when hope and trust and instinct claim a share with prudence in the guidance of affairs, when, in truth, *to dare* is the highest wisdom.[3]

Let there be people and communities of evolutionary consciousness.

The memory is still fresh of my discovery of a bold and noble religious tradition that had managed to break the leg-iron that had shackled

---

3 "The Union," 1829.

it to the presumptive authority of gods and scriptures that rose from the mythic consciousness of another time and place and that oblige many otherwise modern persons (and many other not-so-modern persons) in our time to afflict human society with archaic, sometimes barbaric, foolishness—and worse, including faith-based hate.

Looked at from a perspective of freedom that has finally transcended that consciousness, those traditions can be seen to hold wisdom and truth. But Unitarians (and their Universalist allies) were no longer attempting to revive a bygone era or return to a supposed past perfection from which humanity was thought to have fallen. This is the revolutionary spiritual breakthrough: you understand yourself to be creating a future that has never been, not reconstructing a former glory. We have this power to create. In his dizzying *Beginning of Infinity* the brilliant physicist David Deutsch compares the course of evolution not driven by human intelligence and intention, including tedious millennia of human experience, with what has been achieved and will be achieved "by intelligent beings who wanted those transformations to happen." Compared with intentional human-driven evolution, he calls the scale of the former transformations "negligibly small." [4]

It's harder to do this than might be apparent. This is summed up as well as I've ever seen it by Channing. Members of my Unitarian Universalist religious community quote Channing frequently but I've never seen this passage cited. As you'll see, the Unitarian movement was shaken from torpor by Ralph Waldo Emerson and his Transcendentalist movement. Channing, who had himself inspired and guided the younger Emerson, was alternately thrilled and disturbed by his own spiritual offspring. Channing was once described by the historian Perry Miller as "a discoverer of passages which he himself refused to explore beyond the threshold." [5] Emerson had encountered the same threshold and passed on through, and for this, he had been roundly condemned by the Unitarian establishment. But something deep in Channing understood and resonated. In 1841 he wrote to James Martineau, the

---

4 *The Beginning of Infinity: Explanations That Transform the World.* New York: Viking, 2011.
5 Perry Miller, editor. *The Transcendentalists.* Cambridge, Mass.: Harvard University Press, 1950, p. 22. Reprinted MJF Books.

British Unitarians' closest approximation to Emerson:

> Old Unitarianism must undergo important modifications or developments. Thus I have felt for years. . . . Its history is singular. It began as a protest against the rejection of reason—against mental slavery. It pledged itself to progress as its life and end; but it has gradually grown stationary, and now we have a *Unitarian Orthodoxy.* Perhaps this is not to be wondered at or deplored, for all reforming bodies seemed doomed to stop, in order to keep the ground, much or little, which they have gained. They become conservative, and out of them must spring new reformers, to be persecuted generally by the old.[6]

You keep a revolution alive by keeping it revolutionary. You don't need to belong to my Unitarian Universalist faith, or any other, to find in these pages whatever application your place and time and circumstance require.

---

6 *Memoir of William Ellery Channing, With Extracts from His Correspondence and Manuscripts, in Three Volumes.* London: John Chapman, 1843, vol. II, p. 409. (First published in Boston in 1842, year of his death; republished in 1874 by the American Unitarian Association.)

F U N D A M E N T A L
Life vs. Fundamentalism

IN A SLEEPY THEN-ISOLATED South Jersey town which was in those days far from cultural or intellectual stimulation, I grew up increasingly bored with our family's huge and oh so respectable conservative Presbyterian Church.

Island Heights had been one of many late nineteenth-century Methodist summer camp-meetings that operated in South Jersey. There was the occasional diversion. Once we traveled twenty miles north to Ocean Grove, an entire town built on the oceanfront in 1869 to be a Methodist camp-meeting. The town itself was run by the Methodist Church (until the courts put a stop to that and it was fully absorbed into Neptune Township) and ocean bathing, as well as carriages, and then cars, were forbidden on Sundays. It was the most successful of those Methodist summer camp-meetings that had been inhabited by the "shouting Methodist" revivalists and their year-round churches.

The charming streets were (and still are) lined with gingerbread houses and half-houses—in the summer the Methodists would turn up with tent-like extra rooms; the permanent structures housed the kitchens and bathrooms. More canvas tents were leased for the season and the population would swell to fill the 6,500-seat Tabernacle at the center of it all. It's a fabulous wooden structure at the front of which looms a vast American flag made out of red, white, and blue lightbulbs that flash on and off so that the flag seems to be waving in the ocean breeze. We went to hear Billy Graham.

I don't remember much about Graham, though I'd encounter him again later. What I remember as though it were this morning was the song-leader standing there in front of the electric flag, enthusing "Now let's all sing real illustrious!"

We returned to our proper Presbyterian church, but something in that tabernacle must have remained with me. In time I was drawn—at the age of 13 or so—into the fervor of the Assembly of God just down the street from it, drawn into the Pentecostal strand of Fundamentalism, then to its college in Springfield, Missouri. For Pentecostals and Charismatics, spiritual ecstasy is valued highly and experienced richly (though some of its expressions were a bit odd, like the man who, when the Holy Ghost would "come upon him" under the revival tent would get on all fours on the sawdust—hands and knees—and bark; or the stiff and sour white-gloved lady who, whenever a hymn about the blood of Jesus would be sung, would begin to dance in the aisle). Among them I found unembarrassed passion, abandon, and a commanding sense of purpose—virtues progressive people could do with a bit more of. I was drawn briefly into Assemblies of God ministry—until its world closed in around me, cutting me off from the evil world, but so much more disastrously, from myself, from my mind, from my best instincts and intuitions, from my finest spiritual capacities, my own life truth.

But maybe you can imagine something else that was there, too—the fervor of what they called the presence of God, the Holy Spirit—the love they felt, and of which they were unashamed, love for this something they felt, love for what to them is the Ultimate Heart of Reality. They call it Jesus. I don't, not anymore. But I don't love it any less.

I HAD TO FIND MY OWN WAY TO SPIRIT, that transcendent reality. Not that this is as hard as we often make it, inasmuch as Spirit is *always, already* here. You don't have to beg it to come to you; you cannot be apart from it. My relationship with the Heart of Being had to be authentic and real and my own. It could not be mediated through any third party or on the authority of bibles or churches. It is prior to any theologies or opinions we have about it.

So I've had an unfulfilled wish: that across the divide of theology and dogma, there could be a common recognition of a common transcendent experience and relationship with the Heart of Being.

There are these transcendent moments when you see beyond the surface of things the inherent glory of Being.

You are lifted out of the myopia of daily routine, deadlines, ambitions, fears, resentments, habitual ways of seeing—and you are seeing with the eyes of wonder, beyond ego, beyond the surface of things, and you are filled with a luminosity, the light brighter than a thousand suns, and you see the glory of Being, the shining radiance of the Universe of life, and you are drenched in liquid love and lifted to a higher state of consciousness and bliss.

Was it Jesus? Buddha? the Self Absolute? Atman-Brahman? the "ground luminescence" the Buddhists talk about? the Ground of Being of which the theologian Tillich spoke? the *Shekinah* of mystical Judaism? Emerson's Over-soul?

VIRTUALLY ANYONE CAN HAVE A profound religious experience: that's the vast, many-dimensioned nature of reality. But here's the tricky part: how you interpret that experience. *The interpretation we lay on reality creates our reality.* We will interpret it according to our stage of spiritual development. And there are better and worse ways to do it.

It's all about how far our human consciousness has evolved. New, higher waves of consciousness open up when we feel the limitations of where we are, begin to feel that we're suffocating there, *have* to move farther in our journey, urgently *must* evolve into a higher consciousness. And we as individuals develop through these same stages as the whole human race, beginning with the most archaic until we stop or get stuck somewhere.

More mature, highly-developed forms of religious orientation find ways to extract deeper meanings lurking in the beliefs, rituals, and myths of the previous stages. Each new, higher stage *includes* value from previous stages, while *transcending* it.

A point, of course, repeated again and again by spiritual philosopher Ken Wilber. Anybody can have a spiritual experience, enter an extraordinary *state* of consciousness. And you'll *interpret* it according to your *stage* of spiritual development.

The brilliant (if obscure) New England Transcendentalist Samuel Johnson understood this when, in 1865, he wrote:

> A traditional faith, no less than a heretical one, rests on the authority of the natural faculties; and the difference is only in the condition and treatment of these faculties. The traditionalist may imagine that he has taken his belief on the "divine authority of the Bible or the Church." He has really been decided by that point of discernment at which his Spiritual Consciousness has arrived. He has obeyed his own undeveloped religious senses. And because he does not know that his attempt to escape the necessity of judging according to his spiritual state, is a failure, he suffers that Consciousness which is the light or the darkness of all that is in him, to remain crude, inert, enslaved, instead of quickening and unfolding it by present light and duty. And so it lies gazing at a dead Bible and a dead creed, self-condemned to inflict its own death on that from which it is seeking life. And there is reaction as well as action in this. For his conscience is none the less stifled and perverted by the errors of the Bible and the creed, for the reason that he has taken them upon his own authority and interprets them by his own state.
>
> Much as Christians have insisted that they rest on an infallible Bible, they have never really shaped their creeds by the Bible, whether fallible or infallible; but always primarily by the actual condition of things within and without themselves, putting their trust in this, and making the Bible mean essentially what this demanded.[1]

The great nineteenth-century Unitarian Transcendentalist Theodore Parker had the same intuition:

> The conception which a man forms of God, depends on the character and attainment of the man himself.[2]

Levels or stages in the evolution of consciousness have identifiable characteristics. The earliest, *archaic* stage marks the beginning of the human journey. For the human race, that's where the threshold between great apes and humans was crossed. Or it's the primal consciousness

---

1 "Real and Imaginary Authority," *The Radical*, November 1865.

2 Theodore Parker. *Discourse of Matters Pertaining to Religion.* Boston: Charles C. Little & James Brown, 1842, p. 101.

of a newborn who simply, unreflectingly responds to bodily stimuli. Gradually the child learns to distinguish between herself and the world, but first sees the world as an extension of herself that she can manipulate. So here is a *magical* stage, and it has a parallel in religious conceptualization where rituals gain magical powers. Characteristically things here turn on the individual ego, and gods are invoked for personal gain (personal salvation, personal attainment) without regard for others' interests. At this stage, one might seek association with the most powerful of power-gods. Its consciousness and sphere of concern might begin to expand to include a clan, tribe, or ethnicity—so long as it's one's own.

Next comes a *mythic* stage. Here a larger aggregate of persons can be joined by a central myth, and by conformity with specific rules and laws. In the unglued Hellenistic world, St. Paul marvelled at this quality in the Christian gatherings, and clearly it was a factor in his conversion. Later he would comment in his letter to the Galatian Christians that here, "there is neither Jew nor Greek, slave nor free, male nor female, for you are all one in Christ Jesus." The shared myth had transcended ethnicity, gender, and class.

But communities united by myth can be exclusivistic, parochial, seeing the world in us-*vs.*-them terms. And if you should fall away from the official myth or doctrine, be very afraid. Membership or even salvation can be at stake. Growing cognitive capacities may not extend to the questioning of that dogma. One will probably rely very heavily on the presumptive authority of sacred texts and bibles, or institutions, leaders, or teachers thought to be divinely ordained.

When intellectual independence arises, so, too, can a *rational* stage. The European Enlightenment was such a moment, and now science and critical thought could trump dogma. There's a new, world-centric sense of universal human rights and dignity. But what often goes missing here is any sense of transcendence. This developmental stage characterizes many pockets of my own religious community, Unitarian Universalism. In one congregation I served, an older couple would go apoplectic if the word "spiritual" broke the rational quiet.

A *pluralistic*, relativistic stage began to dominate aspects of Western culture in the 1960s. Its postmodernism opens awareness to many factors, points of view, and cultures, and moral choices are rarely simple. One can observe the cultural embeddedness of one's own tradition or beliefs. And human relationships gain new significance. But it can also tend toward narcissism, where *it's all about me.*

Beyond that stage of development lies something that is only now emerging: an *integral* stage. Consciousness rises from world-centric to kosmocentric, where *kosmos* refers, remember, as it did for the Greeks and for Emerson, to the whole of Being, the totality of all that is. The Divine is seen and experienced as expressed in all being, but as an infinite, unmanifest fountain of potential from which the universe sprang, and from which the world that is to be will flow. Integral thinker Dustin DiPerna puts it well: "The experience of an individual's *I-am-ness* is recognized and felt as the same *I-am-ness* that exists within every other living creature."

Throughout this progression of development, profound experiences of consciousness, *states* of consciousness, are available. But what do they mean? All depends on your interpretation, and *that* can't be any more advanced than the developmental stage of your consciousness.

IMAGINE YOURSELF WITH A fundamentalist friend: he, rapt in ecstasy with his Jesus. And you with your own spiritual experience. Will he rejoice in *your own* transported vision of beauty, with no Jesus, died and resurrected or otherwise? Will he embrace you as a friend who shares the highest of treasures?

Actually, you're probably headed for disappointment. He will know, absolutely, that your transcendent experience cannot be real, because right in *Acts 4:12* it says—we must be saved "by the name of Jesus Christ of Nazareth," and "Neither is there salvation in any other: for there is none other name under heaven given among men, whereby we must be saved." Plain enough. Leaves *you* out. The biblical God is a *jealous* God—says so right here in the Bible, whose authority he isn't about to question—who will tolerate worship of no competitor.

If your imagined friend is an *Islamic* fundamentalist, your problem will still be the same. Or Hindu, or Jewish, or Buddhist (yes, there are fundamentalists in those traditions, too).

You just *think* you've had an authentic spiritual experience. But your true-believer knows better, yessir. You must be possessed of demons. Or maybe just deluded.

I understand why. He has entered the safe enclave of the saved in the midst of a wicked world. All else is demonic deceit. For him there's far too much ambiguity, too much danger, if the train isn't running down the steel rails of an infallible Bible and damn-near infallible church's interpretation of the Bible. Or Koran or whatever. He wants the world neatly tied up in the hands of a God he can understand.

The truth is that the human mind just isn't far enough evolved to penetrate the mysteries that Fundamentalists claim to understand. Our humanity and our truth and our God are evolving. To enter the life of Spirit is to be engaged in your own evolution and with it the evolution of human consciousness. There is no standing-still stagnation of dogma and presumptive authority here.

And religion will either be a lock on the past, or an engine of evolutionary consciousness.

FUNDAMENTALISM IN AMERICA BEGAN when, in the 19th century, scholars started looking at the Bible critically, with the same critical disciplines they would apply to any ancient document. They found that the Gospels, written decades after the death of Jesus by people who never knew him, consist of an artful stringing together of little bits and phrases taken from older sources, so arranged as to create the basis for a new religion and to make of their founder a God-Man sent to fulfill Old Testament prophecies, constitute his followers as the new Israel, and finally restore the Kingdom of God on earth. It wasn't so much the religion *of* Jesus at all, as it was a religion *about* a Jesus made into a god. In the Hebrew Bible, scholars found four historic layers, representing different eras of the evolution of the religion and history of the Jews. They found flaws of inconsistency, contradiction, and historical error. The liberals started seeing Jesus as more of a social revolutionary than a savior.

The Fundamentalists felt their faith undermined, and they singled out many enemies of the true faith—Darwinian evolution, communism, socialism, and of course modern biblical scholarship.

At first the fundamentalist movement tried to gain control of American denominations and save them from what it called "apostasy"—the new liberal thought. It tried to run the liberals out of the churches. When that effort wasn't entirely successful, it organized new denominations and new kinds of churches. Eventually, its ideas about the Second Coming and the end of the world developed into a new "Dominion Theology"—the conviction that fundamentalist Christians must take over the government by whatever means necessary to bring in the reign of Christ—and then came the 1980s, and the campaigns of Ronald Reagan and Pat Robertson, and now the fundamentalists had a new political power. The fundamentalism that for awhile was running the United States of America is a freeze-dried state of consciousness embodying ancient fears, superstitions, and mythology. It embodies a universe of us-and-them, of a stern and punitive Father-God, of warfare against the legions of darkness, of the exclusion of pariahs who don't happen to be, say, heterosexual. It is perforce anti-intellectual, anti-science, authoritarian. Its God is something Other, capital O, out there, looking down on his pitiable fallen creatures. You can find it everywhere, in Protestantism, in Catholicism, in Islam.

As I write, that dominionist-Christianist fundamentalism has taken a startling new turn, which—even more startling—has barely been noticed. It's called the "New Apostolic Reformation" (NAR) movement.

Now a little background. Within Pentecostalism there was always a fascination with the "apostolic" period, when (according to the New Testament) apostles and prophets roamed the earth, performing miracles, uttering prophecies, and generally acting as commanders in the advance of the new religion. In those circles no part of the Bible was more beloved than the Book of Joel, the prophet. The more extreme the gathering, the more you'd hear language and phrases from Joel about the "end times." And a very marginal strain of Pentecostalism called itself "apostolic," or "latter rain" (a phrase from Joel). But these notions already dominated a few gatherings of fundamentalists. While I was a student at that Assemblies of God Bible college in Springfield, Missouri, I sometimes attended a small house-church not affiliated with a denomination, founded on apostolic latter-rain beliefs. During my Pentecostal days I would sometimes travel to Philadelphia to attend the Philadelphia Gospel Temple, which was affiliated with a tiny denomination called "The Apostolic Church." Once the pastor introduced a visiting apostle, down from the headquarters in Canada, I think. These gatherings felt benign and consisted mostly of ecstatic spiritual experience; nowhere did I encounter either the thuggish bigotry or the political aspirations that's so alarming about the movement now. There was speaking in tongues and there were "prophecies," but the prophecies consisted of memorized King James Bible verses fervently uttered.

What I didn't notice, later on during the 1980s, was that some of these, together with alumni of the "Charismatic" movement among mainline churches (I once attended those gatherings, too) had coalesced under the leadership of self-appointed prophets and apostles to prepare for the end times. The prophets and apostles hadn't yet shown up when I would attend their gatherings: I have only warm recollections of nondenominational charismatic services at a Presbyterian church somewhere in eastern Pennsylvania or at events run by the Full Gospel Business Mens' Fellowship. In all these strands of Pentecostalism, there was zeal to "spread the Word," and the drama of life was painted in mythic terms of the armies of God confronting demons, all meant quite literally. If wider ambitions showed themselves, the drama was conceived mostly in terms of believers' private lives, and evangelism. I heard the preaching; I read the texts; and maybe I shouldn't be surprised with where more recent generations of believers have gone with the notion of "spiritual warfare."

But that was then (by which I mean late 1960s); things are different now, and subsequent movement leaders have bigger ambitions. Once known as a mainline-evangelical expert on church growth, Peter Wagner left Fuller Theological Seminary and set himself up in Colorado Springs, where he coined the name for the new movement. He set up networks: the International Coalition of Apostles; the Apostolic Council of Prophetic Elders; and the International Society of Deliverance Ministries to cast out the pesky demons that make people gay, or Democrats, or whatever; faith healers; and more, as well as a training network and a special accrediting outfit for apostolic schools. They teach *dominion;* they even teach that the wealth of the "wicked" (the not-them) is "stored up for the righteous," and the "enemy" camp is there to be plundered as a means to implement theocracy.[3] Churches must be cleansed of infidels and entirely reorganized. In "Apostle" John Eckhardt's words, "We are receiving an anointing to war and overcome the enemy."

That once-marginal strand has taken new form, now with a distinctive doctrinal turn. Fundamentalism had generally taught "Dispensationalism," the idea that in the end times, believers would be "raptured" out of the world while the wrath of God is unleashed for either three and a half or seven years. Only then would Christ return, accompanied by his previously-raptured saints, to establish the eternal kingdom of God on earth. That's not what the New Apostolic Reformation folks teach.

They are driven by the belief that instead, believers (not just *any* believers, of course, just pure apostolic-type believers) are to take control of the seven pillars of world society. Thus Christianist dominion over the arts, business, education (and science), family, government (and finance), media, and religion. Now maybe, dear observer of the current scene, some of this is beginning to look familiar. It's all about the Second Apostolic Age, which, they say, began in 2001. Now the "prophecies" predict floods and famines, specify leadership roles, and decree the launch of new organizations and structures. Their megachurches still preach to the struggles of everyday folk; after all, if things aren't going at all well, you'd better find out if you've been living under a curse.

They've got a few challenges to overcome in taking dominion, and these are literal demonic beings who control particular domains of life.

---

3 In 2006 C. Peter Wagner himself proclaimed that "God has declared through His prophets that the wealth of the wicked will be released to the Kingdom of God." Why? To fund a theocratic takeover: "I declare that this wealth will be distributed for the extension of the Kingdom of God by the apostles that God has set in the church." The wealth transfer would involve human agency, the wealth to come from the "godless": "I decree that vast amounts of wealth will be released supernaturally, even from godless and pagan sources . . . The enemy's camp will be plundered . . . Resistance will be impossible. Jesus will put all things under His feet."

One of the leading "apostles" says she was given the ability to see the literal demon Jezabel in command of the Democratic Party, with the assistance of three lesser demons. This insight might shed a touch of light on the behavior and tactics of a few of the apparently fanatical Christianist political figures on the current scene: yes, they are fanatical. What they're engaged in is not rational political discourse, but "Strategic Level Spiritual Warfare."

If you believe you are God's army and you have read the Book of Joshua recently, you will be prepared to stop at nothing to achieve what your divine King has sent you to do. You will combine adherence to the presumptive authority of premodern scriptures (with their barbarisms and mythology still intact) and very aggressive political intentions sometimes wrapped in stealth so as not to scare the public. They have to take complete control of the arts, business, education, family, government, media, and religion: the Second Coming cannot happen until they do—or so they're convinced. If you don't know the strategy, far-right efforts can seem quite innocent.

They claim to love America, but to them the best of all possible worlds is bronze-age Israel; the America they love is some version of John Winthrop's theocracy. Do they genuinely love our Constitution? Their intention is overthrow of our government and the establishment of theocratic dominion. They do not believe they owe it to unbelievers to be honest about their intentions.

In August 2011, Texas Governor Rick Perry held a big prayer-and-fasting day at Reliant Stadium in Houston. Without exception the major media missed entirely what was going on.[4] Perry was the NAR movement's choice to lead the next phase of Christianist dominion as President of the United States. That's who most of those odd-seeming co-sponsors were. The following week, Perry announced for the Presidency. But Perry isn't the only one of the Republican candidates involved with the NAR, though he is the most deeply involved. There's Sarah Palin, too, and Michelle Bachmann, and Ted Cruz (his father

---

4 The Perry factor was covered at the time of the Reliant Stadium event by Forrest
   Wilder in the *Texas Observer* of August 3, 2011. Covering the movement consistently
   is the Talk2action organization at http://www.talk2action.org/.

is a Dominionist preacher). Rick Santorum and Newt Gingrich have hooked up with the movement. And throughout the Tea-Republican Party, many more. The new prophets and apostles believe that they have been chosen by God to take "dominion" over government and, if necessary stealthily, every aspect of human society.

YES, PRIMITIVE RELIGIOUS EXPRESSION can be dangerous. Under Sharia law, women who commit such offenses as venturing out of their homes unaccompanied by their husband can be tortured. Gay people are routinely executed in Iran. That wasn't the case in Iraq, until now—but now Shia militia have a new target for brutal attacks and executions. Many gay people are fleeing or going into hiding, while women lose the rights and freedoms they had won before the American invasion. There are fundamentalists—whether of the NAR persuasion or not—who would do the same in America, if they could.[5] That's not even to mention what we see on the daily news, the religious warfare in the Middle East.

Islamic fundamentalism divides reality starkly into two absolutely separate and mutually exclusive spheres—the land of Islam (dar al-Islam) and the land of unbelief. Followers of the teacher Sayyid Qutb like Osama bin Laden—see the world as a cosmic battlefield between those two worlds, where anyone who resists Muslim domination must die. Their religious practice is puritanical in its severity.

A Hindu fundamentalist might dwell on magical rituals, sacrifices, and incantations to get something for themselves from various gods and goddesses. But this fundamentalism, too, can go virulent, as in 2002, when fundamentalist Hindus in Gujarat, India carried out a well planned and brutal attack on Muslim communities there.

---

5 Modern Christian theocracy advocacy in America began with Rousas John Rushdoony and his Reconstruction Movement. Rushdoony liked the discipline of John Calvin's Geneva where women pregnant out of wedlock were to be drowned along with their unborn babies. Rushdoony wanted a mandated death penalty for gay Americans as well. And blasphemers, heretics, apostate Christians, people who cursed or struck their parents, females guilty of "unchastity before marriage," "incorrigible" juvenile delinquents, and adulterers. Subsequent Dominion Theology advocates were, when before the larger public, more circumspect in their rhetoric, but the views of many among them were no more moderate than Rushdoony's.

So—THERE YOU ARE WITH your fundamentalist friend.

Both your fundamentalist friend and you are capable of transcendent religious experience—he through a special relationship with Jesus Christ,—and you without any such special means at all. Maybe you were just meditating or deep in contemplation. Maybe it just settled upon you, in a moment of crisis, or no crisis at all, just going about your business, looking out at Nature, whatever.

What about that transcendent experience of the glory, the *Shekinah*, the transcendent wonder and light. *What was it?*

My fundamentalist friend isn't prepared to grasp that at the Heart of all Being—whatever that experience was about—that Heart of All Being—whatever HE, SHE, IT is, *that is ultimately who we are.*

Maybe it was the profound depth of that transcendence that drew me across the threshold. Maybe it was the feeling of suffocation where I was—because we break through into that next level of consciousness only after we've faced the limits of the place where we've been, only after it gets bad enough. But it can happen. Outworn, constricting theologies can be let go. People can grow. I know.

THAT IMAGINARY FUNDAMENTALIST friend: I would like to ask him:

If you believe that your own human perceptions are so benighted and depraved that only an authority external to yourself, an infallible scripture revealed by God himself, can instruct you on what is true—if that is where you begin—and your Scripture warns that you are a fallen creature, now condemned to eternal punishment unless somehow you can find your way to the mercy of a savior who, through unimaginable suffering, bore the weight of your wickedness for you—the God-Man who will give you salvation if you just believe, and become a disciple —

Then tell me: do you believe that the Universe is really ruled by a God who, having created a flawed creature, is prepared to toss the vast majority of humanity—who don't believe the right things, adopt the right theology—into an eternal trash-heap, there to suffer forever?

Our experience of reality is surely bent around our interpretation of it, our expectations and beliefs about it. And the problem begins with one singularly bad idea:

presumptive authority

authority you cannot question, dare not doubt.

Why is it that so many people seem willing to believe the unbelievable?

But suppose we begin somewhere else. Suppose the fundamental thing is something else.

Suppose you are that magnificent achievement of Nature, that evolving splendor, the Universe becoming aware of itself in the human mind, the highest, yet striving manifestation of this Universe of Life.

There is a difference between a religion of *presumptive authority* that is true because it is true, everybody knows it's true and nobody dares question it; and one of immediate, unfolding truth recognized by an inner knowing. Emerson stated it well in his magnificent, heretical 1838 Address to the Harvard divinity students:

> Meantime, whilst the doors of the temple stand open, night and day, before every man, and the oracles of this truth cease never, it is guarded by one stern condition; this, namely; it is an intuition. It cannot be received at second hand. Truly speaking, it is not instruction, but provocation, that I can receive from another soul. What he announces, *I must find true in me*, or wholly reject; and on his word, or as his second, be he who he may, I can accept nothing.

Suppose you start with that: immediate experience of transcendence, however it happens. But the experience requires interpretation because we humans are driven to find meaning. This is important. In authoritarian, dogma-driven religion grounded in presumptive authority, the experience is interpreted as confirmation of the correctness of the doctrines, the authority of the official interpreters.

Suppose you start instead with your journey, your experience of life, the truth of your life. The experience of transcendence—passed through the fire of life-experience and of critical thought. Suppose those things are the fundamentals with which you start. Suppose we bring all our best capacities—intellect, vision, intuition, virtue—into this quest.

My spiritual quest led me beyond the parameters of the old shibboleths and forced me past its boundaries. In the end shunned and disowned because I could not be an appropriate product of Central Bible College or Gordon-Conwell Theological Seminary, I was also liberated and given a painful gift. I was alone with nobody to turn to. I had to find that what I needed, I already had. It's ways, already here, in the heart and soul of us. Nobody else can give us that.

FIND TRUE IN ME. LIKE WHAT we experience in dreams. I had expended plenty of energy arguing down the inevitable misgivings about the presumptive authority I'd always believed. And then I had a dream.

> *I am touring the city where I shall be working for the Church. Now we come to the Church, and I am given my housing. A bed right in the cathedral sanctuary. I lay there in the night, looking up at a vast, cavernous dome. It looks like the vault of heaven, a sea of crystal glass, ornate and grand. Having nowhere else to go, I lay there, I keep looking, contemplating the dome above. It's old; the bronze needs polishing. The crystal glass that covers the entire ceiling is turning color. Now I notice the cracks. It is going to collapse of its own weight and I will die. I am terrified. I run from the cathedral.*

NOW, ANOTHER STORY ABOUT a fundamentalist who makes an urgent exit from the "cathedral" of his family's faith.

PRIMITIVE RELIGION, PRIMITIVE SOCIETY

THINK ABOUT THE HISTORY of slavery in America.

It was a Southern institution but the whole of the nation was in thrall to it. The few real foes of slavery in the United States Congress were ridiculed and shouted down, branded as shrill-voiced radicals. Among those at the intellectual center of this greatly outnumbered Abolitionist movement were Ralph Waldo Emerson, Theodore Parker, and their Transcendentalist circle.

In an effort to maintain peace, the Congress had agreed not to discuss slavery. In his quest for the Presidency the great Daniel Webster had bent his conscience to support the Southern Slavocracy and, with his support, the Fugitive Slave Act had been passed by the Congress, forcing the recapture of escaped slaves and their return to the South. Since the writer belongs to that progressive religious movement called Unitarianism, it must be said that a shameless *Unitarian* president, Millard Fillmore, signed the Fugitive Slave Bill into law. It is instructive to ask:—What was the role of *religion* in this time?

The radical Unitarian Theodore Parker and his Transcendentalist friends, along with some Quakers, Unitarians, and some anti-Calvinist evangelical Christian followers of the evangelist Charles Finney, formed a vocal religious minority against the evil. From the rest of the pulpits, an ear-shattering silence, or outright support for slavery. The Catholic church told its followers to obey the fugitive slave law simply because it was the law. The Calvinists found some divine purpose in slavery, or perhaps some divine punishment. And throughout the South, ways were found—it wasn't so hard, after all—to show that the Bible actually supported slavery, to show that abolitionism itself was the sin against the divine order, and with a straight face, Southern clergy preached as much. After all, did not the Word of God say plainly, in *Exodus* 21:20-21:

> When a man strikes his slave, male or female, with a rod and the slave dies under his hand, he shall be punished. But if the slave survives a day or two, he is not to be punished; for the slave is his property.

Ralph Waldo Emerson had crisscrossed the Northeast to condemn the Fugitive Slave Law, Webster's betrayal, and popular notions of black inferiority. But even in the North, Emerson was called a fanatic and a fool, and, in the words of a Boston newspaper, "the idol of this collection of human vermin." At Cambridge, he was interrupted by

> a considerable body of students from Harvard College did what they could to disturb the audience and insult the speaker, by hisses

and groans, interspersed with cheers for Webster, Clay, Filmore, Everett, and "Old Harvard!"[6]

Wendell Phillips invited him to speak at the Anti-Slavery Society's annual meeting at Tremont Temple. Pro-Union rowdies swarmed the meeting and Emerson had to wait out a lot of shouting before he could begin his address but when he did he declared that no compromises could be made on the moral issues dividing North and South.

> As to concessions, we have none to make. The monstrous concession made at the formation of the Constitution is all that can ever be asked; it has blocked the civilization and humanity of the times up to this day.[7]

That was about as far as he would get. The proslavery people responded with hisses, groans, and yells to "put him out." Calls for order were ignored and the police refused to act. The meeting ended with the police clearing the galleries.

AT THIS MOMENT THERE WAS, in Virginia, a slave-holding Methodist preacher named Moncure Daniel Conway. He, too, preached the pro-slavery theological line, and saw the institution as benign. For awhile he believed a new idea recently worked out between some handy pro-slavery theologians and some handy pro-slavery scientists that proposed separate divine acts of creation for the separate races, whereby the ones with white faces were actually humans with souls, and the rest were not.

Now, throughout the North, nobody believed in this unique multiple-creation theory. In theory, they thought slavery a bad thing—*but not their concern* and not particularly important. They looked the other way as the evil continued unchallenged, and didn't mind that Southern postmasters were permitted and even expected to burn any literature from northern Abolitionists that might pass through their post offices.

And so I want you to note a piece of mail that made it through. Why, after all, would a postmaster in Safford County, Virginia, question a

---

6 Len Gougeon and Joel Myerson, ed. *Emerson's Anti-Slavery Writings.* New Haven & London: Yale University Press, 1995, p. xl.

7 Gougeon and Myerson, p. xlix.

letter from Rev. Moncure Conway? Still, that postmaster might have wondered why it was addressed to the notorious Mr. R. W. Emerson in Concord, Massachusetts. Quite simply, Conway wrote:

> I will here take the liberty of saying what nothing but a concern as deep as Eternity should make me say. I am a minister of the Christian Religion,—the only way for the world to reenter Paradise, in my earnest belief. I have just commenced that office at the call of the Holy Ghost, now in my twentieth year. About a year ago I commenced reading your writings. I have read them all and studied them sentence by sentence. I have shed many burning tears over them; because you gain my assent to Laws which, when I see how they would act on the affairs of life, I have not courage to practise. . . . [8]

I was riveted by that letter before I knew the rest. This is what he said about a great moment of turning in his life: it was

> A spiritual crisis, as I have said . . . Through a little rift I caught a glimpse of a vault beyond the familiar sky, from which flowed a spirit that was subtly imbreeding discontent in me . . . Was it for this I was born? . . . It was no fancy that now in my maturer life Emerson had set free in my heart a winged thought that sang a new song and soared—whither? [9]

— And he has to ask. He hadn't wanted to ask; nobody around him was asking, because he had the approval of his family and community and enjoyed both wealth and prestige, a respected Methodist preacher who, like anybody else important and wealthy enough to do so, owned slaves. This was the way God had set things up—the church said so, the community said so, *the Bible said so*—but now he had to ask. He had to undergo burning discontent.

He had gone off for a walk that day. Something had been bothering him, he didn't know what, and on the way out the door he'd picked up a British magazine from the table, and now he faced a crisis, because an article in that magazine by someone he'd never heard of named Emerson had spoken to some very deep part of himself he hadn't been

---

8 Moncure Daniel Conway. *Autobiography of Moncure Daniel Conway.* Boston: Houghton, Mifflin and Company, 1904, I.109.

9 Conway, *Autobiography*, I.78.

acquainted with, and now it resounded and shook him and turned him around.

The day came when that glimpse of a vault beyond the familiar sky from which flowed a new spirit, that winged thought that sang a new song and soared—presented its real-world demands on Mr. Conway. All this flowed through some portal into his soul, and now that portal was real and he was going to have to enter it and pass through. In truth, it meant being misunderstood, leaving a fortune and a lot of prestige and all his security and undergoing real danger.

But he turns up in Boston, three years later, and so do two neighbors of his. He knew both of them. One was a Captain Suttle, a well-respected politician and slaveholder. The other was Anthony Burns. Anthony Burns, the escaped slave, captured under the Fugitive Slave Law and held at the Suffolk County Courthouse in Boston, which had been taken over for the purpose by the federal government. Charles Suttle, his owner, come to demand his return in a kind of mockery of American justice called a fugitive slave *hearing* where the accused was not permitted to speak and was automatically guilty, an affair that was presided over by a United States Fugitive Slave Commissioner.

By and large the people of Boston were enraged that their Court House, the court house of a free people in a free state, should be used as a prison for a man who, under Massachusetts law, should be a free man, and who, here, in the cradle of liberty, was being held as property.

Seven or eight blocks away at Fanuiel Hall, that hall that has been called the "cradle of liberty," five thousand people gathered to hear Theodore Parker challenge the crowd to go down to the court house, immediately, storm it, and forcibly rescue Anthony Burns. Among them was a young divinity student who had recently been torn away from his old life by the powerful leverage of Truth and had enrolled at Harvard—Moncure Daniel Conway of Safford County, Virginia.

In his autobiography, he writes:

> The Southern students at Cambridge assembled to offer their sympathy to the owner of Burns. I was notified, but replied that my sympathies were with the fugitive.[10]

---

10 Conway, *Autobiography*, I.175.

But his mind hadn't been completely settled yet, so he'd gone to an abolitionist rally and heard Henry Thoreau. He heard a Unitarian minister who displayed a facial injury he had just received in that failed attempt to rescue Anthony Burns from the courthouse. At the same rally—in his words:

> A very aged negro woman named "Sojourner Truth," lank, shrivelled, but picturesque, slowly mounted to the platform, amid general applause, and sat silently listening to the speeches.[11]

Conway watched that scene, where William Lloyd Garrison had just burned the Constitution because it sanctions slavery. And now Garrison invited a young Southern heckler to come to the stage to speak his mind. Here's how Conway describes it:

> The young man complied, and in the course of his defence of slavery and affirming his sincerity, twice exclaimed, "As God is my witness!"

From across the stage Truth bellowed:

> "Young man, I don't believe God Almighty ever hearn tell of *you!*" Her shrill voice sounded through the grove like a bugle . . .

MONCURE CONWAY TURNS UP again later. In Concord, a regular visitor and trusted friend of the Emersons. In Boston, with the radical antislavery preacher Theodore Parker. And then in Washington, D.C. as minister at the First Unitarian Church, where his preaching drove the spineless Millard Fillmore, the former President who had signed the Fugitive Slave Act into law and a Unitarian, to abandon his speciallycushioned pew; and I found him in Cincinnati, where he held the Unitarian pulpit in this tense border city. And then I found him in London, where his preaching distinguished him as a reformer at South Place Chapel (now called Conway Hall) for thirty-three years. *Religion as an engine of the evolution of consciousness.*

WHICH BECOMES UNMISTAKABLY clear when Emerson speaks of the

---

11 Conway, *Autobiography*, I:184.

antislavery struggle. In his 1844 Address on the Emancipation of the British West Indies, he declared:

> If the black man carries in his bosom an indispensable element of a new and coming civilization, for the sake of that element, no wrong, nor strength, nor circumstance, can hurt him: He will survive and play his part. . . . The might and right are here: here is the anti-slave: here is man: and if you have man, black or white is an insignificance. . . . I esteem the occasion of this jubilee to be the proud discovery, that the black race can contend with the white; that, in the great anthem which we call history, a piece of many parts and vast compass, after playing a long time a very low and subdued accompaniment, they perceive the time arrived when they can strike in with effect, and take a master's part in the music. The civility of the world has reached that pitch, that their more moral genius is becoming indispensable, and the quality of this race is to be honored for itself. For this, they have been preserved in sandy deserts, in rice-swamps, in kitchens and shoe-shops, so long: now let them emerge, clothed in their own form. . . .

adding

> It cannot be disputed, there is progress in human society. There is a blessed necessity by which the interest of men is always driving them to the right; and, again, making all crime mean and ugly.

In "Uses of Great Men," in *Representative Men:*

> One's own culture, the unfolding of his own nature, is the chief end of man. A divine impulse at the core of his being impels him to this. The destiny of organized nature is amelioration *[advancement or progress]*, and who can tell its limits?

Emerson had come to understand slavery in the context of his evolutionary spiritual vision. He well understood that slavery had been assumed *forever*, in virtually all cultures. And now, higher human possibility required that it must go. In the space of his own century (1780-1880), it was being abolished virtually everywhere. It doesn't happen automatically: it requires those willing to stand at a sometimes uncomfortable Edge, a place he hadn't sought but could not refuse.

THE LEVERAGE OF TRUTH

WE KNOW WE ARE LIVING in a time when the course of events and the advance of human possibility is still distorted by powerful public lies.

Most of the time we just have to maintain a wise trust in the durable leverage of Truth (Eric Erikson's phrase). But there are moments when in the midst of, and in spite of, the tenacious force of a public lie, we get some intimation of the strength of Truth.

MONCURE CONWAY'S CALLING AND DESTINY exacted a price, wrenching him away from hearth and home and inheritance. And the cost went beyond Monc Conway himself.

By and large, the women of the South had far less love of this system that enslaved people than their husbands. These enslaved people had become part of their households and they had come to care for them and respect them; but women had no voice. There were, among the wives of slaveholders, some who wept when a family was broken up forever by the sale to separate buyers of various family members. It was these women who cared enough, and dared enough, to violate the laws against teaching slaves to read. And Moncure Conway's own mother was one of those whose soul would be tried in the balance of the higher law that had overtaken her son. After the War began, Margaret Conway, too, left home, left her husband and her inheritance, moved North, joining both her son and the abolitionist movement.

BUT THE STORY DOESN'T STOP there; something else happened that week in Boston when Anthony Burns went to trial. Generally, Unitarians had hardly been exemplary during the crisis. Octavius Brooks Frothingham, the Transcendentalist minister son of one of the pillars of the cautious, stodgy, old Unitarianism, reflects that

> the Abolitionists were poor, humble, despised people, of no influence; [people] one could not ask to dine, who were not respected.[12]

12 Octavius Brook Frothingham. *Boston Unitarianism 1820-1850, A Study of the Life and Work of Nathaniel Langdon Frothinham*. New York: G. P. Putnam's Sons, 1890, p. 197.

No, it was respectable people who sat in Unitarian pews, including merchants who were amassing wealth from the slave trade and whose mills and ships relied on Southern cotton.

It was during this time that Theodore Parker, around whose unrestrained presence thousands of radicals, former slaves, and reformers gathered at the Twenty-Eight Congregational Society, frequently came into conflict with the minister of the old Federal-Street Church, Dr. Ezra Stiles Gannett—the very man who had taken the place of William Ellery Channing after the governing board silenced the anti-slavery Channing. It was to that church that many of the wealthy and powerful retreated on Sunday mornings, to be reassured and comforted. Among its members was George Ticknor Curtis, the federal Fugitive Slave Commissioner. You see what that meant. Parker had, in his congregation, former slaves who had somehow escaped and made their way to Boston. And so in one particularly dramatic Unitarian ministers' meeting, Theodore Parker confronted Dr. Gannett with the fact that Dr. Gannett had been urging a member of his, Gannett's, church to kidnap members of Parker's. He was talking about Fugitive Slave Commissioner Curtis whose job was to apprehend escaped slaves and send them back to their owners.

And now comes Anniversary Week, when numerous organizations, including the Unitarians, held their annual meetings in Boston, so everybody in Boston, it seems, has house-guests. And Dr. Gannett has one, a Unitarian minister named John Parkman, come for the annual ministers' meeting, but Dr. Gannett doesn't seem to know that his guest is a member of Theodore Parker's Vigilance Committee, which rescues fugitive slaves from this system.

A curious thing happened this week. This was the week Anthony Burns was arrested in his Boston home and held at the Court House.

And Dr. Gannett's house-guest, Rev. Parkman, skipped the ministers' meetings to attend Anthony Burns' trial. The first couple of days he'd come home and express his outrage over what was going on, and wind up in an argument with Dr. Gannett, just home from the ministers' meetings. Gannett would offer adamant defenses of the slave system, even calling the Abolitionist movement "the hellish spirit alive and active here in our very midst, even in New England."[13]

Dr. Gannett's daughter asked him what he would do if a fugitive slave came to his door, and he replied that he would send the fugitive slave away unaided and unsheltered rather than break one of this nation's laws.

Maybe you can imagine the tension. It was getting ugly and finally Parkman asked that the topic be discussed no more. He simply couldn't bear to hear his good and even great host utter such inexplicable idiocy.

For three days an awkward kind of calm held. Then came Friday, a day of infamy. It was the day Anthony Burns, manacled and chained and surrounded by hundreds of federal soldiers, was led through the streets of Boston past an unbelieving crowd who shouted their protests and hung black crepe, and was delivered finally to a ship in Boston Harbor that would return him to Virginia. Many protested, but many more Bostonians stayed home, thinking, like Dr. Gannett, that this unpleasant business had to be done to uphold the law of the land.

Rev. Parkman saw all this, this day of infamy, and returned to the Gannett home. I'll give you the rest of the story in John Parkman's own words, from a letter he wrote to Ezra Stiles Gannett's son, who had become a Transcendentalist:

> On the day when Burns was given up, the first person whom I met on entering his house was Dr. Gannett. 'Is it true that he has been surrendered?" he asked, in those plaintive tones which all who knew him well remember. On my replying, 'Yes,' he threw himself into a chair, buried his face in his hands, and then, in a voice broken by sobbing, burst out, 'O God, forgive this guilty nation! What will become of us?' [14]

Again his daughter asked him what he would do if a fugitive came to his door. "I have thought about that," he told her. "I should shelter him and aid him to go further on to Canada, and then I should go and give myself up to prison." He had felt the persistent leverage of truth.

Dr. Gannett didn't do *anything* at first. That Sunday he preached the sermon he'd already planned.

---

13 William C. Gannett. *Ezra Stiles Gannett: Unitarian Minister in Boston,1824-1871.* Boston: Roberts Brothers, 1875, 287f.

14 W.C. Gannett, *Gannett*, 288f.

But after a few weeks he took to the pulpit with a sermon called *Relation of the North to Slavery*. It was an amazing day at Federal-Street Church. The conservative Dr. Gannett did an utterly courageous thing.

What he said drew the attention of Fugitive Slave Commissioner Curtis, who sat in his pew glowering and sour-faced that Sunday morning—sat there glowering just as Dr. Channing's standing committee had done in those same pews that day in 1842 when Channing defied them and turned the service into a Memorial for the great Abolitionist Charles Follen. But Commissioner Curtis remained unmoved, grew bitter, attacked Dr. Gannett in pamphlets, even managed the desperate presidential campaign of Daniel Webster, who, in hopes of winning the presidency, had thrown his great weight behind the Fugitive Slave Bill.

BUT THE STORY IS, FINALLY, NOT REALLY about Commissioner Curtis or Rev. Gannett or Moncure Conway.

It *is* about the leverage, in this world, of truth.

What was happening within Moncure Conway, within Dr. Gannett, was happening within others. Visiting Concord to tell the good Mr. Emerson how deeply Emerson's writings had transformed his life, Conway was told, "When the mind has reached a certain stage it may be sometimes crystallized by a slight touch." Truth was in the air and, one by one, a growing multitude came to see it.

I don't mean the kind of "truth" people mean when they use that incomprehensible expression "what's true for me" and "what's true for you" as if there really isn't any such thing as Truth at all.

And I don't mean truth the way the old systems of unquestioned religion and myth mean it when they say *this is true because it's true and to hell with the evidence.*

I mean Truth in the way Emerson meant when he said,

> The truth is in the air, and the most [sensitive] brain will announce it first, but all will announce it . . . later. . . . [The mind of the morally sensitive person] is righter than others, because he yields to a current so feeble as can be felt only by a needle delicately poised.[15]

---

15 Emerson, essay "Fate," 1851.

Think of Gandhi, who titled his autobiography *The Story of My Experiments With Truth.* He was finding his way to truth, whose glow appeared ever more clearly before him; even as it's always there before us, even if it takes us awhile and some struggle to find our way there. And Gandhi knew it couldn't be long until that Truth would ring true with many others, who would join him. It unfolds in a moment of history; it reveals itself within the stream of time when someone, somewhere, ventures forward where no one has ever been.

WHAT GREATER DOCUMENT IS THERE THAN the one that declares "We hold *these truths* to be self-evident, that all men are created equal, that they are endowed by their Creator with certain unalienable Rights, that among these are Life, Liberty, and the pursuit of Happiness"? Yet already you could rephrase it just a bit and it would be even more true. All *men?* And indeed, only men could vote until 1920. I felt the weight of that when for a year I served the Universalist congregation in Orlando, and knew that the two female ministers who founded it in 1910 *couldn't vote.* But these words are immortal.

The force of those words was greater that its 56 signers knew. And even after civil war and struggle to reach beyond outmoded notions of truth that had enslaved millions, outmoded ideas that many took to be the purpose of God as revealed in Scripture —still, a full century later, it didn't yet mean you could vote in Mississippi.

Such Truth has no leverage *in the abstract.* You find its meaning in action or it's lost to you. In action it deepens into new realms.

Truth of this kind *sings.* Just as a great Truth was gripping Moncure Conway, many of the hymns in our UU hymnal were being written. James Russell Lowell was writing this:

> *Though the cause of evil prosper, yet 'tis truth alone is strong;*
> *Though its portion be a scaffold, and upon the throne be wrong.*
> *Yet that scaffold sways the future.*
> *New occasions teach new duties, time makes ancient good uncouth.*
> *They must upward still and onward who would keep abreast of truth.*

And such Truth *commands.* That is why Eric Erikson's biography of Gandhi is titled *The Leverage of Truth*.

Emerson once asked, [16]

> Where shall I hear words such as in elder ages drew men to leave all and follow,—father and mother, house and land, wife and child? Where shall I hear these august laws and moral being so pronounced, as to fill my ear, and I feel ennobled by the offer of my uttermost action and passion? The test of the true faith, certainly, should be its power to charm and command the soul.

Consider the astonishing spiritual achievement of Martin Luther King. He drew heavily from Gandhi's idea of *ahimsa* (taking upon one-self—from a position of strength—suffering and the consequences of others' karma) and *satyagraha* (nonviolent resistance born of soul-force). What was happening in his movement was a profound development in the consciousness of those activists. Now, they moved in a realm where few of us ever venture. It was tough sledding: in the last four years of King's life, the movement seemed to backslide into mere anger and rage, which we know well. It was coming unglued and King was living with depression, so great was his burden. But something powerful and I will say transcendent was at work, fueling a quality of daring, and care, and sacrifice that these times, once again, require.

I was reminded of the magnitude of that as I listened to an Amy Goodman *Democracy Now* broadcast[17] on the Freedom Rides. The story involved Diane Nash, a young Student Nonviolent Coordinating Committee organizer. The White House was in a political pickle over the Freedom Rides and the political impact on the Kennedy Administration in these Southern, still-Democratic states. And the Attorney General demands (she is interviewing John Siegenthaler, who was the assistant to then- Attorney General Robert Kennedy):

> "Who the hell is Diane Nash? Call her and let her know what is waiting for the Freedom Riders." So I called her. I said, "I understand that there are more Freedom Riders coming down from Nashville. You must stop them if you can." Her response was, "They're not going to turn back. They're on their way to Birmingham, and they'll be there shortly."

16 Emerson, "Divinity School Address," 1838.

17 *Democracy Now* broadcast, February 1, 2010.

You know that spiritual, "Like a tree standing by the water, I will not be moved"? She would not be moved. And I felt my voice go up another decibel and another, and soon I was shouting, "Young woman, do you understand what you're doing? You're going to get somebody—do you understand you're going to get somebody killed?" And there's a pause, and she said, "Sir, you should know, we all signed our last wills and testaments last night, before they left. We know someone will be killed."

Can you imagine yourself in that picture? Can I? I tremble to think. I've engaged in civil disobedience and I've been injured in the process but my life was never in danger.

The truth is before us, and it calls to us, and new Truth reveals itself at the frontiers of our advancing journey.

And if we will listen attentively, and if we dare to advance toward it, leave what must be left behind to answer to its command, we may feel rising about us, from out of us, a bold new sphere of values, a realm of grand possibility, a new order grander and fairer than ever was before. It calls, it beckons, it commands.

IN CONTRAST—THE MOST DAMNING uses of religion are told in daily headlines of war and bigotry.

During a sabbatical leave from Unity Temple Unitarian Universalist Congregation, in Illinois, I served two small Unitarian congregations in the United Kingdom. Britain was plagued with floods, results of the real effects of climate change; and its cattle, sheep, and pigs were undergoing a massive outbreak of foot-and-mouth disease, to halt which they were being slaughtered in their hundreds of thousands, bankrupting farmers and filling the skies with acrid smoke from the burning carcasses. Meanwhile, the railways had been afflicted with deadly accidents.

And so this, from the clerk to the Outer Isles presbytery of the Free Presbyterian Church of Scotland, addressed to the First Minister of the Scottish Parliament:

> We view your action, Sir, as a gross betrayal of all that the martyrs stood for and we believe that there may well be a connection between it and the troubles which afflict our nation at present,

not least of which is the sudden appearance of the virus causing Foot-and-Mouth Disease.

Such is our apprehension of the Divine displeasure that we appeal to you as First Minister to call for a national day of humiliation and prayer, in the hope that the Lord's judgments may be turned away from us.[18]

The offence against heaven? Both the First Minister and the Queen (she got a similar letter) had paid a visit to the Pope, whom the Westminister Confession of Faith of 1649 calls "that Antichrist, that man of sin, and son of perdition, that exalteth himself, in the Church, against Christ and all that is called God." He wanted a day of national day of humiliation and prayer "in the hope that the plague will be stayed and that further judgements will be averted."

Nobody much agreed with the clerk of the Outer Isles presbytery. A few believed American televangelist and Republican politician Pat Robertson when he told his vast television audience that Scotland is "a dark country" overrun by homosexuals: "In Scotland, you can't believe how strong the homosexuals are," he declared, adding that in tolerating gay people, the nation was offending its Christian heritage.

I wondered if, by Scotland's Christian heritage, Mr. Robertson meant the time when, in 573 CE, at the Battle of Aedderyd, the pagans of Strathclyde were slaughtered by the Christians of Cumbria and the pagan king Gwenddolau found that even Merlin's help wasn't enough to save those 80,000 pagan humans.

I recalled Robertson's warning to Orlando if it permitted Disney World to conduct a "Gay Day": "I would warn Orlando that you're right in the way of some serious hurricanes,and I don't think I'd be waving those [gay pride] flags in God's face if I were you." He added that acceptance of homosexuality is "the last step in the decline of Gentile civilization"; hence "a condition like this will bring about the destruction of your nation. It'll bring about terrorist bombs; it'll bring earthquakes, tornadoes and possibly a meteor."

Now, the trouble with that last one is that a lot of people believe it (even if the only storm that followed Gay Day in Orlando was a hur-

18 Iain Maciver. "Papal visits to blame for disasters, say Wee Frees." *The Scotsman*, March 12, 2001.

ricane that struck Robertson's homebase Virginia Beach).

The Free Presbyterians could only assign guilt for Foot-and-Mouth Disease. Peter Wagner outdid them when Europe was later hit with further divine judgment, Mad Cow Disease. He writes:

> God commanded me to go to the platform, and as I unburdened myself, I began to weep profusely. When I regained control, I made an apostolic proclamation, in the name of the Lord, that mad cow disease in Europe would immediately stop!" [19]

And, he insists, it did.

MODERATE AND PROGRESSIVE RELIGIOUS people will draw entirely different values than fundamentalists do from the same scriptures and myths. But the myths were born not in minds concerned with symbolism and metaphor; but in more primitive minds with more literal meanings. It cannot surprise us if they are still read that way by most people. Regression to a primitive past is not the answer. Religions must transform, must evolve, now. They must become engines of evolution, not chains binding us to the barbaric worst of what humanity is capable.

A CLASH OF FUNDAMENTALISMS

AS I WRITE, THE WORLD SEEMS LOCKED into a clash of fundamentalisms on a titanic scale. Fundamentalist Muslims strapped with bombs, who expect delivery of virgins upon martyrdom, are enraged that fundamentalist Israelis have deprived Palestinians of their homeland—this on orders from the same Jahweh who long before had told Joshua to march into the "promised land" and slay all the unbelieving men, women, and children, and their animals, and take the land. You can read about the massacres in Ai and Jericho in Joshua 5-9.

The "Christianist" version of the apocalypse was being taught in the fundamentalist churches and college I attended in the 1960s; evangelists then were thrilling audiences with their inside line on the end of the world. They were quite convinced that the prophets of ancient Israel

19 C. Peter Wagner, *7 Power Principles I Learned After Seminary* (Ventura CA: Regal Books, 2005, p. 96.

were *actually* talking about the United States of America, or "Communist Russia," or "Red China," right now, in 1963! I was told of the day, in a Pentecostal home, when they heard the news of the establishment of modern Israel. Shouts of "Jesus is coming" filled the house. Now, they're attaching these "biblical prophecies" to different political figures, like Saddam Hussein, or the late Yasser Arafat, or the latest U.N. Secretary General. Fundamentalist American Christians, meantime, await the Second Coming—in *Jerusalem*, in the conviction that it cannot happen until—according to their reading of biblical books like Revelation and Daniel—the ancient kingdom of David and Solomon is restored and Israel occupies the rest of its "biblical lands," as promised to Joshua and to Abraham, leaving no room for any Palestinian homeland. Their political power is vast, exceeding, during the administration of George W. Bush, the influence of the Israel lobby, including AIPAC, the American Israel Public Affairs Committee—not alone because they represent roughly six times as many voters as AIPAC, but because their message was, during the Bush administration, directed to a witless fundamentalist president. They've already managed to clear away, in Saddam Hussein, the "Babylonian" obstacle to the second coming, and to hell with the consequences.

In their millions, they read, and watch, the *Left Behind* series of novels and videos identifying the "Antichrist" with the Secretary General of the United Nations. In the most popular "bible prophecy" scenarios, the Jews will get a final chance to accept Christ as Lord and Savior, a belief that allows these Christian Zionists to avoid the appearance of wanting to convert Jews to Christianity: they'll get their chance to convert when Jesus comes back. Still, having rejected him the first time around, they have forfeited their status as the "Chosen People" and voided, or at least sullied, the Covenant. If—at the end—they continue to resist Christian conversion, they will burn like any other unbeliever. Which is precisely why St. Paul refers to the *Christian church* as the new Chosen People of God bound by the *New* Covenant. In the presence of Jews, Christian Zionists try to soften the implications of the New Testament's antisemitism.

Among the most influential of these is dominionist televangelist

Pastor John Hagee, pastor of an 18,000-member Texas church and founder of Christians United for Israel (and another NAR endorser of Rick Perry). His 2006 book *Jerusalem Countdown* argues that a bloody military confrontation with Iran is also necessary before Armageddon, the battle described in Ezekiel, chapters 38 and 39, and the Second Coming. Hagee's nominee for the biblical Antichrist is the head of the European Union, but he's also said the Antichrist will be a Jewish homosexual.[20] In a BBC World Service interview, he said this:

> I believe in my mind that the Third World War has begun. I believe that it began on 9/11. I believe that we are going to see an escalation of the Islamic influence all over the earth use their financial power and terrorism to bring nation after nation to its knees. And finally, they are going to come after Israel in waves of human attackers with the purpose of destroying the Jewish State. And at that point in time, this battle is described in Ezekiel 38, 39. God, in His sovereign grace, is going to stand up and defend Israel, and the enemies of Israel are going to be decimated.[21]

Worse—many of America's fundamentalists—including many in places of great power—see the United States as God's special chosen nation which must, through its political and military might, prepare the way for the Second Coming.

Hagee puts that clearly:

> At this point in America's history, we are plainly rejecting the Word of God because, according to Joel 3, we are helping to divide the land of Israel. We, through billions in foreign aid, are pressuring Israel to abandon the covenant land that God has given to the Jewish people forever. America is in the valley of decision and we are making the wrong decision. Pray for the peace of Jerusalem and pray for the security of America.
>
> If America lifts her hand of protection from Israel, God will lift His hand of protection from America. He has the power to crush our economy, to allow our enemies to bathe our streets in our own blood and to make a Super Power a prophetic footnote

---

20 In his 16 March 2003 sermon "The Final Dictator."

21 Richard Allen Greene, "Evangelical Christians plead for Israel," BBC News, August 11, 2006; "American evangelists see God at work in Israel," *The Age* (Australia), Aug 9, 2006; "Evangelicals unite for Israel," *Aljazeera Magazine*, July 26, 2006.

in the world tomorrow.[22]

At Hagee's first national conference of Christians United for Israel in Washington, in August 2006, one could find not only Gary Bauer and Jerry Falwell. There were the rightwing Republican senators Rick Santorum and Sam Brownback; Israel's ambassador to the United States, Daniel Ayalon; and Ken Mehlman, who was chairman of the Republican National Committee. "This is a religious war that Islam cannot and must not win," Hagee has said. "The end of the world as we know it is rapidly approaching." During the first half of 2006, the Bush White House convened a series of off-the-record meetings about its policies in the Middle East with leaders of Christians United for Israel. This is the road to Armageddon. Hagee has also joined Christian right evangelicals in condemning the Evangelical Climate Initiative, signed by 86 evangelical leaders acknowledging the seriousness of global warming and pledging to press for legislation to limit carbon dioxide emissions.

We want to keep quoting our Bibles and Korans, but maybe it's time we lay them aside, turn to our higher spiritual capacities and stop harking back to the conceptions and convictions of an outmoded stage of consciousness.

REVOLUTION

A HIGHER QUALITY OF consciousness, beyond ego and beyond ethnicity and beyond religious myth—a worldcentric, and beyond that a Kosmocentric consciousness—awaits humanity, and it calls to those who will hear, and turn, and commit. It isn't confined by a premodern grasp of the nature of the Universe or of our own humanity—it's truly evolutionary. It asks of us not less than everything. It demands a radical change in the terms and conditions of life. There must be those communities of people who will begin to live in a new way. There must be leaders who dare to live and lead in that new way.

Can awakened people in our time be vehicles for the coming of a spiritual revolution? Wherever they are, communities of consciousness must be in earnest about this; must not be too skeptical about the centrality of their role in what can and must happen in our time.

---

22 *John Hagee Ministries Magazine*, January/February 2006, pp. 4ff.

Can the primitive laws of nation and conquest, domination and division, greed and waste, depravity and futility, be transformed, turned to music, the strains of a higher consciousness?

It is time for a revolution of Consciousness. The alternative could be something like Armageddon.

IT'S AS THOUGH EACH LIFE IS A DEEP well, and way down there, way below the surface, the individual wells are all united, all flow into a deep underground river.

There is no other way down to reach the great underground stream that connects them all—except by going down into the well of your own inner depths. And there you learn that *your story is everyone's story.* And you are united to the whole world of life.

And then we are not looking at life *only* from our own personal experience, but through wider and wider circles of life and humanity. And then we might imagine what it is to be poor, without healthcare, tortured, intimidated and controlled by a faraway power. And then we might have the moral imagination that can imagine both the consequences of greed and arrogance and the likely outcome of the actions that flow from our worst impulses—and *imagine, too,* our highest and noblest possibilities and the kind of world we might create.

THE CHALLENGE OF THE TIMES is a contest of passion. If we dare engage it, unembarrassed, unapologetic—a spiritual revolution will have been set in motion that no reactionary force can stay or overcome. It will be the most magnificent energy ever yet set loose upon the earth.

II

MY MOTHER'S SON
In the family Bible

Annie Dillard
from Holy the Firm[1]

So this is where we are. Ashes, ashes, all fall down. How could I have forgotten? . . . Didn't I fall from the dark of the stars to these senselit and noisome days? The great ridged granite millstone of time is illusion, for only the good is real; the great ridged granite millstone of space is illusion, for God is spirit and worlds his flimsiest dreams: but the illusions are almost perfect, are apparently perfect for generations on end, and the pain is also, and undeniably, real. The pain within the millstones' pitiless turning is real, for our love for each other—for world . . .—is real, vaulting, insofar as it is love, beyond the plane of the stones' sickening churn and racing to the realm of spirit bare.

· · · · · · · · ·

Each thing in the world is translucent . . , and moving, cell by cell. I remember this reality. Where has it been? . . . Everything, everything, is whole, and a parcel of everything else. I myself am falling down, slowly, or

---

1 Annie Dillard. *Holy the Firm*. New York: Harper Colophon, 1977, pp. 43-44, 65-68.

slowly lifting up. . [I] see all that time contains, all the
faces and deeps of the worlds and all the earth's contents,
every landscape and room, everything living or made or
fashioned, all past and future stars, and especially faces,
faces like the cells of everything, faces pouring past me
talking, and going, and gone. And I am gone.

For outside it is bright. . . . It is the one glare of holi-
ness; it is bare and unspeakable. There is no speech nor
language; there is nothing, no one thing, nor motion,
nor time. There is only this everything. There is only
this, and its bright and multiple noise.

AFTER DAD DIED, MOM began doing things she had never done: like
air travel, and drinking margaritas. Then Mom sold the house where
she had lived for fifty-six years and Dad had spent his last fifty-three,
and my sister and brother-in-law, a mile away by the Barnegat Bay in
South Jersey, took her in. And while she was living with them, Mom
was found one day reading a little book none of us had ever seen. It
had been authored by our Mom herself as a high school senior in 1935,
and even though she seemed to know that *she* was its author, now the
contents seemed entirely new to her.

I don't know when the word Alzheimer's first came up. Mom was
losing a few words and some long-term memories. Soon she would
have to stop driving. I would ask her about people and events in the
past—elders know these things—and more and more often she would
laugh and say "You know I don't remember very much." Still, she could
laugh, I don't know how. The missing words multiplied until a complete sentence was impossible. But still she was her same dear, funny
self. Until that summer, really. Now she was confused, frightened, and
crying, pleading with Pat and Al not to leave the house.

In June, with a lot of anguish and after a careful investigation of nearby facilities, Pat, exhausted and over her head, moved our Mom to the best nursing home she could find. The worst was about to begin. Mom spent a lot of time crying but couldn't say what was wrong, couldn't put her finger on the source of anguish. While we sat in the nursing home she said to me, "We could go out . . . What does that mean?" Was she missing home and wanting to return there, but unable to get clear in her mind that *that* was it, that there had been a place called home?

Here is a great grief and a great joy: the loveliest of good lives, the kindest, the sweetest, whose gentle laugh can never be forgotten—reduced to confusion, and terror, and helpless oblivion, dying, finally, in a state unrecognizably remote from the person we knew.

BUT THE LITTLE BOOK. WE'D NEVER known the dreams and convictions she cherished and had once committed to the little book. She describes herself—in 1935—as an "anti-war fanatic" and makes a strong case. She speaks of her hopes of higher education, shattered by the Depression. She wants to travel the world as an ambassador of peace. She wants to be a broadcaster. She wants to leave the world better than she found it. But, she writes, "I have been advised not to be a nurse."

After she earned an RN she served as a public health nurse for her entire career. She devoted herself to her work, even though the pay was appalling; she ran about Ocean County tending to the county's clients who, when they needed her, called her at home.

She never traveled the world or crossed an American border. After Dad was gone, while I was living in London, I almost persuaded my sister to bring her across the sea. She really ought to have seen the great monument on Great Portland Street—near Florence Nightingale's—to her great-great (there may be more "greats" in there) grandfather, Sir Joseph Lister. We waited too long.

Her forebears—mine—lived in Yorkshire, England. Some crossed the Atlantic between 1820 and 1830 and settled around Philadelphia and then New Jersey. I found *that* in another book she'd kept and never told us about, a very old family Bible. By the time we found it in the attic of the old house, she didn't know what it was.

While we were picking through rooms crammed with 56 years of living,—attic, basement, garage, all stuffed—there it was. A stash of photographs and a family Bible. Nobody knows who maintained it or put it there.

There were hundreds of photographs. There were some I knew, and some I'd never met, and many I never knew of. There was my grandmother's mother—as a child! There were ladies in enormous hats, dour gentlemen, going back to the 1890s, and mixed in, pictures of myself at various stages of life. Time was telescoped, collapsed. Here we all were. This is my family.

IN THE BIBLE, THERE WAS A REGISTER of births, and deaths, and marriages. First there was John Lister, born in 1786 in Hoccondwicke, Yorkshire.

I followed the names in each list. Sometimes the year of birth was also the year of death; sometimes it was two years after, or five, or ten. Some lived long lives but for each there was a death date.

Farther back I found the most extraordinary thing that my grandfather had added to the Bible: an

INDEX TO THE GERM-PLASM

going back to the 1890s and registered with the Eugenics Record Office. I knew this had been kind of a fad, the purpose of which was to breed better human beings. The problem— eugenicists held—was not a matter of social structure, but of the individual—defective "germ-plasm"; the solution was encouraging the breeding of people with "good" genes and discouraging breeding by people with "bad" ones. The idea goes back at least 3,000 years, when the Israelites marked the Amalekites, Palestinians, as corrupting the Jews through intermarriage, since they had been created evil and were worthy of extermination.

With the mantle of "science," some eugenicists lobbied—successfully—for legislation to keep social and ethnic groups separated, to restrict immigration, and to sterilize the "unfit." Anti-miscegenation laws forbidding interracial marriage were one consequence, lasting in 18 states until struck down by the Supreme Court in 1967. Indiana enacted the nation's first law providing for sterilization on eugenic grounds in 1907; Connecticut followed, then *most* other states. Among the "grounds" eugenicists wanted to warrant sterilization: the "feebleminded, insane, criminalistic, epileptic, inebriate, diseased, blind, deaf, deformed; and dependent." The concept of preserving the purity of the germ-plasm was adopted and pushed to its horrific logical limits by the Nazis. In 1936, Germany's University of Heidelberg awarded honorary doctorates to American eugenicists.

In America, a Eugenics Record Office operated at Cold Spring Harbor on Long Island, New York from 1910 until 1944—along with the Cold Spring Harbor Laboratory. The First International Congress on Eugenics met in 1911, leading to the founding of the American Eugenics Society. In the 1920s, "Fitter Family" contests were held. An astonishing array of distinguished Americans, among them religious leaders, supported the eugenics movement's goals. Oliver Wendell Holmes wrote the appalling *Buck v. Bell* sterilization decision in 1927—"It is better for all the world, if instead of waiting to execute degenerate offspring for crime or to let them starve for the imbecility, society can prevent those who are manifestly unfit from continuing their kind . . . Three generations of imbeciles are enough."

My grandfather was, apparently, among the believers. In the family Bible there were tables of things you had to fill out. I learned that Dr. Leon Goble, my great-grandfather, was of phlegmatic temperament, whereas my grandfather was of nervo-phlegmatic temperament. Under "Special gifts or peculiarities of mind and body" I learned that Henrietta Goble "thinks she is sick all the time" and that James J. Goble, born in 1799, was a "tobacco fiend" and died of dropsy of the heart. Several were described as "narrow minded." I learned that Beula Lamb was cheerful and was paralyzed at 36.

Apparently after family approval as eugenically fit, there were the marriages.

All these had lived and loved and worked and wept and died and I had never heard most of their names.

Nevertheless I was aware of this fact: It was because they were where they were and did what they did when they did that I am here, and had it been otherwise, I would not be.

And this extremely improbable existence of mine is also precarious. Despite all the care they took to assure eugenic fitness, with the few exceptions of those born later in the twentieth century, they got sick, and died, are all gone, vanished.

HOW VERY EXTRAORDINARY TO be here! How improbable, and how utterly astonishing! What some exploding star cast out billions of years ago, taking human form on a little planet, passed through these long-vanished lives in Yorkshire, England, and has come down to *this*.

My grandfather believed in eugenics. So did the Nazis. We've learned a lot through the anguish of the last century. And two-thirds of the way through it, the bitter tale was disrupted by the inbreaking of the "green" wave of consciousness, and we wondered how the Nazis ever got away with what they did, how a somewhat earlier generation could have tolerate talk of "degenerates such as Jews and Negroes"? Now we wonder how those American eugenicists could have imagined that the quality of a person was a matter of genes? There is an inexorable forward movement, the evolution of consciousness. There are reversals, to be sure. I write as one called the Tea Party movement exerts a powerful backward drag toward times and conditions I will call barbaric. That is how this forward movement goes. Old gods and outworn universes don't sign off easily. It is a long journey, and demands of us everything.

SEVERAL YEARS BEFORE, WHEN I HEARD that the finite flame that was Dad's life was burning very low, it was clear that my tickets to fly from Chicago could not get me there in time, and after preaching a tribute to him on Sunday at Unity Temple, I got in my car. I was only in Ohio when my cell phone rang—while a zealous local police officer was writing me a speeding ticket on Interstate 80—and my brother Tim gave me the news that Dad had gone. This didn't deter the officer from asking if I was carrying any weapons, in his best threatening tone.

In New Jersey I came across Route 70. A sign read "Pemberton."

Dad's hometown, and his father's, and his sister's, all of them gone. Gone, leaving me feeling very exposed.

At the end of the journey was the house on Central Avenue, where Mom and Dad lived for 53 years. Every visit took me back to the simplicity of childhood, happy days on June evenings with my mother and father out by the honeysuckle bushes and I'm chasing fireflies.

WE EMPTY THE HOUSE. I KEEP a few mementos. Pat brings me boxes of my past; things written and recorded and photographed and long lost. I send them to the trash. I drive home, and pull Sam Keen off the shelf, and turn to this:

> Your past
> just disappeared.
> Now what?
>
> The future begins when I cease to rehearse old scenes in which I recited lines written for me by the directors. When I become my own playwright I act in a drama I helped to create. The play begins when I become the author, the authority, of my own life.[2]

Amazing and improbable that I am here; here because they were there; but they won't write the script and each of us changes the drift of the master script somehow. (I'm the one who got them scouring their minds and questioning their gods about what it means to be gay. They will do with it what they will; I'll go on writing my script.)

Sam Keen concludes:

> We are shaped more
> by what is not yet
> than by yesterday.
>
> The vacuum more than the thorn
> in the flesh makes us who we are.
> the not-yet may be a place of hope or despair.
> Stay hungry for the future, but be nourished
> by past and present. We are moved by

---

2 Sam Keen. *Beginnings Without End.* New York: Harper & Row, 1975, p. 123f.

the promise of a fulfillment that is forever
slightly beyond our grasp.

MY MOM'S FATHER WAS A DENTIST and a devout Presbyterian—except
for when he was a devout Baptist. It all depended on which minister
he was most displeased with, and then he'd move his men's Bible study
from Washington Street to Main Street and back again. And such a
Calvinist. A dentist who refused to use Novocaine. (I just wanted you
to know what we went through.)

Both sides of my family, staunch Republicans, united in their
loathing for Franklin Roosevelt. My grandfather once refused to shake
President Wilson's hand because Wilson was divorced.

My father's side of the family had been even *more severe* evangelical
Republicans. Dad believed in the Vietnam War because an American
victory would mean Christian missionaries could go and covert all those
poor doomed Southeast Asians from Buddhism or whatever they are
over there to Christianity and they could go to heaven.

In so many ways they pretty much resembled their cultural sur-
roundings. *Their* Bible was the only one worth reading, and it contained
all truth. Their America, their church, their South Jersey—not to be
confused with *North* Jersey, which was heavily Democratic. Dad was the
head of the household—mowed the lawn but didn't do dishes, always
drove the car, always held onto the TV remote, though he'd be asleep
on the couch.

Without saying much, Dad could be chilly and severe. Mom was
utterly loyal, always deferring to him, never contradicting him. Sometimes I could see the wrenching conflict on her face, but she remained
silent.

At first, *their* world was *my* world, with its values and beliefs. Their
gods were my gods. If they were evangelical Presbyterians—my form
of revolt was to become an outright fundamentalist.

That was all a long time ago.

ROBERT KEGAN, IN HIS *In Over Our Heads*, talks about life as a big school. The curriculum consists of our growth through orders of consciousness until we arrive at one where we stay. Unless we keep growing!

MY MOM WATCHED IN ANGUISH as I disappointed Dad. I felt his disappointment, though never hers. I didn't turn out different in order to disappoint him. The world changed. I found in my own soul different realities that had to be reckoned with. I had to abandon the household gods, evangelical Presbyterian sorts of gods, fundamentalist gods. Leave them behind.

THAT'S THE HARDEST PART. It made me a fish out of water—which is a fish who has nothing to suspend it and has to move toward something that can.

To Robert Kegan, a fish out of water is "a desperate, expiring creature cut off from what it needs to survive." But *that* is also the story of the evolution of our species.[3]

You won't find that fish exulting in this marvelous evolutionary triumph onward and upward, into a creature that can live on land. Mostly they're looking desperately for another pond to jump into.

I found a few transitional ponds. Then, when later on I found my religious home in Unitarian Universalism, I remember telling someone, "Now if I change my mind, if I evolve some more, I'm still home. I don't have to find another home." Here was a spacious pond that understands what we're in this world to do—evolving our consciousness, and supporting each other in doing that. Never standing still.

When Carl Jung went his own way, he disappointed both his mentor, Sigmund Freud, and his father, who didn't understand. In a dream, Carl Jung is looking at the glittering roof of the cathedral, and he sees God the Father sitting on his golden throne high above the world, and then, from under the throne—I'd really better quote Jung here—"from under the throne an enormous turd falls upon the sparkling new roof,

3   Robert Kegan. *In Over Our Heads: The Mental Demands of Modern Life*. Cambridge: Harvard University Press, 1994, p. 105.

shatters it, and breaks the walls of the cathedral asunder."

Jung continues:

> I felt an enormous, an indescribable relief. Instead of the expected
> damnation, grace had come upon me, and with it an unutterable
> bliss such as I had never known. I wept for happiness and grati-
> tude. . . . A great many things I had not previously understood
> became clear to me. That was what my father had not understood,
> I thought: he had failed to experience the will of God, had op-
> posed it for the best reasons and out of the deepest faith. . . . He
> had taken the Bible's commandments as his guide; he believed
> in God as the Bible prescribed and as his forefathers had taught
> him. But he did not know the immediate living God who stands,
> omnipotent and free, above His Bible and His Church, who calls
> upon man to partake of his freedom, and can force him to renounce
> his own views and convictions in order to fulfill without reserve
> the command of God. In His trial of human courage God refuses
> to abide by traditions, no matter how sacred.[4]

WE WILL HAVE TO DISCOVER A SELF larger and more encompassing. We
have to be the authors of our own book.

Sometimes that calls for a changing of the gods. A very traumatic
thing to do.

There had been in my former Chicago church a young man who
came out as a gay man to his parents in a letter, and then he went home
for Christmas. They had changed the locks. Their gods told them to
do it.

I wondered what Mom and Dad would do. I had heard Mom talk
about "homos." When my brother-in-law announced that *he* was gay, I
heard Mom say, "Michael was such a nice young man before his illness."

When I *did* journey to New Jersey and tell them, noting the books
on the shelf by Anita Bryant, my Mom utterly astonished me. "What
matters is that you're happy," she said. "What matters is what you do
with your life," she said, adding, "I'd been wondering." By my next visit
the Anita Bryant books had been replaced by some gay-friendly titles.

---

4 Carl Jung. *Memories, Dreams, Reflections,* ed. Aniela Jaffe, trans. Richard and Clara
   Winston. New York: Random House, 1963, p. 39f.

How could they do it? For a long time that huge Presbyterian church provided Mom and Dad with no support in that kind of expansion of consciousness. I don't know where it came from. (Though it must be said that, in May 2011, the General Assembly of the Presbyterian Church, USA finally voted to change its constitution and allow out gay people in same-sex relationships to be ordained—this after thirty-three years of debate and many negative votes.)

There is a quality about Being Itself—a property it has;—a capacity in Nature to evolve and grow in complexity and depth.

I could go home again to the slightly overgrown honeysuckle, and there was a comfort with my Dad and my Mom that I couldn't have predicted. Even if who I am was not fully understood, it was accepted—*except* for my Unitarian Universalism, which they found a deep mystery. My sister, now a Quaker, confided with me about a conversation with them in which they expressed concern for my eternal salvation. They didn't know what to make of a wildly changing world, a divorced and remarried Quaker daughter, a gay Unitarian Universalist son.

SPIRITUAL WRITERS THROUGH THE ages have often spoken of a Self so big and expansive that it can look on the identity you present to the world and see it with detachment, as if you were looking at it from a distance—look at the values and beliefs of your culture from a bigger place — and remind you that you are more than that, more than you know. When you look from that bigger place, seeing yourself from *there*—who is it who is doing the looking?

MOM HAD THAT QUALITY. There was more to her than she knew how to talk about. She could embrace what she couldn't understand.

This trait—it reminds me, strangely, of William Ellery Channing, really the founder of American Unitarianism—and of his children.

Channing's spiritual children were the Transcendentalists— Emerson, Parker, Margaret Fuller. He knew it and they knew it. But Channing was a committed, biblical Christian. He firmly believed in the miracles of the Bible—not a very Transcendentalist point of view, and today, not a very Unitarian one. He feared for their souls, *even while* he believed they had seized on some great truth and he deeply honored them. He wanted them to speak freely from, as he put it, "a full heart." Even though they made him a bit nervous.

Mom and Dad, and Dr. Channing, held their fears about their offspring in this same way. It's explained by Samuel Johnson—he was one of those spiritual children of Channing, too, another great Transcendentalist minister. And he said:[5]

> The limits of Dr. Channing . . . were of the head, not of the heart; and the ever forward look of the prophetic man inspired all younger and freer minds.

There were times when my mother made some pretty startling statements that showed a degree of vision, and ability to comprehend, that her Presbyterian church didn't give her. Where has she gone? Is all that lost?

I don't know. I have dropped the old materialist assumption that death is the end of the cessation of our being: such materialism flows from an outdated grasp of "matter," which turns out, like this whole Universe, to be—as the great physicist Niels Bohr put it—to be "not only stranger than we think, but stranger than we *can* think." And everywhere, an intelligence—which some dare call consciousness.

But wherever she is, it seems unlikely to me that whatever may await across the threshold of death can be very much like our earthbound existence. Too much of *that* identity and sense of self relies on the processor that occupies the center of our heads.

I should know. I have diabetes.

It struck—the kind known as Type 1—in my mid-50s. I learned very quickly that the brain runs on sugar. And now the plant that makes the insulin that regulates and uses the sugar as fuel—in my pancreas— had gone out of business. So I must constantly test my blood sugar (lots of needle pricks in the fingers) and administer insulin—not too much, not too little. Too little, and the blood glucose does devastating damage.

5 Johnson, Samuel. *Theodore Parker, a Lecture.* Ed. John H. Clifford and Horace L. Traubel. Chicago: Charles H. Kerr & Co., 1890, 20.

you lose limbs and eyes, among other things. Too much insulin—and this is what's pertinent here—and the brain doesn't work.

Before I started using a highly refined device known as an insulin pump, I relied on injections, and on far-less precise hand-computing of how much to inject. Overnight—when I was asleep and unable to sense that I was getting into trouble—blood sugar could plummet.

Then, I couldn't understand anything at all. I would hallucinate. These were the most terrifying experiences of my life. I often wonder if that's what Mom's times of confusion and fear were like.

I was reminded of this eighteen months after my last pre-pump episode—when I had another. Unlike all previous episodes, I was alone. Steve, my dear friend and housemate, wasn't there to bring me out of it by feeding me sugar in the form of orange juice and glucose tablets. This wasn't easy—once, my hallucinations told me that if I drink the juice, we all die.

This time, I was alone. So this time it went on and on, possibly for hours. So I'd reverted to a more primitive stage of consciousness. Specifically, it was a return to the "magical" stage when things in the environment are invested with magical powers.

The radio was on, tuned to the NPR station in Albany. I hardly understood the interviews, or Garrison Keillor's poetry reading. It was those disembodied speaking voices themselves: they held the key to my fate. The decision whether to let the voices go on—or shut them off, which I seemed to understand I might do—would determine the future. Now the voices on the radio had some godlike power.

I think I'm alone in an isolated universe I've dropped into—a usual feature of this sugar-starved state. By now I've crawled off the bed onto the floor and into the guest room, looking at shirts on hangers above me that I can't reach because I can't achieve the balance necessary to stand. Is this to be my fate? Forever to stare up at these unironed shirts? Will I ever escape this fate?

The horrible isolation is interrupted by a noise from below. Something has disturbed Scooby, downstairs, who now bumps into something, reminding me of another existence sharing this space. I know who he is. I try to call his name: "Come here, Scooby," but my speech is slurred beyond recognition. I work at it until I get enough of it out, and his head appears at the bottom of the stairs, visible from the hallway floor where I've now dragged myself after many contorted movements in the guest room. The sight of him greatly expands my universe, and though he wanders off somewhere, I am reassured and reminded that there is more. Maybe I can get there. Maybe I can get to where he is. Can I get down those stairs? Can I put on some clothes and rejoin that world, or at least appear to do so by going down those stairs? I drag myself back into the bedroom, where I see a bottle of glucose tables on the dresser. I cannot quite, at first, reach them but after some effort, I knock that bottle down and open it and pull out a grape tablet. They have a strange, tiny appearance, but no matter, I've got one, and put it on my tongue—they're extremely tasty—but should I be tasting this, eating this? So I take it off my tongue and hold it, contemplating it, then back to my tongue, then back and forth until I decide it's all right to eat. Some brain power returns. I manage to put on some shorts and go get downstairs and, now standing in the kitchen, eat some bread, with some jam, and now I remember the orange juice, which I drink, and now I'm coming back. But the sickening feeling that I can so quickly revert to a lesser stage of consciousness comes with the awareness and can haunt me for days afterwards.

I DO KNOW THAT THE CURRICULUM of life is not about better genes and germ plasm. It consists of our growth through orders of consciousness. The time to come may be a cataclysm or it may be a saving transformation and it's going to depend on what *we* do *now*.

I HAVE CONTEMPLATED CHANNING'S death. This is the account of another of his Transcendentalist spiritual children, Octavius Brooks Frothingham:

> He was taken ill in a hotel, in Bennington, Vermont, October 2, 1842. As the vital flame in him burned low, he said, "I have received many messages from the spirit." His whisper was his last communication. With declining day his countenance sank. Being

assisted, he turned to the window at the east. The curtains were drawn back, and the light fell on his face. He gazed over the valleys and wooded hills, and none but God and the spirit knew when his soul passed to that prospect which the horizon could not bound.[6]

THAT IS NOT HOW MY MOM DIED that Thursday morning. Her face had been wrenched in the terror and confusion of Alzheimer's Disease; her cries would haunt the core of me. When my sister reached the hospital where she'd been taken the night before, she found the emaciated body, her face no longer wrenched as the night before, but calm. Her suffering was over.

When I went that July day, I hadn't been sure she'd even recognize me, but when we found her where she had wandered in the secure section of the nursing home, her face lighted up. She reached up and hugged and kissed me. Two or three weeks later she would be beyond recognizing my brother Tim when he came from San Francisco.

WHERE IS SHE?

The ancient mystics and spiritual sages—and not a few modern ones as well—have understood that these cells and particles that hurt and decay are not the ultimate reality. *They* arise *out of* an intelligence, a Ground of Being that is primal consciousness.

And we—we separate individuals are entities with brains in which a kind of self-referential quantum measurement takes place, an astounding contraption that measures and compares and analyzes, and that provides us with memory and a sense of individual identity and personality. But we partake in one Life, one Mind, one Being from which these cells and particles arise, from a realm of possibility, the Great Unmanifest *made manifest* in particular forms and ways in each of us, in the moments and choices of our lives.

We live, as Emerson put it in his essay "The Over-Soul," within

that great nature in which we rest, as the earth lies in the soft

---

6 Octavius Brooks Frothingham. *Transcendentalism in New England: A History*. New York: G.P. Putnam's Son, 1886, p. 363.

arms of the atmosphere; that Unity, that Over-soul, within which every man's particular being is contained and made one with all other . . . Meantime within [us] is the soul of the whole; the wise silence; the universal beauty, to which every part and particle is equally related; the eternal ONE. And [in] this deep power in which we exist, . . . the act of seeing and the thing seen, the seer and the spectacle, the subject and the object, are one.

The world is changing fast and so is what's required of us. Can we see beyond the realm of separated cells and particles and the small-*s* individual "self"—and genuinely sense and feel that all of Life is one, to sense and feel the soul of the whole that is not diminished by disease, not extinguished by death?

A new consciousness is rising now and every one of us shares in it. We won't always have the tools to understand it, but we have to try. And when we cannot—then let our limits, like those of Dr. Channing, like Dad's and Mom's—let them be limits of the head, and not of the heart. What if we were to trust the creative powers that are at work in us and in this time, and commit to them? Because what is at stake is this whole world of life.

To take our place in that work—to commit ourselves to it without reservation—is to make our lives worth dying for.

GOOD CHRISTIAN
ENCOUNTERS UNTHINKABLE

AYEAR AFTER I WAS GRADUATED from seminary I sent a short article to the seminary newspaper. I thought they'd like it. Thought that if they didn't like it, they'd print it anyway since I had been editor the previous year. Presently there appeared, not my article, but an editorial:

> A few weeks ago, I received a letter from a recent alumnus of this seminary. He had an article that he wanted printed in *Qoheleth*. The article was essentially the confessions of an homosexual.
>
> But perhaps "confessions" is not the right word. The tone of the article was that of so much of the current talk on the subject: he considered homosexuality to be only an alternative sexuality, and that it could be biblically justified. He referred to it as something beautiful. His tone was cordial, not abrasive. . . .
>
> After discussing the letter with some friends, I decided that, homosexuality being biblically untenable, the confessions of a brother, printed for the public to read, could cause him future embarrassment after the Lord has dealt with him—as He always does with all His children—concerning this sin. Yes, sin. The article, therefore, does not appear in this paper.

Not that this school would be anyone's idea of a proper place to come out. I'd figured out about myself during my senior year—1972-73—and kept this new realization quiet, except for four friends with whom I dared to share it. One subsequently came to my room with tears streaming down his face. Was going to lay hands on me and cast out the demons. I declined his intercession. The Holy Ghost had already had the ten years of my Pentecostalism to cast out demons and hadn't bothered. A second friend—my closest—replied to my disclosure: "I guess that's the evidence that you've been predestined for damnation. Not your fault—nothing anybody can do about it." Next morning, when I met him for our daily 6:30 a.m. jog, he began to run—into the dorm, down the hall, up the stairs to his room. For the remaining months of school, he never again acknowledged my presence, not even when there was no one else in the room but us.

The third was good humored in his acceptance. But the fourth— well, that's the experience that radicalized me.

The fourth was an evangelical Presbyterian from Pittsburgh (lots of Presbyterians from the conservative Pittsburgh Presbytery would go to Gordon Conwell Seminary rather than the Presbyterian seminary in Pittsburgh). "Gay? Gay Christian?" he said. "Yes—I know a couple of Gay Christians back home. They struggle so against their sin that they're always suicidal. I really respect them."

It happened that I was already suicidal, had been all year. If what this guy's religion did for his friends in Pittsburgh, which was why he respected them, was to make them suicidal, I didn't need his religion, or his God. Probably, I'd had too much of it already.

My move from the house of orthodox Christianity had begun in earnest. Its answers, confidently simplistic sureties, only insulted my humanity. I'd had a fairly ample chance to test out that repertoire of answers, since an incident in the *Qoheleth*. A student had presented me with an article about the new Metropolitan Community Church of Boston, which he didn't think I'd want to print. Which I wanted to print and did, which generated heated response. So in a March 1972 issue I ran a lengthy editorial defending the MCC church, which I'd never attended, and arguing for its validity. All in the third person. And spent the rest of my senior year alternately having people View With Alarm my struggle, and eating lunch at quickly-emptying cafeteria tables. And listening with bemused interest to the raging debate, which struck me as vastly silly. Modestly, I propose that my editorial was the seminary's Event Of The Year.

What was going on inside wasn't silly.

I didn't want to live. Here was the problem: This orthodox Christian

God imposes upon me the life of a gay person in this world, knowing already that He (the certified orthodox God is always He) had long ago drafted laws against such things, condemning the pervs to hell.

The dilemma might be inconsequential to some, but not to a born-again South Jersey boy who got saved at a Billy Graham crusade back in 1957 and then proceeded to join the Pentecostal church. Now, I'd really been into this. As a teenager bored with the very proper Presbyterian church, here was something . . . *exciting.* Here, you got to speak in tongues, heal people, things like that. And have passionate (purely spiritual, surely!) embraces with young men with whom you were praying at the altar. Funny how long it can take to figure out why you like a thing.

The Assemblies of God church was followed by Central Bible College, an Assemblies of God institution in Springfield, Missouri. I did this right, you understand. Fasted, prayed, preached, stuffed literature into people's hands in parking lots and even knocked on their doors. I even sacrificed a quality education in order to be a true believer attending this true-believer school. Here, one's own identity was supposed to be lost in Christ's identity. So struggling with one's sexual identity would have been kind of out of order anyway. Once, encountering a student I didn't know in a hallway, I introduced myself. "Hi—I'm Jay," I said. "My name isn't important, only the name of the Lord Jesus Christ, praaaise JEEEzus!" he responded. I noticed that Friday and Saturday nights were worse than other times. Seemed like writing papers, praying, and reading the Bible just didn't make it at all on a Saturday night. I wasn't very happy. To make matters worse, the theological case for this faith was wearing very, very thin.

Meanwhile, CBC, and for that matter the Assemblies of God itself, turned out to be the venue of sex scandals more spectacular and imaginative than ordinary fantasy could conjure, mostly involving faculty and preachers—a hint that something was fundamentally wrong with this. I got disillusioned with this allegedly supernatural religious movement in its headquarters city and left before graduating, stuffed everything I owned into the used Mercury I'd bought at Bighearted Bill's Friendly Rambler and headed back for New Jersey. (I got to Springfield, Ohio before the car would go no farther.) I finished a couple of courses by correspondence and got the degree in the mail. I've never seen the place since. I found an apartment, nasty but cheap, in Union City, New Jersey and went to work at the Interchurch Center in New York City. Here, I learned another side of the Vietnam War, which heretofore I'd patriotically supported. At the Interchurch Center, draft resisters were welcomed and given a platform. And that Communist troublemaker, Martin Luther King, showed up in Newark and made a speech, a few phrases of which turned up on the evening news, and I heard it. And I knew he was right. That was March 27, 1968. From there he headed to Memphis, where the sanitation workers' strike wasn't going well. King died on the fourth of April. Within a week, the Interchurch Center was closed so we could all stay home and watch his funeral from Atlanta— which I did, through a lot of tears. A corner was turned.

After a few months at the Interchurch Center I got a job with the Pentecostal youth evangelist David Wilkerson, who specializes in drug addiction. Eventually he fired me for being a "Communist sympathizer," because I hadn't liked one of his films in which he accused youth today of being a bunch of rebellious communist lesbians, bla bla. But before that incident, he cornered a bunch of us to inquire of each one directly, "Do you have, or have you ever had, any homosexual tendencies?" I said No, and I thought No. It couldn't be. He hated to ask, he said, but even though his center claimed an eighty percent cure rate for drug addiction, he told us he'd never seen anyone delivered of the demon of homosexuality. Subsequently, he's made some extravagant claims to the contrary. I don't believe him.

So here was good Christian. A Pentecostal one, even. Such a good Christian. Besides all the rest, a virgin!

And now I was in this evangelical seminary, confronting a long-neglected reality, a reality shut out so effectively, so long. I wanted a man. I was in love with a classmate (that, of course, went nowhere). By now I'd concluded that the Assemblies of God was a touch too narrow a context for me, and I'd affiliated with the American Baptist Churches. Now, told by an American Baptist placement officer that he'd never place a man in a church who wasn't married, I was faced with the fact that I wasn't ever going to be married. Now it was a career crisis, too.

And what the hell kind of God was this, doing this to me? I had some principles. I would not deal with a God who didn't. A long spiritual journey thus began to see whether a genuine relationship with this Reality—one that wasn't constrained by the orthodoxies and legalisms of the house of orthodox Christianity—wasn't possible. The journey would lead through an agony like death, which is the way I think resurrections are supposed to go. Before I'd get anywhere, I'd have to learn a new language for divinity. Not the language of Calvin, whose entire *Institutes* this seminary had made me read. An inner language of dreams, speaking with the immediacy of a Reality not housed off in the heavens or glued to the pages of a holy book, but closer than my breath.

> *I sit at my desk, which isn't in my student's cubicle but outdoors, by the sea, in a park. Behind me, facing my back, is a park bench. I am afraid, because of what is on the bench.*

> *It's an old man, dressed in tattered rags, all torn and baggy and grey. The old man is gray; the park bench is gray. He is the picture of death, desolation, bad fortune, ruin. Old, alone, and destitute. On his face, just above his eyebrow on the side of his forehead, a big, open sore. An ugly sore that goes right through to the bone. It cannot be hidden. He is telling me his story.*

> *It is a sad story that he whines; misfortune has befallen him. But I am repelled. His story is punctuated every now and again, after a few more paragraphs of sad narrative, with: "Now that you have gained these insights into me, how do you feel about me?"*

> *I avoid answering. I'm in the grip of fear. Scared to look at him. Scared not to look—what if he should reach forward and touch me? Then, I would become like him! In*

his voice, I recognize my own . . .

    Crying and yelling, I wake up. Try to prevent myself
falling back into this dread dreaming sleep. The effort fails;
I fall back into dream-scene at the desk, and this time, I
wake up screaming in tongues[1] and crying, waking others
down the hall. What was I becoming? What was I afraid
of becoming?

THE THERAPIST SAID I'D have to tell him my dreams and fantasies. Otherwise, his time and mine would be wasted. So I could decide, now, to speak up or get up. The fantasies were pretty hard to own up to. But the dreams began to come in a flood.

The therapist has a solution to propose. The Navy. That's right, join the Navy. They'll be a father for me; that'll straighten me out. That is not at all what I've heard about the Navy.

But the dreams have a declaration to make. They have a transformation to declare.

    A disreputable person comes down the street fresh
from perpetrating some indecency or crime. A cop stands
across the street. I am both frightened and disgusted by the
unseemly character, and the cop calls to him, taking aim
with his pistol. This "shadow" character grabs me as a
hostage! He takes me behind a lamp post: no place to hide
now. If the cop shoots, he gets me. He doesn't shoot, which
is good since this pole is little protection. I do not enjoy the
company of this character, nor do I enjoy being his hostage.
I am afraid and ashamed. And then I look at him. See
something familiar. Something that I somehow like. Halt-
ingly, I dare to embrace him, and he is transformed into a

---

1 A phenomenon attributed by Pentecostals to the Holy Spirit (unless non-Pentecostals do it, in which case it's attributed to demons) and by Carl Jung to the unconscious.

beautiful and warm friend, and we go off together.

I am in the car driving to a party I don't want to attend. My sister sits by me giving directions. In fact, there are lots of other people in the car, all giving directions. I am following their directions, except that they are not agreed as to where we're going. In any case I don't want to go.

We arrive, at length, in front of a city row house on one of those winding, narrow Boston streets near a chaotic intersection. There is a small space to park. As I maneuver the car, everyone has a criticism of the way I locate the car in the space. "You're too close!" "You're too far from the curb" (which is tricky, because it curves).

My sister gets out of the car to go into the house. "Aren't you coming?" she asks me. I stay in the car. She's annoyed and procedes to move my belongings into the house. I am watching the end of the street. A sleezy bar with a few cars parked in front. A black man tries to pick up another man in one of the cars. Another car pulls up. A fat white straight middle-aged man jumps out. "I saw that," he yells, and chases the black man, now sitting in a station wagon. He locks the doors but the straight white man gets in via the tailgate. The black man runs.

Now I'm driving again with my sister. I stop on a boulevard and an old car pulls up. It's the black man, still fleeing. He wants to drive my car and continue his flight. I am happy to let him. I like him and think I'd like to take him wherever he'd like to go.

THE BLACK IMAGES CAME AS a particular surprise to someone who had picketed Brooklyn department stores with Operation Breadbasket, while attending Rev. Herb Daughtry's House of the Lord Church in Bed-Sty. Herb had laughed at the sight of his sole white parishioner wearing a sandwich sign reading "Soul Brothers Unite." I was no racist, uh uh. Not until my unconscious needed images of something disreputable and associated with shame. But as in racism, so in homophobia and one's own coming out. The dreaded image was the denied Self. We would have to make friends. I would have to get over the dualism so intrinsic to good ol' orthodox Christianity that specializes in setting up splits between light and darkness, God and the Devil, male and female, soul and body, heaven and earth.

You see what happened. I learned to do this in dreams. I'd been reading Jung, about embracing the shadow and experiencing some profound transformation. And it worked. There has never been a more profound terror than the moment before the embrace. You think you are plunging to your death.

Salvation came from inside, where the truth is. The Authorities were wrong. What I was, it turned out, was good. Once, sitting in my monastery-like dorm room, I read a story buried deep inside the *Times* about some homosexual rights movement (then, the *Times* wouldn't use our chosen names, *gay*, or *lesbian*, but insisted on *homosexual*, and rarely printed any news about gay people, but here it was, a story about some homosexual rights thing somewhere). I read it and, to my surprise, I was sobbing so much I had trouble finishing the story. What stories they printed in 1973 weren't very long, and I was already sobbing. I knew what it was. *My people.* These are my people. Yes.

I wanted to meet some gay people. I figured I'd go to that church I'd defended. The old Mercury was up on cinder blocks and the school was deep in the northern exurbs of Cape Ann. I'd have to get a ride with somebody. Ulp. So I had a friend drop me off at Park Street Church, downtown Boston's temple of evangelicalism founded in the nineteenth century as an orthodox reaction to the Unitarian revolution in New England (the second sermon ever preached there was titled "The Uses of Real Fire in Hell"). The orthodox were particularly concerned about the powerful presence of Theodore Parker, who drew thousands to his Twenty-Eighth Congregational Society to hear his Transcendentalist spiritual vision and, flowing from that, his condemnation of slavery and greed. During a revival on March 6, 1858 the following prayer was uttered at Park Street: "Lord, we know that we cannot argue [Mr. Parker] down, and the more we say against him, the more will people flock after him, and the more will they love and revere him. O Lord, O Lord, what shall be done for Boston if thou dost not take this and some other matters in hand."

But I wasn't headed for Park Street Church. I walked across Boston Common to the opposite corner, to the Arlington Street Church, the historic Unitarian Universalist congregation once served by William Ellery Channing, that now rented its smaller chapel to the Metropolitan Community Church. I went cautiously for the steps. Scared of being recognized by some evangelical writing a paper about perversion.

I was greeted by an actual gay person, then another, and sat toward the back of the crowded chapel. A second layer of transformation was happening: while I shored up my new perception that I was okay, I was surrounded by others whose kindness, decency, and goodness I could not doubt. Whatever was being said back at school about homosexuals was being said about *them*. It was rubbish.

I went back the next week. Easter Sunday. Met a man who understood my struggle. We arranged to meet again. No punitive lighting-bolt came from above to protest what we shared. I returned to school notably happy.

They hadn't seen me happy before. Until this, they'd gotten to play the role as caring and compassionate, like Christians are supposed to be. It had worked as long as I played the part of miserable sinner. But now, I wasn't miserable. Now, I was a problem. For the balance of the school year, until graduation, I was isolated from my classmates. But with the exhilaration of a newfound sense of integrity, I didn't mind.

KEYNOTE TO A REVOLUTION
What Emerson said; or, Soul, soul, soul!

Ralph Waldo Emerson
From the Divinity School Address of 1838:

Meantime, whilst the doors of the temple stand open, night and day, before every [one], and the oracles of this truth cease never, it is guarded by one stern condition; this, namely; it is an intuition. It cannot be received at second hand. Truly speaking, it is not instruction, but provocation, that I can receive from another soul. What he announces, I must find true in me, or wholly reject; and on his word, or as his second, be he who he may, I can accept nothing. . . . The doctrine of the divine nature being forgotten, a sickness infects and dwarfs the constitution. . . . And because the indwelling Supreme Spirit cannot wholly be got rid of, the doctrine of it suffers this perversion, that the divine nature is attributed to one or two persons, and denied to all the rest, and denied with fury. The doctrine of inspiration is lost; the base doctrine of the majority of voices, usurps the place of the doctrine of the soul.

And from his essay, "The Over-Soul":

*The Supreme Critic on the errors of the past and the
present, and the only prophet of that which must be, is
that great nature in which we rest, as the earth lies in
the soft arms of the atmosphere; that Unity, that Over-
soul, within which every [one]'s particular being is contained and made one with all other; that common heart,
of which all sincere conversation is the worship, to which
all right action is submission; that overpowering reality which confutes our tricks and talents, and constrains
every one to pass for what he is, and to speak from his
character, and not from his tongue, and which evermore
tends to pass into our thought and hand, and become
wisdom, and virtue, and power, and beauty. We live in
succession, in division, in parts, in particles. Meantime
within [us] is the soul of the whole; the wise silence; the
universal beauty, to which every part and particle is
equally related; the eternal ONE. And this deep power
in which we exist, and whose beatitude is all accessible
to us, is not only self-sufficing and perfect in every hour,
but the act of seeing and the thing seen, the seer and the
spectacle, the subject and the object, are one. We see the
world piece by piece, as the sun, the moon, the animal,
the tree; but the whole, of which these are the shining
parts, is the soul. . . . Only itself can inspire whom it
will, and behold! their speech shall be lyrical, and sweet,
and universal as the rising of the wind.*

Hafiz

A 14th-century Sufi poet loved and translated by Mr
Emerson:

The
Great religions are the
Ships,
Poets the life
Boats.
Every sane person I know has jumped
Overboard. [1]

EMERSON WAS BORN A BIT over two centuries ago—in 1803, to be exact. Like his father, he entered the Unitarian ministry. Before Emerson, Unitarianism was comparatively "liberal" in that it didn't accept the Calvinist ideas that human beings are inherently fallen, depraved, and incapable of any good; and it didn't see Jesus as a God walking about on earth—hence the name, *Uni*tarian, in contrast to *Tri*nitarian. Still, many saw Jesus as a notch above regular humans, a special messenger from God and the only way to God. They based their beliefs on the absolute authority of the Bible, which they believed to be divinely inspired and without error. After a couple of years of turmoil, Emerson quit. So come with me to a perfect Summer day six years later, in Cambridge, Massachusetts, where at the age of thirty-five, he is about to deliver himself of a spiritual manifesto that will rock the Unitarian movement and, with it, the religious world.

I NATURE

ONE PERFECT JULY EVENING in 1838, a small audience packed into an even smaller chapel in Cambridge listened in astonishment to a description of the summer day just passed. The speaker began:

1 But, not having Emerson's translation, I offer Daniel Ladinsky's, from *The Gift: Poems by Hafiz the Great Sufi Master*. New York: Penguin Compass, 1999, p. 177.

In this refulgent summer—

Reading Emerson, you will have to handle a bit of nineteenth-century language. Try using "refulgent" in a sentence at least once each day. (Oh Mrs. Jones, why that's just *refulgent* of you!) But in fact, *Refulgent* means saturated with glorious sunlight —

> — In this refulgent summer it has been a luxury to draw the breath of life. The grass grows, the buds burst, the meadow is spotted with fire and gold in the tint of flowers. The air is full of birds, and sweet with the breath of the pine, the balm-of-Gilead, and the new hay. Night brings no gloom to the heart with its welcome shade. Through the transparent darkness the stars pour their almost spiritual rays. Man under them seems a young child, and his huge globe a toy. The cool night bathes the world as with a river, and prepares his eyes again for the crimson dawn. The mystery of nature was never displayed more happily. The corn and the wine have been freely dealt to all creatures, and the never-broken silence with which the old bounty goes forward, has not yielded yet one word of explanation.

In New England the summer brings what Henry Thoreau called *"the tonic of Nature."* When Emerson's 200th birthday came around in 2003 I had just returned to New England from a decade in Chicago. I'm a city boy but the endless expanse of poured concrete that is Chicago and its suburbs was a suffocation of the senses and the soul.

Yes. There is a correspondence between nature and mind, nature and soul. Nature draws us *beyond itself to That from which it flows.*

One day years ago, sitting beside Great Pond, somewhere toward the middle of Connecticut, with its profusion of life, noble and great and glorious (even though I could never find the place again), my mind opened to Mind with a capital M. My life opened to Life with a capital L. Was I changed? What had until now been closed in me was opened wide. It was all already there. I saw what I had not seen, felt it, knew it.

When he was 10, young Waldo Emerson, a student at Boston Latin School, walked one winter evening across the Boston Common and saw: not a few stars, not a blanket of wet snow, but the Kosmos. It made him an amateur scientist which he remained for life, a charter member of the American Academy of Arts and Sciences; and he became a scientist of Spirit, the most brilliant, luminous religious thinker America ever produced. In the crowded chapel that night in 1838, hearing the great address, was Theodore Parker, who went home and wrote in his journal,

> I shall give no abstract, so beautiful, so just, so true, & terribly sublime was his picture of the faults of the church in its present position. My soul is roused, & this week I shall write the long-meditated sermons, on the state of the church & the duties of these times.

Which he did, and the moribund church of their day shook again. Theodore Parker, who, two decades later, dying, left as a testament to what Emerson had meant to him, this:

> The brilliant genius of Emerson rose in the winter nights, and hung over Boston, drawing the eyes of ingenuous young people to look up to that great, new star, a beauty and a mystery, which charmed for the moment, while it gave also perennial inspiration, as it led them forward along new paths, and towards new hopes. America has seen no such sight before; it is not less a blessed wonder now.

II NATURE AND SPIRIT

THEODORE PARKER WELL KNEW what this meant, this correspondence of nature and soul. This religion that Emerson preached, this religion of soul:— it led Parker to stand, alongside Emerson, resisting the Fugitive Slave Law, in the struggle to end slavery and ensure civil rights for black Americans, in denouncing the Mexican War and the savage mistreatment of native American Indians. He knew: I *must*. I *must*.

So Emerson said this: The mystery of Nature draws us into a quiet ecstatic awareness of *that from which Nature flows.* "The mind opens," he says, and we ask, "What am I? and What is?"—so "asks the human spirit with a curiosity new-kindled but never to be quenched." There appears to us, then, "a more secret, sweet, and overpowering beauty" when our heart and mind open to the sentiment of virtue, and we are instructed in what is above us. We learn that our being is without bound. We cry: "I love the Right; Truth is beautiful forevermore; Virtue, I am thine." It was directly from this ecstasy that his moral vision and moral courage flowed.

This was not the religion of his father, the esteemed minister of First Church in Boston, William Emerson. No, *that* was certainly a religion of culture and learning, but it was acutely uncomfortable with this bit about *soul*. The old New England Unitarians didn't want to get mixed up with soul or passion or ecstasy anymore than the old orthodox Calvinists did. They were all about obeying the Bible, that external, presumptive authority—not soul, not intuition, not our own mind. These were dangerous.

Emerson came to call the religion of his fathers "corpse-cold Unitarianism." He'd been drawn away from *that* by his own revelatory experiences of Nature, and by some of the people in his life, among them, his Aunt Mary Moody Emerson who, though quite Christian herself, valued rapture and inspiration as the fountain from which light and eloquence must flow, if it's ever going to flow. She loved eloquence and poetry but warned her nephew never to write poetry that was merely *pretty* but did not come from the divine Muse, drenched in holy imagination. All this drew him further away from the old religious authority to a wilder inspiration.

I LIKED THAT ABOUT EMERSON, too, when I started reading him, when I was a minister in a denomination devoted to the authority of the Bible and the concept that inspiration lay all in the past, sealed and complete. Emerson and his friend Thoreau opened up new continents in my mind. I had my own Aunt Mary Moody Emerson in the form of the Pentecostals who inhabited the earlier years of my life. Their theology was a mix of primitive mythology and superstition—quite a disaster—but they were not afraid of Spirit and passion. And for that I'm grateful.

Emerson, too, outgrew his aunt's theology, but would never settle for less than her live, first-hand experience of Spirit, in his own quiet way.

III ONE:—SPIRIT, NATURE, AND MORAL VISION

A WILDER INSPIRATION. SO WHILE the old-line Unitarians joined the Calvinists in sitting out the antislavery struggle, Emerson became a central light in it, its spiritual center. His speeches were sometimes drowned out by mobs, and sometimes, the authorities deliberately let the mobs in to disrupt this dangerous revolutionary.

His was a revolution that began inside the heart and soul of a person. He said that there are, at work in Nature, laws that execute themselves. There is, he said, "in the soul of man . . . a justice whose retributions are instant and entire. He who does a good deed, is instantly ennobled. He who does a mean deed, is by the action itself contracted," made small and mean.

And why is this? because:

> "The world is not the product of [many separate powers], but of one will, of one mind, and that one mind is everywhere active, in each ray of the star, in each wavelet of the pool . . . whilst a [person] seeks good ends, he is strong by the whole strength of nature."

One will, one mind. *One.* This word *one* leaps from the pages of almost everything Emerson said. Like this, from his essay, "The Over-Soul":

> The Supreme Critic on the errors of the past and the present, and the only prophet of that which must be, is that great nature in which we rest, as the earth lies in the soft arms of the atmosphere; that Unity, that Over-soul, within which every [one]'s particular being is contained and made one with all other; that common heart . . . Within [us] is the soul of the whole; the wise silence; the universal beauty, to which every part and particle is equally related; the eternal ONE.

What does this word, ONE, signify, and why is it so prominent in our Unitarian Universalist religious language? The Unitarians were thinking of it when they chose their name. Quite separately in history, the Universalists, too, were thinking of it.

YOU CANNOT LISTEN TO THE DIVISIVE rhetoric of the Christian right or of the Islamicist fundamentalist rhetoric of division and separation without longing again for the sense of this great word, ONE. Honestly, I don't believe that human civilization on this planet has very many years to survive unless we come to that unitary consciousness.

The lack of it is the product of our cosmology, what we understand the nature of this Universe to be. It's the religion of a dying order: the religion of separation, of alienation. It pervades the atmosphere and is embedded in our bones. Children grow up into violence and alienation, sick at heart and mind.

Without a sense of the *Kosmos*, without an awareness of our integral part in it—we ourselves are lost.

Now from the frontiers of science comes an understanding of the nature of the Universe that sounds like the Transcendentalism of Mr. Emerson.

The great physicist David Bohm was among many in our day speaking of a new vision of reality, an imaginative view of the relationship between mental and physical, between mind and matter, two aspects, finally, of one reality. Matter and Spirit, or Matter and Energy, if you prefer: Energy enfolds Matter and Meaning; while Matter enfolds Energy and Meaning. Space and time all seem to flow from a universal, unbroken field, a ground beyond time.

And David Bohm wrote,

> The mind may have a structure similar to the universe and in the underlying movement we call empty space there is actually a tremendous energy, a movement. . . . [G]etting to the ground of the mind might be felt as light." [2]

IV WHERE TO START: SELF WITH A CAPITAL "S"

COMING INTO THAT INNER light is *an ecstasy*. That is where the ecstasy of Nature's beauty naturally draws you. But then, another revelation: This perception awakens in the mind what Emerson calls the religious sentiment, and he says,

> Wonderful is its power to charm and to command. . . . It makes the sky and the hills sublime, and the silent song of the stars is

---

2 Quoted in Renee Weber, ed., *Dialogues with Scientists and Sages: The Search for Unity.* London: Routledge and Kegan Paul, 1986, p. 48

> it. . . . This sentiment is divine and deifying. . . . Through it, the
> soul first knows itself. It corrects the capital mistake of the infant
> man, who seeks to be great by following the great, and hopes to
> derive advantages *from another*,— by showing the fountain of all
> good to be in himself, and that he, equally with every other, is an
> inlet into the deeps . . . When he says, "I ought;' when love warms
> him; when he chooses, warned from on high, the good and great
> deed; then, deep melodies wander through his soul from Supreme
> Wisdom. Then he can worship, and be enlarged by his worship.

It sounds so lofty, so unattainable, so immediately he corrects the
mistaken fear that all this is above you, beyond your reach. He says
this sublime religious experience is never far from any of us, and is
greater, and stronger, than all our errors and missteps. Whoever you
are, wherever, in whatever state: The doors of the Temple stand open.

They stand open before everyone, and the oracles of this truth are
guarded by just one condition: this is an intuition, it's got to be your
own and first-hand. "It cannot be received at second hand."

So don't set out for a church or temple to get religion, to get spirituality; no: go to be *provoked* to *open yourself* to something that you cannot
get from another soul. You must find it just where it is, in your own
soul. And so *you* have to judge, judge for yourself, judge between what
is real and what is false. I must speak my own working grasp of truth
with passion and so must you. We must be open to inspiration from
the only place it ever comes, from the deepest wells of our Selves.

V RELIGION

NOW HE'S GOING TO SPEAK DIRECTLY to the graduates. Did I tell you?
The occasion for all this is that he has been invited to speak to the
graduating class of what is now Harvard Divinity School. This is the
next generation of Unitarian ministers. Seven graduating students, plus
a bunch of faculty and townspeople and one of last year's graduates who
has walked all the way to Harvard Square from West Roxbury because
he knows his walk is going to be worth it, Theodore Parker. And Waldo
Emerson is going to tell these new ministers about religion and being
ministers of religion.

You are going to be preaching from pulpits, he tells them, from pulpits that have been devoted to the idea that all these grand splendors of the soul apply *only to one* person, Jesus, and in this narrow, self-dismissive delusion, men and women have long been shut off from *their* fullest, divinest selves. You must correct the delusion.

Jesus saw with open eye the mystery of the soul and was ravished by its beauty and lived in it and had his being there *just as you might.* He said:

One man was true to what is in you and me.

This he said in the hearing of all the old doctors of religion at Harvard, and they shuddered, and in their minds they began writing their pamphlets condemning was they were hearing. Blasphemy! Heresy! Infidelity!

But calmly, with the sweetest of smiles, Mr. Emerson went on, he wasn't finished. It was getting quite warm in the chapel.

The problem with the church now, he says, is that it exaggerates the importance of the *person* of Jesus and made him a demigod, and has set up a kind of religious *monarchy*—Christ the *king*, etcetera —, built on power and fear that injures the soul. And religion ought to be about soul.

So Mr. Emerson has to declare:

That is always best which gives me to myself. . . . That which shows god *in* me, fortifies me. That which shows God *out of* me, makes me a wart and a wen [*that's a skin cyst!*].

Isn't Mr. Emerson just a bit optimistic about humanity? We have lived through and after the Holocaust, terrorism, and corrupt, lying government, and incomprehensible greed.

But then I remember the man I saw, on the BBC World News, the man in East Timor whose neck was nearly severed by an axe wielded by the Indonesian army during one of those waves of repression. With his misshapen neck bearing witness to what he had undergone, he said he was willing to let the Truth and Reconciliation process go forward and to forgive those who hurt him, so the new nation might have freedom and independence. How is this possible?

The primitive tribal behavior of war and cruelty we understand well, it's still a part of us, but how do we understand the noble and the good? How do we understand forgiveness, or love? But that is why we are human, Nature's highest achievement to date. We are capable of self-reflection, contemplation, and moral inquiry and vision. It is to *that* that Emerson calls them.

So Mr. Emerson declares a religion of inspiration *now*, or, as he says it, "Men have come to speak of the revelation as somewhat long ago given and done," and this he calls an *injury* to faith. No, it's with the beauty of the soul that they must begin, and if they do, it will beget a need to impart the love and beauty they see. "Always," he says, "the seer is a sayer." However you express this beauty, this truth, this love, you will become its priest or poet.

Now he turns to the church as it is now. Oh oh.

> In how many churches, by how many prophets, tell me, [is a person] made sensible that he is an infinite Soul; that the earth and heavens are passing into his mind; that he is drinking forever the soul of God? Where now sounds the persuasion that by its very melody imparadises my heart . . . ? Where shall I hear words that in [earlier] ages drew men to leave all and follow? . . . Where shall I hear these august laws of moral being so pronounced as to fill my ear, and I feel ennobled by the offer of my uttermost action and passion?

Where?

What kind of religious communities do we mean to create, and sustain, and be? What is supposed to happen to people when they come through the doors? What do we think is even *possible* in our religious gatherings?

HE COMES TO HIS CONCLUSION. His final plea is this:

> Now let us do what we can to rekindle the smouldering, nigh quenched fire on the altar. The evils of the church that now is are manifest. . . . The remedy . . . is, first, soul, and second, soul, and evermore, soul.

THAT'S IT; THERE YOU ARE.

The most influential of Unitarian theologians, Andrews Norton, a member of that Cambridge faculty, published a series of pamphlets calling Mr. Emerson's remarks "the latest form of infidelity." The religious world shook and rattled for awhile as Mr. Emerson retired to Concord to continue his quest for farther reaches of truth, and to write some more. In his parlour would gather a truly radiant assortment of men and women who might have remained obscure and mediocre, but for their having been kindled in that flame; but they were drawn into that fire, and they changed the world.

Mr. Emerson wasn't invited back to speak at Harvard, not until 1862, twenty-seven years later. It didn't matter. Divinity school students, and ministers, and throngs of laypeople were reading his essays, going to hear his lectures. For most of the rest of his life he lived on the outskirts of Unitarianism, quietly, powerfully, by the force of soul, gradually drawing the Unitarian movement, and with it the Universalist, up a more daring pathway, igniting a new and transforming fire on its altar. Within a decade of his death in 1882, the names of those who had denounced his bold words were not remembered; no one could tell you who that theologian was who called his gospel "the latest form of infidelity;" there were no monuments to those who had ridiculed him. Unitarianism and Universalism too were born anew, rekindled.

And still there is no more urgent message for this world: we've got to arrive at this sense of ONE, beyond these separate egos of ours—this sense that we all participate in one great always-unfolding whole, or human civilization on this planet cannot have very long to survive.

The road to that consciousness of ONE, —

That road—is the soul within us. The remedy to the greed and the division, to the exploitation that threatens life on earth, is nothing less, nothing more complicated, nothing other than what, that day in Cambridge, Mr. Emerson said it was: it is, *first, soul, and second, soul, and evermore, soul.*

V

G - D
Of language and spirit

William James Potter
A radical Unitarian minister in New Bedford,
Massachusetts, 1871.

*No definition of religion, I think, will satisfy the philoso-
phy of the subject which does not in some way denote a
contact which the finite mind has with the vitalizing and
sustaining Energy of the universe. It is not necessary
that the definition should embrace the idea of a personal
Deity, not necessary that it should attempt the impossible
problem, which most theological systems do attempt, of
defining the Infinite; but it must, in order to cover all
the facts, in some way recognize the Infinite,—in other
words, recognize that the human soul is conscious of a
life that is not bounded by its material organism nor by
any limits which itself can measure, but opens outward
into the whole infinity and eternity of things, and is a
natural, inherent part of the universal order.* [1]

---

1 From "Religious Sentiment in the Light of Science," 1871, 19f. This work can
currently be found in Volume II of the collection *Essays and Sermons of William
James Potter (1829-1893),Unitarian Minister and Freethinker* edited by Edited by W.
Creighton Peden and Everett J. Tarbox (Edwin Mellen Press, 2003).

J. Krishnamurti

From *On God: At the end of a lecture about God, someone asks Krishnamurti a question:*

QUESTIONER: "You never mention God. Has he no place in your teachings?"

KRISHNAMURTI: "You talk a great deal about God, don't you? Your books are full of it. You build churches, temples, you make sacrifices, you do rituals, perform ceremonies, and you are full of ideas about God, are you not? You repeat the word, but your acts are not godly, are they? Though you worship what you call God, your ways, your thoughts, your existence, are not godly, are they? Though you repeat the word God, you exploit others, do you not? . . .

So you are very familiar with God, at least with the word; but the word is not God. . . . I don't use that word for the very simple reason that you know it."

And on another occasion, a questioner asks,

Q: "Tell us of God."

K: "Instead of my telling you what God is, let us find out whether you can realize that extraordinary state, not tomorrow or in some distant future, but right now as we are quietly sitting here together. Surely that is much more important. But to find out what God is, all belief must go. The mind that would discover what is true cannot believe in truth, cannot have theories or hypotheses about God. . . . When the mind is full of belief . . . it is burdened, and a burdened mind can never find out what is true. . . . You yourself must see the importance of relinquishing . . . all the accumulations of centuries, the

superstitions, knowledge, beliefs; you must see the truth
that any form of burden . . . dissipates energy. For the
mind to be quiet there must be an abundance of energy,
and that energy must be still. . . . Because the mind has
abundant energy that is still and silent, the mind itself
becomes that which is sublime. . . . When the mind is
completely still, . . . then that energy is love . . ." [2]

At a reception I was once introduced to someone by an Episcopal clergy friend—a Trinitarian—who explained "Jay's a Unitarian. Unitarians believe in one God at most."

One *God?* But whatever do you mean by *God?* Well, what you're about to read is not what I learned as a kid, not what I was taught in that fundamentalist college and evangelical seminary.

In that world we talked about a god *out there*—wholly separate from you and me. Some kind of super-person out there who created everything and who could draw near to me or abandon me because it, or as they said, *he*,—is separate from me.

I lived with that for a long time but in my gut it didn't feel right, didn't ring true. And then I read Emerson.

I came to sense that these cells and neurons and tissue, and this mind, give expression to an evolutionary impulse at the heart of everything—give form to that intelligence and energy, make manifest some something that lies beyond the capacity of our science to detect or measure. We're palpable expressions, we make manifest, something that is unmanifest, and it's everywhere, and it's here, closer than your breath. And the startling insight that thoroughly contradicted my Presbyterian and then fundamentalist and then evangelical earlier beliefs was something that the Hindu Chandogya Upanishad declares: *Thou art That.* You—you're it. There's only one. You. Along with seven billion others, you're it.

It wasn't long before I left the household of Christian faith. I applied

2 J. Krishnamurti. *On God.* New York: Harper San Francisco, 1992, pp. 51, 62-4.

for a transfer of ministerial credentials from my former denomination and became a Unitarian Universalist. My friends were baffled. How can this be a religion, they asked? It didn't deal in the traditional religious language, the categories in which traditional religious people think and speak. It didn't have saviors and miracles and heavens and hells. It was about spiritual experience, first-hand spiritual experience of your own, interpreted in light of how we're coming to understand the universe; and it was about the life of this world. It's about the choices we make and the deep source of our choices and actions. But what about Christ and Satan and salvation and God and all?

WHAT IF YOU GO OUT TONIGHT and you look up and you see that the stars have rearranged themselves before your very eyes so that they spell out "G-O-D?" And millions of people are seeing this before their very eyes. If they could be sure this wasn't some form of mass hallucination—ah! at last! the final definitive proof!

But—proof of *what?* No matter how many people saw it, and no matter how thoroughly documented, the sighting of the stars rearranging themselves to spell God couldn't *define that troublesome word.* All that throng of people out there under the stars would know is that something pretty darn weird had happened.

In one of Krishnamurti's little books of lectures, the one called *On God,* at the end of the lecture about God, somebody asks him, "You never mention God. Has he no place in your teachings?" And you just read what he said to that.

ONCE, IN THAT PREVIOUS RELIGIOUS life of mine, I was working with an ever-so-slightly progressive evangelical minister in Brooklyn in a pretty conservative Swedish church. He said to me: you know, you can say pretty much anything you want so long as you get enough of the important words in—God and Christ and Salvation and so on. Then they won't notice what you're actually saying.

Language is a funny thing: so essential to communication, so apt to get in the way of communication. Gustave Flaubert nailed it when he wrote:

> The truth is that fullness of soul can sometimes overflow in utter vapidity of language, for none of us can ever express the exact measure of his needs or his thoughts or his sorrows; and human speech is like a cracked kettle on which we tap crude rhythms for bears to dance to, while we long to make music that will melt the stars.[3]

In 2002 the newly elected president of the Unitarian Universalist Association, Bill Sinkford, stirred up a controversy about religious language. In the *Boston Globe*, the headline was "Words of 'reverence' roil a church;"[4] and in the *New York Times*, it was "A Heated Debate Flares in Unitarian Universalism."[5] It seems to have started with a sermon in which he said, among other things:

> [W]e have in our Principles an affirmation of our faith which uses not one single piece of religious language. Not one. Not even one word that would be considered traditionally religious. And that is a wonderment to me . . .[6]

Well no, those Principles and Purposes, adopted in 1984 and periodically revised, are simply these:

§ The inherent worth and dignity of every person;

§ Justice, equity and compassion in human relations;

§ Acceptance of one another and encouragement to spiritual growth in our congregations;

§ A free and responsible search for truth and meaning;

§ The right of conscience and the use of the democratic process within our congregations and in society at large;

§ The goal of world community with peace, liberty, and justice for all;

§ Respect for the interdependent web of all existence of which we are a part.

---

3 *Madame Bovary*. Part II, XII: "Preparations."

4 By Michael Paulson, June 28.

5 May 17, 2003.

6 Sermon delivered Jan. 13, 2003, Fort Worth, Texas.

These are followed by a six-point statement of the sources from which we draw—words and deeds of prophetic men and women, wisdom from the world's religions, Jewish, Christian, humanist, and earth-centered traditions. None of the traditional religious words. This bothers Bill, but it doesn't bother me. And it starts, significantly, with this:

"Direct experience of that transcending mystery and wonder, affirmed in all cultures, which moves us to a renewal of the spirit and an openness to the forces which create and uphold life." Well now, *that* I call religious language.

BUT BILL SINKFORD RAISED AN important question. How do we talk about our religious, our spiritual, experience and community? I've read a number of sermons that colleagues have preached in response to all this. Most of them say we really need to start using the traditional religious language again, just investing the old words with new meaning.

YOU MIGHT FIND IT USEFUL TO do that for yourself. But I've seen so many people so severely injured and traumatized by that language. I saw a sign at a Gay Pride march that read "Pat Robertson uses the Bible the way Hitler used gas." Same applies to a lot of abusive statements from the Vatican and the bishops. The words are *loaded*, and with all the freight and terrifying weight of the vaunted authority of church and bible and hierarchy and creed, the words hit like missiles. And these missiles are real, unlike certain alleged weapons that turned out not to be real.

You say the word "God" and a raucous jangle of pandemonium goes off in the heads of your hearers—alarm bells ring, red lights flash—it's really quite something.

For some it's a matter of dread and fear. Those words began to have another kind of effect on *me*. My memories are still fresh. During an intensive period of education at evangelical institutions and deep involvement in their churches, the constant repetition of those words came to have a *numbing* effect. The mechanical repetition may as well have been profanity. It was a mind-numbing repetition of special religious lingo that shut down the thought processes and—worse—shut down any resonance in the gut with anything transcendent, locked you in a tiny room already so fully defined that there was no way out.

I think you can give those words new meaning for yourself but I'm not so sure you can give them new meaning for our time and culture. These words have long-established meanings. And this new time and culture requires a new spiritual vision.

Some prefer to work within the old systems of language and symbol by redefining them. My late colleague Forrest Church has said "God is not God's name. God is our name for that which is greater than all yet present in each." But can we, really, just use the same words and give them new meaning? Some can make the transition, at least partway. Many others will not. Even if we think they're outworn and archaic, these words have long-established meanings. Be very, very careful.

BILL IS RIGHT ABOUT THIS: we *do* need a way to talk about spiritual experience and to interpret it. But do we really think there are, or ever could be, words adequate to what we mean? We'll have to struggle with our language to say what we mean. And that's good. The struggle will keep us from easily mouthing words with no meaning.

MAYBE THAT'S WHY, AMONG the ecstatic and mystical religions, there is glossolalia, tongue-speaking. Maybe *that* is the only legitimate vocabulary of reverence. Not one word of it can be found in a dictionary, can be translated into any propositional concepts. But American Pentecostalism wasn't satisfied with that—they figured these ecstatic utterances had to be translated out into familiar religious concepts. So they followed St. Paul's teachings about the *interpretation* of tongues and supplied an interpretation—usually consisting of memorized King James Bible verses. About as fresh, immediate, and original as the Apostles' Creed. Oh well.

"Of that ineffable essence which we call Spirit," Emerson wrote, "he that thinks most, will say least. . . . when we try to define and describe

[God], both language and thought desert us, and we are as helpless as fools and savages. That essence refuses to be recorded in propositions."

SO NOTE THE KABBALISTIC SPELLING, *G-dash-D*. In an earlier time, Jews were forbidden to pronounce the Divine Name, since any attempt to speak of the Divine was bound to be inadequate, because it is too high, too holy. The divine name was written as four consonants —*Yod, Hay, Vav, Hay,* Y, H, V, H—no vowels, not pronounceable and never pronounced in any reading of scripture. With the Temple destroyed and the act of pronouncing The Name outside of the Temple prohibited, pronunciation of the Name fell into disuse. Scholars passed down knowledge of the correct pronunciation of YHVH for many generations, but eventually the correct pronunciation was lost, and we no longer know it with any certainty. Among Orthodox Jews you can still find those who reverence the Unutterable Name by not uttering it; and who write the Name the way I did in the title, G–d. I think they've got it right.

God is a dangerous word. Once speak the word, and our mental memory-banks are at once filled with all the things we think we know, have been taught, believe.

You can give old words new *meaning*. But it isn't the *words* that count, it's the *meaning*. Anyone can have a profound religious experience. But how will they *interpret* that experience? What meaning will they give to it? That matters maybe even more than the experience.

So many ancient accounts of *God!* As often as not, they are national epics created and repeated in a world quite unlike ours, stories created and repeated for political reasons, to give stability and strength to that political entity. Oh, where did we ever see anything like *that?*

And these stories, and the people who tell them, are always marked by special words—shibboleths—by which you can tell who belongs to the "in"-group and who doesn't—and we repeat those words because they make us feel that we're insiders instead of outsiders, we're saved instead of lost; knowers of the true doctrine.

What meaning do those ancient stories hold for us? We live in another universe.

Slowly we have penetrated the depth of reality and found not gods and dragons of the deep and angels and archangels—but Leptons and Muons held together by Gluons, and we find the Universe pervaded with Light that we cannot see, and we marvel at dark matter, that keeps it from flying apart, and dark *energy*, that drives the expansion of the Universe.

When I hit the desk in front of me, it goes thunk. We like that. We think we have made contact with the essential brass tacks of life—*matter.*

Not really. Not the way ages and generations before us thought. This book you hold, and the chair you sit in, and you and I are made of cells and the cells are made of atoms and, in the subatomic realm— mysterious patterns of energy, and no solid matter at all. Right now, bazillions of protons and leptons are flying *right through* you! And now we know that *atoms*, which I was taught were supposed to be the fundamental building block of the entire universe, constitute only about half of one percent of what's out there. The rest is pretty mysterious.

Our science has penetrated reality and found mysterious communication across the abyss between things, and things we thought *things* vanish with our seeing them. There is more than meets the eye.

But what is this Life that evolves, and what is this All of which everything we know is a part? and what is this Energy and Intelligence that insisted on exploding from nothing into something with form and substance 14 billion years ago? and what are the ethical implications of *that*, and what might it mean in our living? and what does it have to do with our loves and our hurts and our hopes? and what is this Universe that goes forth in a moment from an infinitely small, infinitely dense darkness and void and creates worlds and gives us life?

MAYBE YOU HAVEN'T GOT A DOUBT in the world about the existence, or nonexistence, or whatever, of God. Or —

Maybe you find yourself speaking of God with a ringing ... *ambivalence.*

Maybe you are a theist, which means you believe in a God who is some kind of divine cosmic super-person.

Or, maybe, like so many mystics, or like the theologian Paul Tillich, or like our own Transcendentalists, or like some kinds of Eastern
religions, or like me, you sense that there is something, some central
Life of the Universe, but you are not a theist because you don't mean
some personal super Somebody-out-there; no, you mean something in
which all the universe, and you and I ourselves, *are a part*. Tillich called
it the *Ground of Being*.

Maybe mostly you figure you don't believe any of this stuff. Maybe
you're a materialist.

Maybe you are troubled by your own contradictions.

MAYBE WE NEED TO TALK more immediately about our own firsthand
experience, our own emptiness and ecstasies, our own sense of ultimate
meaning—with less embarrassment, with more poetry—talk about it
in ways that are informed by how we now understand the universe.

NOT SO LONG AGO, AT NIGHT, the dog and I stood in silence for a long
time, out on the hill in back of my house in the foothills of the Berkshire
Hills in Massachusetts, in the great quiet and darkness of Westhampton,
watching as our tiny planet shaded entirely our tiny moon, and in the
dark, through the crystal-clear skies, looked—at least *I* did, Scooby was
likely smelling things—I looked into the depth of space.

What language could I offer? But the vocabulary is quite second-
ary to the reverence and it has to rise naturally from it. And *that*, I am
certain, will communicate far more than outworn, tired words and
shibboleths. Reverence, but not superstition. Look into the depth of
space, and into the depth of ourselves, and do it in the light of what we
now understand about this evolving Universe.

The Reality I am attempting to speak of—isn't the ancient *Tao te
Ching* about right when it says:

> There is a thing inherent and natural,
> Which existed before heaven and earth.
> Motionless and fathomless,
> It pervades everywhere and never becomes exhausted.

It may be regarded as the Mother of the universe.
I do not know its name.
If I am forced to give it a name,
I call it Tao, and I name it as supreme.

And there is another line that says

The Tao that can be spoken is not the eternal Tao;
The name that can be defined is not the unchanging name . . .

I AM PRETTY SURE THAT RELIGIOUS language *should* be a struggle, *should always* be a struggle. If it can be repeated mechanically, it isn't helping us get to the real thing.

We'll have to free ourselves from an archaic universe with its Bibles of unquestioned authority, its heathen tribes versus godly warriors, its dragons of the sea, its angels and archangels; and its God, who is always too small, too neatly wrapped.

We have to let it go. We have to set our minds free to perceive anew and to think new thoughts.

WHEN I WAS ENGAGED IN THEOLOGICAL study, this jolted me once in a dream. I was studying for the ministry of this God I thought I knew quite a good deal about, had thick books of theology explaining. In the dream I sat in the great cathedral of God and heard chanting, the rich, resonant voice of the Divine singing, filling the cathedral. But being curious, I walked about, examining things, looking behind things, until I looked behind the wrong thing, and, right out of *Wizard of Oz*, there was Rev. Dr. Van Dyke—the minister I grew up listening to—chanting into a microphone, and there everybody thought it was the voice of God. The funny thing is, as far as I can remember, I (unlike every other gay man on earth) had never seen *The Wizard of Oz*. I was appalled, and not a little disappointed. The temple-full of worshippers was being duped and deluded.

I wonder if you ever felt that way.

HUMANS ARE BY HABIT AND TRAINING unable to find what we seek. We do what we know how to do, from the scripts we have learned. Wage wars, conquer the heathen, slice up the dragon. Defend against perceived threats to whatever we think we are, to whatever we think is ours.

All these stories and bibles and histories are embedded in us. For most of the human journey, change came very slowly. Only recently (in relative terms), the pace of change has accelerated, and exponentially. But for most of our time on earth, not much new ever showed up. Evolving human consciousness was a long, slow movement. The appearance of anything really new was rare. We aren't well adapted to the staggering rate of change and innovation we now face. So we're apt to favor the old, familiar stuff.

In the evolution of Life there have been astonishing breakthroughs as life invents and transforms itself. And in between the breakthroughs, or when we get tired or afraid, we turn back to what we know, and what we know is only the past.

Our relationships, too, are made of our memories and scripts. And the hurts, the irritations, the pleasures, the flattery, and the brutal words, remain, recorded in the cells of the brain. We live from the past and we construct our visions of the future from the past and we know each other in the past. And in our old bibles we can find all the justification we need for all of it. Meanwhile we poison or proscribe other relationships. Religions are still debating whether certain kinds of people really belong within the human community, and so may be permitted to represent the human community as its priests and leaders. It used to be about race, and now it is about women, gay people; and the circles of exclusion remain, reinforced primarily by our religions.

And out of this past—the whole of the human past, because we are the world, we are each other—out of this past, the affronts, the hurts, the threats, the pain, and the things we did to relieve the pain, out of this disorder of the human soul, has come the entire structure of human society. Is it possible for us, shaped and conditioned as we are by the very structure of human society, with its values and assumptions, to bring about a spiritual revolution? I believe was can, and we must. It is time, and past time.

THE EARLY UNITARIANS AND Universalists started a revolution. They wanted to measure what they believed against the measure of reason, and against their own passionate religious sense. If it didn't make sense, they refused to believe it. If it violated their deep sense of truth and spiritual reality, they rejected it. And so they rejected some of the most destructive doctrines, like the belief that human beings are essentially depraved, fallen, and worthless.

But their revolution did not get to the heart of the matter. Always they returned to the traditional sources of religious Authority—Authority external to ourselves, getting the truth about life second-hand from some respectable source. The Bible. The historic Church. The Apostle Paul. Jesus Christ. Religiously, many of them knew the familiar and comforting feeling that comes with the assurance that the sacred texts of the Bible could not be questioned, could provide all the answers they needed. They were *a little* progressive. Many of them had never had any profound and transforming religious experience of their own, personally—they'd only heard about it. They had opinions, somewhat progressive opinions at that.

And then came Ralph Waldo Emerson. He was not content with second-hand religious experience. He did what you have to do to have first-hand religious experience. He experienced insight. He saw reality deep and wide in transforming moments of insight.

He said, you have to stop looking in all the familiar places for the Next Thing, for the vital energy of Life Itself. Religious experience, he might have said, is not like freeze-dried coffee: you know, you take all the same old stuff, add water, and stir, and it's all there, living and dynamic. It won't work. You cannot turn to Paul or Moses, and take it from them second-hand. There is no authority short of the Source, the Ground, the Mystery beyond all our knowledge and all our words and all our memory. You have to touch it for yourself.

Emerson's 19th-century Unitarian minister colleagues would have none of this. They insisted that he had gone too far; that the Bible must be the final authority and that the miracles in the Bible prove the Bible's divine authority (rather a circular argument, wouldn't you say?).

But he was undeterred. These are the opening words of his first book, *Nature:*

> Our age is retrospective. It builds the sepulchres of the fathers. It writes biographies, histories, and criticism. The foregoing generations beheld God and nature face to face; we, through their eyes. Why should not we also enjoy an original relation to the universe? Why should not we have a poetry and philosophy of insight and not of tradition, and a religion by revelation to us, and not the history of theirs? . . . Why should we grope among the dry bones of the past, or put the living generation into masquerade out of its faded wardrobe? The sun shines today also. There is more wool and flax in the fields. There are new lands, new [humans], new thoughts. Let us demand our own works and laws and worship.[7]

Let us learn—learn, as Emerson wrote—"learn the revelation of all nature and all thought . . . this, namely; that the Highest dwells with [us]; that the sources of nature are in [our] own mind . . . But if [you] would know what the great God speaketh, [you] must go into [your] closet and shut the door, as Jesus said. God will not make himself manifest to cowards."[8]

But what is that? About whom could he be speaking so rudely?

But none of this is of any use to those who would make of all this just some intellectual exercise, superior religious wisdom in the hands of someone who has not been transformed by it. You cannot know about God as a mere idea. God is not something to believe in, but to *undergo.* And you surely don't have to call it "God." You *do* have to know it in your own life and *undergo* it. He goes on:

"God will not make himself manifest to cowards. He must greatly listen to himself, withdrawing himself from all the accents of others' devotion. . . . Our religion vulgarly stands on numbers of believers. . . . The faith that stands on authority is not faith. The reliance on authority measures the decline of religion, the withdrawal of the soul. "

And speaking directly to the graduating theological class of Harvard College in 1838, he dared to say:

> it is an intuition. It cannot be received at second hand.[9]

7 *Nature.* Boston: James Munroe and Company, 1836, p.5.
8 His essay "Over-Soul."
9 "The Divinity School Address."

IT'S TIME TO SEE MORE DEEPLY than the dragons and sea-monsters, the armies of conquerors, the gods with arms and legs and gender, apostles, all male, looking down from the bulwarks of heaven. First-hand spiritual experience is available to all. So you've had an experience—how will you *interpret* it? In some archaic or pre-modern way, fitting it into the myth and dogma of another time and place?

There is religious imagination there, but not the kind or quality that we need. We are fascinated by it because we, in our time, seldom look beneath the surface, the material. But we must look more deeply.

There is more than meets the eye.

Already the human mind, the minds of scientists and those who study the very structure of this Universe, have reached far beyond the stories and myths of ancient religions. They have moved into a realm far beyond the reach of churches and religions. And it is more than a little ironic that it was science that saw once again what only ancient poets and mystics had seen, that this material world is not as it appears, but is a dance of energy, it is all energy, patterns of energy, creating forms, creating the phenomena of matter, matter, which we have gotten used to, used to behaving in a consistent and stable manner, and it does, all our lives, until it disappears into a black hole or is transformed back into energy again in a nuclear interaction.

And: "It is more than a little ironic," writes Ken Wilbur[10] —"that it was science . . . that in the closing decades of the twentieth century would rediscover the self-organizing and transcending nature of evolution itself."

We know the world was not made by gods. We have some idea about the evolution of life. The evolution of cells, of life-forms, of species; the emergence of the human, the development of the brain. Whatever there is to be known—the point is not to have opinions about it, dogma about it—but to come into direct relationship with it. And what relationship will it be? Bitter resentment? passionate love? fear? despair? gratitude?

And then it comes to us again that behind and beyond our ev-

10 *Sex, Ecology and Spirituality: The Spirit of Evolution.* Boston & London: Shambhala, 1995, pp. 523f.

eryday experience there is this mysterious energy (some have called it Spirit); there is Life Itself, and we awaken to a world that is not dead as we had thought, lifeless rock and soil, but a living organism with fire at its heart, and this living earth ceaselessly turning with the planets around the sun in the immensity of space, and all this community of the Universe the artwork of Life Itself, a Universe itself that is self-organizing, as if driven by some sort of intelligence, by a passionate impulse to unfold, evolve. It is inherently creative and intelligent. There is the creative capacity to evolve into ever more complex forms. There is one Life, for all shares the Life of a larger whole.

WHERE TO FIND THIS GROUND of Being? Here. Now. Closer than your breath. It is what remains when everything else is gone, when all the clutter is cleared away. We need only clear away the clutter —

halt the comfortable reliance on authority and past experience,

halt the hurt of past injuries, and fear of whatever we have been taught to fear.

You don't need any messiahs or saviors.

You don't need to struggle and strive.

Let it go. Let it all go.

When the noise and tumult stop, when the striving ceases, when we see the disorder of our own thought and are freed from it, we are in silence, in an immensity of silence and emptiness, and in that silence and emptiness, in that immensity, there is creative energy. There is the Mystery beyond our naming. In this immensity there is the highest state of passion, and there is Love, and this love is undivided, it is Life Itself, it is Revelation, it is Truth, it is Freedom. It is pure Light.

You are held in the embrace of a Love we can only know when all the clutter is cleared away and there is emptiness and silence. You are held in a Love that we can only understand when its fire ignites us.

Though we have dissipated it and wasted it in the terrible struggle to find the answer in the dustbins of our past, you are part and parcel of the energy that spread the stars across the heavens.

Some have said they can explain this great energy, but if you can name it and describe it, you may be certain it is something less than the radiant light you seek. The Mystery beyond the Silence, the pure Energy—cannot be named; words have no meaning here.

In the Silence you will know that you are more than you knew. The Self you will meet in the Silence is far greater than the isolated individual you thought you were and thought you had to protect against the others; the *other*, before whose opinion you need no longer tremble. Only such a spiritual revolution can bring about order in a confused, sorrowing world. And then there can be peace in this world—because when you no longer perceive the other to be really separate from you, you don't need to strive to be kind or generous toward others.

The Silence opens onto a great open expanse of pure consciousness.

And out of this great and luminous Silence comes the fire of soul, and the energy of Life, and flowing out of the silence is the new creation that you seek.

It is for us—for you and me—to clear away the clutter, to open the windows of our soul. That is why the meditator meditates, and enters an "empty-alert" state. Is this not what Emerson meant when, in his first book, *Nature*, he asked "Why should not we also enjoy an original relation to the universe?" and wrote

> Standing on the bare ground—my head bathed by the blithe air, and uplifted into infinite space,—all mean egotism vanishes, I become a transparent eye-ball; I am nothing; I see all; the currents of the Universal Being circulate through me; I am part or particle of God.[11]

KEN WILBER[12] HAS BEGUN TO speak of "the three faces of God." That is, we can speak of God—or whatever your (inadequate) language calls it—in the *first* person, or the *second*, or the *third* person.

By *first-person* he means: "God" or Spirit as the great I AM, Being Itself, the Absolute Self, the Ground of Being. It's of that Divine face

---

11 *Nature*, 13.

12 For more on this, see Ken Wilber, *Integral Spirituality: A Startling New Role for Religion in the Modern and Postmodern World*, Integral Books, 2006, 154-162; or, more accessibly, his *The Integral Vision*, Shambhala, 2007, 198-205.

that the Chandogya Upanishad speaks when it declares to everyone, *Thou art That!* It's what most truly, authentically, we are. It's the message of Emerson's essay "The Over-soul." It's our truest identity. The Divine is not something out there, remote from our selves. It isn't the neo-orthodox theologian Karl Barth's "Wholly Other." It's right here, always, already, here, and we are its expressions, manifestations of what many Eastern religious traditions call the Unmanifest. We are one and we can feel each others' existence as part of our own. It's what we are, looked at from within.

God in the *third* person is the evolutionary Kosmic process itself, looking as if from without.

The experience of either of these can leave the ego intact. It's the *second* face that shatters it: Martin Buber called it the *I-Thou*. Yes, I am a part of it, but it is infinitely greater than I, and in this face-to-face encounter, I surrender and submit. When you speak in the *second* person, you *address this Mystery*, you stand before it in wonder, or gratitude, or worship (or, sometimes maybe anger, or bewilderment). This doesn't require seeing yourself as standing before some personal deity, some super-person in a cosmic control-room. Yet now there you are, face-to-face—this is not just something cerebral. Now something you can truly call *worship* is possible.

This is pictured in an old biblical myth:[13] there was a beloved king named Uzziah who ruled for fifty-two years in Jerusalem. He extended Israel's borders and defeated its enemies. He brought prosperity. Eventually he was as taken by his own grand image as everyone else was. His ego defeated *him* and he began to presume a self-importance that was not his to claim. For this, the story goes, God punished him with and unpleasant disease, of which he died.

This is the prophet Isaiah's personal witness:

> In the year that King Uzziah died I saw the Lord sitting upon a throne, high and lifted up; and his train filled the temple. Above him stood the seraphim; each had six wings: with two he covered his face, and with two he covered his feet, and with two he flew. And one called to another and said:

---

13 Uzziah's reign, humiliation, and death: II Chronicles 26. Isaiah's epiphany: Isaiah 6.

"Holy, holy, holy is the Lord of hosts;
the whole earth is full of his glory."

And the fountains of the thresholds shook at the voice of him who called, and the house was filled with smoke. And I said:

"Woe is me! For I am lost; for I am a man of unclean lips, and I dwell in the midst of a people of unclean lips; for my eyes have seen the King, the Lord of hosts!"

The ego is a constant companion we must befriend, but it makes the worst and most despotic of kings. The grandest day in Isaiah's life was the anguished day of the king's death. And then he encountered, face to face—this second face of the Divine. When you do, you stand in the precise ground where prophets and poets and seers have stood, speechless, stumbling for words, just as they were.

VI

CHURCH & STATE & FAITH-BASED HATE

William Blake
from *The Everlasting Gospel* (1818)

The Vision of Christ that thou dost see
Is my Vision's Greatest Enemy:
Thine loves the same world that mine hates,
Thy Heaven doors are my Hell Gates.
Both read the Bible day & night
But thou read'st black where I read white.

. . . . .

Thou Angel of the Presence Divine
That didst create this Body of Mine,
Wherefore hast thou writ these Laws
And Created Hell's dark jaws?
Tho' thou was so pure & bright
That Heaven was Impure in thy Sight,
Tho' thy Oath turn'd Heaven Pale,
Tho' thy Covenant built Hell's jail,
Still the breath Divine does move
And the breath Divine is Love.

. . . . .

And tho' you cannot Love, but Hate,
[You] Shall be beggars at Love's Gate.

What was thy Love? Let me see it;
Was it love or dark deceit?

THERE IS AN ATTRACTIVE ENERGY that holds the Universe together. Within the human community we know it as love.

It requires space for each thing, whatever it is, with a certain respect for its nature, and space to exist according to its own nature. The freedom of each is conditioned by its meaning or destiny within the whole fabric of being.

Life is an interdependent web and we're all a part of it, all responsible for finding our place and our way, for figuring out how to love this whole universe of life. When there is space for everyone to take their place within the whole, each of us will have a more interesting and fulfilling time of it.

Love is more than a feeling and so is hate.

I REALIZE I HAVE USED RATHER a strong expression: *faith-based hate.*

I have turned to fairly stark language to portray a stark fact of life. Whether it's found in Wahabist Islamists, in al-Qaeda, or way closer to home, it remains a monumental factor in human experience.

If both love and hate are more than a feeling, then—when we face the hard reality of the consequences of what we do or do not do—then, at least by the sternest measures, maybe we're all guilty. It's a complicated and demanding world.

We may want to escape the human responsibility of being here, showing up, taking our part, finding our way and our place in this world, treading the path of love and not the path of hate.

The Christians and Jews and Muslims I count my dear friends have stood again and again for love and not hate. But then again, this is about *how* you look at an ancient tradition. It's about whether, fundamentally, your faith-perspective is a backward look, or one intent on creating the future. This is not about Christianity, or Judaism, or Islam. It is about what you get when the pressures and the felt needs and even the barbarisms of the ancient past dominate your vision. It's about faith-based hate.

WHAT WAS IT, IN COLONIAL America, when the European settlers fell easily into speaking of the native American Indians as "barbarian, primitive, pagan, savage, idolatrous, heathen, and superstitious?" Or as they said at the Jamestown settlement, Indians were "chayned under the bond of Deathe unto the Divell," or when Indians were referred to as "heathen dogges"?—and, once so labelled, the Indians were in danger, and a colonial leader wrote "better kill a thousand of them than that we Christians should be indangered or troubled with them; Better they were all cut off . . . and so make way for Christians." Good Christians, all; earnest, well-meaning. Is this hate?[1]

IN THE CHRONICLES OF THE Transcendentalist spiritual movement during the era of American slavery there are a lot of accounts by firsthand witnesses and participants. They take me, like some sort of time-and-space traveling machine, into the heart of a human dilemma.

Here is one account, by a 24-year-old student for the ministry who, too ill to attend seminary, has gone South for his health. He's in St. Augustine, Florida, in 1827, and the student, the young Ralph Waldo Emerson, wrote this in his journal:

> A fortnight since I attended a meeting of the Bible Society. The Treasurer of this institution is Marshall of the district & by a somewhat unfortunate arrangement had appointed a special meeting of the Society & a Slave Auction at the same hour & place, one being in the Government house & the other in the adjoining yard. One ear therefore heard the glad tidings of great joy whilst the other was regaled with "Going gentlemen, Going!" And almost without changing our position we might aid in sending scriptures into Africa or bid for four children without the mother who had

---

1 Forrest G. Wood. *The Arrogance of Faith: Christianity & Race in America from the Colonial Era to the Twentieth Century*. Boston: Northeastern University Press, 1990, pp.35-36.

been kidnapped therefrom.[2]

A whole Christian culture did this. Among the stars of our story is Moncure Conway, whom we met in the first chapter, a smart man, certainly—a lawyer; an earnest man, certainly—a Methodist preacher. He and his denomination in Virginia preached a gospel of slavery, slavery as God's will and purpose, against which abolitionism was a great sin. Monc Conway has a conversion and turns up in Boston alongside Parker, Emerson, Phillips, Garrison, and Frederick Douglass. He leaves behind a multitude of earnest religious people who have no conversion.

The British Unitarian Harriet Martineau, during her famous travels in America, complained in 1837 that, with one exception, "I never heard any . . . reference made to grand truths of religion, or principles of morals." Instead of preaching about virtues like "striving after perfection, mutual justice and charity, and christian liberty," the ministers spent all of their time "pretending to find express sanctions of slavery in the Bible . . ."

Shortly before the Civil War the Rev. B.M. Palmer claimed that God had entrusted the black race to the care of the white—a "trust providentially committed to us"—which meant that the South was obligated to "conserve and to perpetuate the institution of slavery as now existing."[3] How very caring. Was this love, or was it hate?

HATE, LIKE LOVE, IS NOT so easy to define. I suppose we spend our lives trying to define them.

Call it what you will. Consider its consequences.

THEY DIDN'T MEAN ANY HARM. Jonathan Edwards owned slaves until the day he died. Was it hate that drove him? Or hate that kept him unconscious of what he was doing? There are times when I am severely tempted to cast judgment on agonized souls whose consciousness never quite arrived at where we now can earnestly wish it had.

---

2   R.W. Emerson. Journal entry for Feb. 25, 1827. *Journals and Miscellaneous Notebooks.* Belknap. III, 117.

3   Wood, *The Arrogance of Faith*, 64.

But it isn't the *perpetrators themselves* that we must condemn. History will find *us* guilty, too, of some lack of consciousness. It is the *thing*—this factor in human failure—faith-based hate. It casts blinders over the eyes of the sincere and pious. It subverts the deeds of well-meaning people and makes them wicked.

M.K. Gandhi said that

> it is quite proper to resist and attack a system, but to resist and attack its author is tantamount to resisting and attacking oneself. For we are all tarred with the same brush and are children of one and the same Creator, and as such the divine powers within us are infinite. To slight a single human being is to slight those divine powers, and thus to harm not only that being, but with him or her, the whole world.

IT TAKES A LOT OF VIGILANCE TO escape faith-based hate. Ancient religious traditions preserve, as we know, ancient visions of the world, and the unevolved consciousness of the ancient world. In the Apostle Paul, the message was consistent and undeniable: servants were to obey their masters in all things; defiance toward civil authority was also defiance toward spiritual authority. Isn't that the word of God? The pro-slavery churches said so, and after that, the pro-segregationist churches.

And there's the Curse of Ham. Not many years ago, the whole South and many at the North believed it. Ham was the son of Noah, and because one of his sons, Canaan, looked upon his father naked, all of Canaan's descendants were cursed with perpetual enslavement, forever. And then the curse was extended up one generation to all Ham's sons. I don't remember how this was handled in Presbyterian Sunday School. I think those Presbyterians were sufficiently enlightened to leave that myth where they found it and to teach us, instead, to sing

> *Jesus loves the little children, all the children of the world*
> *Red and yellow, black and white, all are precious in his sight*

And for that I'm grateful, since the Bible says of Noah's sons, "By these were the nations divided in the earth after the flood."[4] It was believed

---

4 Genesis 10:32.

that they were the founders of the yellow, black, and white races. It was believed that because of his sin, Canaan was turned black. It's even more explicit in the Book of Mormon.

It's *just what they believed*. Do you call that hate?

This disastrous idea—the curse of Noah upon the descendants of Ham—was concocted by white religious people out of three verses in the Hebrew Bible—just fifty-one words in the King James. Very few in the Christian world even challenged it. Was that hate?

Many *slaves* believed it. Frederick Douglass did at first, until he got his hands on a book of great speeches and read, and read, and read sublime utterances about freedom. Later he wrote, "I have met many religious colored people, at the South, who are under the delusion that God requires them to submit to slavery and to wear chains with meekness and humility."[5] Well, did the fact that some of the slaves themselves believed it —make it true, and not a lie?

This Curse of Ham rubbish even surfaced in the debate about interracial marriage that flared during the presidential campaign of 1864. The editor of the New York *Daily News* invoked the Curse of Ham and filled three full columns with "scientific" testimony to prove it.[6] Jefferson Davis used it to defend both chattel slavery and the foreign slave trade: *that's* why the accursed race of Ham was brought to our shores.

Distant past? The white-supremacist Citizens' Council's pamphlet about the Curse of Ham, called "A Christian View on Segregation," consisted of a minister's address to the Mississippi Synod of the Presbyterian Church, just after the Supreme Court's desegregation decision *Brown v. Board of Education* of 1954.

Well—it's just what they *believed*, you see.

SOMETIMES MATTERS CAN BE made worse by an unfortunate marriage of church and state. What can we say of the Crusades and the Inquisition? What can we say of the complicity of Pope Innocent XII with the

---

5 Frederick Douglass. *My Bondage and My Freedom.* New York,, Auburn, Miller, Orton & Co., 1857, p. 159.

6 Wood, 98.

Third Reich—altogether consistent with two millennia of Christian anti-semitism? When church and state are wed, public policy begins to flow from the unquestionable, presumptive authority of creeds and bibles and bishops. There's no room for questions.

These are the bitter fruit of faith-based hate when it is coupled to the marriage of church and state.

Now—you may know that, in 1967, the United States Supreme Court overturned laws in seventeen states that banned interracial marriage. It was the culmination of a case that began in 1958, when a Virginia judge ordered an interracial couple, Richard and Mildred Loving, to leave the state for twenty-five years as punishment for violating Virginia's anti-miscegenation law. Here's what Judge Bazile wrote: "Almighty God created the races white, black, yellow, Malay and red, and He placed them on separate continents, and but for the interference with His arrangement there would be no cause for such marriages."

Faith-based hate. On the twelfth of September 2004, the Pentecostal televangelist Jimmy Swaggart[7] (famous for denouncing other evangelists for sexual improprieties and then being caught, repeatedly, with prostitutes) told his large audience in Baton Rouge and on his TV "ministry" seen in all fifty states and Canada (where broadcast of the statement was judged to have breached Canadian human rights standards):

> I'm trying to find the correct name for it . . . this utter absolute, asinine, idiotic stupidity of men marrying men. . . . I've never seen a man in my life I wanted to marry. [Cheers, hoots, applause.] And I'm going to be blunt and plain: If one ever looks at me like that, I'm going to kill him and tell God he died. [More cheers, hoots,

---

7 Swaggart had gleefully denounced Jim Bakker (whom he called "a cancer on the Body of Christ") after *his* earlier scandal, and exposed the scandal of fellow Assemblies of God evangelist Marvin Gorman. At first he refused to acknowledge and "repent" for his breach; then he made his famous, tearful confession on television. His television audience plumetted, as did his Baton Rouge church membership and Bible college student body. The Assemblies of God revoked his credentials to preach. So you might think he's faded away. You'd be wrong. Instead, he now owns 78 American radio stations, broadcasting his gospel 24/7; and his television reach includes both Spike and Discovery cable channels, and broadcast stations in the U.S. and Canada, as well as Sky television in the United Kingdom. His "I'm going to kill him and tell God he died" was part of his campaign for an amendment to the Louisiana state constitution banning same-sex marriage. Voters passed it 4-1.

applause.] In case anybody doesn't know, God calls it an *abomination*. It's an *abomination*. It's an *abomination*. They oughta have to marry a pig and live with them forever. I thank God that President Bush has stated we need a constitutional amendment that states that marriage is between a man and a woman.

I could go on, but why do it? You could add many more examples yourself.

FIFTEEN HUNDRED YEARS ago, in the latter days of the Christian Roman Empire, now crumbling into chaos—marriage was one of the secular functions assumed by the stable bureaucracy of the church. It was made a church sacrament valid only if performed before a clergyman, in a church.

In this matter of *marriage*, the *marriage between church and state* has kept the lines blurred ever since.

Right now, many religious institutions, believing they hold a stake in the definition of civil marriage, *and driven by some fury not at all accounted for by the content of their arguments*, are telling us that marriage must not be extended to same-sex couples because marriage is a *sacrament* ordained by God that has remained unchanged for three thousand years. (In 2008, California, Florida, and Arizona joined twenty-six other states that have passed constitutional amendments banning same-sex marriage; others have passed statutes. Thirty-one states put the marriage rights of the gay minority to popular vote and thirty-one times the gay minority lost. Why would any gay or lesbian person live in such a hate-zone, or pay taxes to it? The pattern held until a dramatic shift in 2012, when four states put marriage equality on the ballot and marriage equality won. [8])

The arguments are absurd; they ring oddly hollow. They don't explain the fury with which they're argued. They're enhanced in sermons coming from fundamentalist pulpits, and heard by millions of impressionable congregants inclined to trust their preacher's words, by junk-science "facts" and made-up statistics churned out by Dr. Paul Cameron, a roundly discredited (and unlicensed) psychologist who was

---

8 Find the lists at the end of this chapter.

thrown out of the American Psychological Association in 1983 and has been pretty universally condemned for his shoddy and misleading work. He now runs the Family Research Institute in Colorado Springs.

I listened to one of those sermons, from First Baptist Church of Central Florida in Orlando, and had an email exchange with the preacher. I told him that to swallow whole this junk science smear of a whole class of people, and to repeat it, is to smear that class of people. I asked him if he had any sense of the damage that does to those people. Not surprisingly, the "dialogue" ended there.

It's faith-based hate. Part of its arsenal is a denial of the evolving nature of marriage.

The truth is that marriage *has* changed and evolved as our understanding of human complexities, and freedoms, and dignity have evolved, and it's a good thing that it has, because for long ages, marriage was a work and property contract that upheld the principle that the husband was lord and master in the marriage. Until the Married Womens' Property Acts of the nineteenth century, marriage meant—for a woman—signing over all she owned to her husband. This principle, which was then essential to the definition of marriage, was expressed in 1765 by Lord Blackstone, who consolidated British common law. He wrote: "In law husband and wife are one person, and the husband is that person." The changes took a long time—between 1840 and 1893—because they touched off a death-of-the-family panic. A New York legislative committee argued that allowing married women to control their own property would lead "to infidelity in the marriage bed, a high rate of divorce, and increased female criminality," while turning marriage from "its high and holy purposes." The *Times* of London screeched that the reform would "abolish families in the old sense."

And—until *1967* it was illegal in seventeen states to marry someone of another race.

Yes, marriage has changed, fundamentally, in many ways, and it's a good thing it has, and it's time to change it again.

And how odd to be told that marriage has not changed in three thousand years by a former Massachusetts governor Romney, whose Mormon great-grandfather had five wives and whose great-great-grandfather had thirteen, according to Mormon records! The arguments, apparently, don't need to be rational. It's really about something else.

What do we call it when, against all evidence, we are told in a *Boston Globe* op-ed that gay and lesbian people are responsible for the poor quality the author attributes to heterosexual marriages? The author of the op-ed, by the way, was Shaun O'Malley, the new archbishop of Boston.[9]

He goes on to say that opposition to the right to marry simply doesn't imply opposition to the civil rights of gay people. So what were those lobbyists from the Archdiocese doing in the legislative chambers in Boston in the 1980s, when, after seventeen years, we were still trying to pass a basic civil rights amendment affecting employment, housing, and credit? I was there for the UUA trying to lobby *for* it. *They* were there doing everything they could to defeat it. To claim to have supported the civil rights of gay and lesbian people is dishonest.

What is it when logic is contorted to reach a predetermined conclusion? Is procreation the *sine qua non* of marriage or isn't it? Once, the Catholic church refused marriage to people who were too old to bear children. Now, couples are not asked about their ability or even willingness to do so. Meanwhile, many same-sex couples *do* raise children. But still the argument is dragged out. Why?

When it seeks to deny to same-sex couples the ability to collect the pension or social security benefits, say, or access to the emergency room, and about 1400 other protections—it is disingenuous in the extreme to tell those who are relegated to second-class status that they should—and I quote Shaun O'Malley—"be reassured that the church wants all people to live in harmony and mutual respect and to have everyone's legitimate civil rights guaranteed." The denial of these things, and the whitewashing of the facts, cannot be done "with charity."

WHEN WE HAVE EXHAUSTED the contorted logic and the non sequiturs and dubious assertions of ominous threat—*what is left*, behind the sentimentality and the pious mask—but the latest manifestation in the

9 Thursday, March 11, 2004.

saga of faith-based hate. It is the never-failing fountain of convoluted logic and twisted arguments.

The hateful signs at the Massachusetts State House and the epithet yelled at me on the street in liberal downtown Northampton not long ago speak more truth about the grounds of queer peoples' second-class status in this society than all the platitudes of the churches about harmony, charity, and respect.

WHEN WE HATE—DO WE always *mean* to hate?

What *is* hate? Is it a feeling? Who is guilty of it? What does it do to us?

IT HAS LONG BEEN SOCIALLY ACCEPTABLE to bash gay folks. How does a hate become popular, pervasive?

In Victor Klemperer's *LTI: The Language of the Third Reich*,[10] the Jewish professor at Dresden University until forced to live in a "Jew House," who barely escaped the death camps, analyzes the massively clever manipulation of language to bring about a state in which sheer hatred of Jews could become the entire engine behind the Nazi juggernaut and the fanatical popular embrace of it (the cruder and less well-sorted the individual, the more fanatical). In the chapter "The Jewish War," you observe something of how this was achieved—so that the most innocent of the young, brought up in this perverse universe, even while aware of the contradictions and cruelties and eager to see the end of the Reich, knew and never questioned that all this war, and all this horror, and every social ill, was the fault of the Jewish pigs, who were due nothing better than contempt. The "language" was more than words, and included symbols of various kinds, beginning with the star which must never be hidden. It's a language which, as Klemperer has it, "writes and thinks for you."

I don't have to dwell long on the question, *Could this be accomplished again, in this cosmopolitan country, with all its cultural and intellectual*

10 Victor Klemperer. *LTI—Lingua Tertii Imperii. The Language of the Third Reich.* London and New York: Continuum, 2000, 2006. First published in 1947.

assets? In fact, I wake every morning to some new attempt, aimed at another target, queer people, gay, lesbian, transgendered people. Only the perpetrators this time aren't quite as good at it.

Nevertheless, it is there, and it is effective. *Family. Protecting the family. Family Defence Act. Morality. Special privilege. Actively homosexual. Homosexual activists. Homosexual Agenda. Demean the traditional family.* The language writes and thinks for you.

SHAME ON RELIGIOUS PEOPLE who practice, rather than challenge, this popular sin of bigotry. All this took a particularly stunning turn when the lead spokesman for the anti-same-sex-marriage crusade in Western Massachusetts, when confronted with charges of staggering hypocrisy, could not be found to answer to the charges. The Roman Catholic bishops of Massachusetts conducted rallies throughout the state in early 2004 to oppose same-sex marriage. In Western Massachusetts, Springfield bishop Thomas Dupre visited parishes, too, to promote a constitutional amendment defining marriage exclusively in hetero-sexual terms. Then he vanished. Two men who had kept his secret for years were finally persuaded by the sheer hypocrisy of Dupre's crusade to go to the Springfield *Republican* with their story. When they were boys—one of them a twelve-year-old refugee—Dupre had introduced them to sex and pornography. The abuse had continued for some years. The *Republican* confronted him with their allegation; he resigned and checked himself into an undisclosed facility.[11]

My first reaction was anger for the stunning duplicity. But the anger shifted quickly to an anger and a sorrow for the tragedy of his life—a life so arranged that it required hypocrisy to survive. We must always

---

11 The anti-same-sex-marriage rallies were reported in William Zajac, "Bishop pushes for gay marriage ban," *Springfield Republican*, Jan. 13, 2004, in Michael Paulson and Raphael Lewis, "Weaker church tested on marriage," *Boston Globe*, Jan. 18, 2004, and in Jenn Abelson and Jack Hagel, "Gay-marriage opponents rally across state," *Boston Globe*, Jan. 26, 2004; the scandal was reported in William Zajac, "DA to present abuse case against Dupre," *Springfield Republican*, March 4, 2004 and Kevin Cullen, "Grand jury eyes charges for bishop; Hampden DA points to abuse accusations," *Boston Globe*, March 5, 2004. The Associated Press also reported the story on March 4.

ask the ways in which institutions shape the lives, for good or for ill, of those who live and work within them.

IF WE KNOW THAT AN UNENDING succession of wars and crusades and witch-hunts have flowed from faith-based hate, then I think we ought to own it as our mission to reach out to its victims and guard against its destructiveness. And vow to be honest about our own feelings, and to become as conscious as we can of the consequences of *our* actions and *our* inaction. Love and hate are more than sentiments.

I CALL THE COURAGEOUS *GOODRIDGE* decision of the Massachusetts Supreme Judicial Court an act of love.

The extraordinary uproar over the Massachusetts Supreme Judicial Court decision in November 2003 in *Goodridge v. Department of Public Health*—declaring that there is no constitutional basis for denying marriage to same-sex couples—owes to a peculiar anomaly in American life, because America professes to believe in the separation of church and state. And the problem *behind* the problem of the seething battle over same-sex marriage is the unfortunate *marriage* of church and state in the institution of marriage. The consequences ought to be a wake-up call that it's time, at last, to separate the legal status of civil marriage from the religio-sacramental realm.

This church-state entanglement has been with us so long we seldom notice the incongruity. The distinction between *civil* and *sacramental* has remained blurred, with the result that religious institutions think that they hold far too much of a stake in the definition of *civil* marriage.

Somehow this marriage of church and state has gone on relatively uncontested. State Rep. Matthew Patrick of Falmouth seemed absolutely anguished over the conflict between the prospect of the proposed "Defense of Marriage" amendment watering down the state's Bill of Rights,—torn between that, and churchly claims to the right to define marriage, saying: "To me, a marriage between a man and a woman is a sacrament under the laws of the church."[12] (Rep. Patrick decided for

12 Raphael Lewis. "In lawmaker poll, few back limiting marriage; Political debate shifts to accommodate SJC." *Boston Globe*, Dec. 1, 2003.

the Bill of Rights, and voted against two constitutional amendments banning same-sex marriage.)

The attempt to preserve this tangled relationship has resulted in appalling statements by public officials and from the Archdiocese asserting that the Courts have no role in protecting the Constitutional rights of citizens when legislatures fail to do so, or when popular opinion runs against dignity and equality. To so argue is to set oneself against *Oliver L. Brown et. al. vs. The Board of Education of Topeka*, by which the Supreme Court ruled, despite adamant public opinion to the contrary, to end segregated school systems, because separate is not equal. It is to repudiate *Loving v. Virginia*, by which the Court, in 1967, overturned very popular laws in 17 states banning interracial marriage.

Both decisions were probably more unpopular than *Goodridge*. Two years before *Loving*, a Gallup poll found that 72 per cent of Southern whites and 42 per cent of Northern whites still wanted to ban interracial marriage.

THE DAY THE MASSACHUSETTS SUPREME Judicial Court's decision *Goodridge v. Board of Public Health* took effect, City Hall at Northampton, where I was minister of the Unitarian Society next door, was awash in couples, friends, activists and press. One hundred thirteen couples applied for licenses that day in our little city of 32,000—surpassed only by Cambridge and Provincetown. By the waterfall at Smith College where they first kissed, I pronounced, for the first time, the words "by the authority vested in me by the Commonwealth of Massachusetts" to two women. It was a simple ceremony: they'd had a fancy wedding at our church years before, and now they were parents of a beautiful little girl. This marriage had already passed the test of time. What they wanted now was the protections everybody else assumes, and wouldn't, without a furious battle, surrender: surviving spouse benefits of many kinds, protections for home and property, children and health, and many having to do with circumstances you don't like to think about. But that simple phrase had an astonishing power and eloquence in every one of a dozen same-sex marriage ceremonies I've conducted.

The dilemma Massachusetts same-sex couples faced on tax day made immediate and real the meaning of the Defense of Marriage Act (DOMA), signed shamefully by President Clinton. State returns were filed jointly, but what about the federal ones? What Massachusetts did was barely the beginning of the revolution. A succession of courtrooms loomed to press the validity, elsewhere, of marriage made in Massachusetts. *Goodridge* said as much: "The history of constitutional law 'is the story of the extension of constitutional rights and protections to people once ignored or excluded'"—itself quoting *United States v. Virginia*, involving sex discrimination on the part of state institutions.

But whatever storms cloud their future, the couples I married, and the ones I know about, are ready for it. Virtually every one is already of long duration. They've waited for this recognition without any great anticipation it would ever come. Some wanted elaborate ceremonies. Others wanted only the simplest of rites, accompanied by a Massachusetts marriage license and the hundreds of protections it brings. But the enormity of the moment escaped none of them. The first of the male couples has, since their marriage, tirelessly crisscrossed Western Massachusetts to campaign against the discriminatory amendment to the Massachusetts Constitution.

As of this writing, over twenty thousand same-sex couples have married in Massachusetts. A Lake Research Partners survey in 2009 found that 74 percent of Massachusetts voters favor same-sex marriage.; only 23 percent were opposed. In the Spring of 2009, Massachusetts was joined by Vermont, then New Hampshire, then Maine when those states' legislatures all acted in rapid succession. In Vermont, the legislature overrode a Republican govern's veto. An even bigger surprise: the Iowa Supreme Court unanimously legalized same-sex marriage. In Connecticut the state Supreme Court ordered the recognition of same-sex marriages in November 2008; the case was argued by Attorney General Richard Blumenthal, subsequently elected to the U.S. Senate. Rhode Island awaited the end of a Republican governor's term; his successor, Gov. Lincoln Chaffee, supported same-sex marriage. Powerful Roman Catholic Church opposition slowed the process, but marriage equality passed both houses of the legislalture with surprising majorities in the Spring of 2013, and Chaffee signed the bill into law in a big public ceremony outside the State House in Providence. I had the honor of conducting Newport's first legally recognized same-sex marriage ceremony: a couple who'd been "engaged" for 35 years, members of Channing Memorial Church.

In New York, same-sex marriage had been passed in the state Assembly but was defeated in 2009 by a Democratic controlled Senate. But in 2010, New York's new Democratic governor Andrew Cuomo made its passage a serious priority, and in June 2011 the now Republican-controlled Senate passed it on a 33-29 vote (with four Republicans in favor and one Democrat opposed). With New York recognizing same-sex marriage, the number of Americans having that right doubled. In 2004 a Quinnipiac poll showed 37 percent of New Yorkers favoring marriage equality; in 2011 support had risen to 58 percent. The vote was witnessed on television screens by a throng that crowded the Stonewall Inn, site of the 1969 revolt against police brutality against gay people. Sixty-two year old Danny Garvin had been there in 1969; he came back to the reopened Stonewall to watch the tide turn.[13]

In Maine, a coalition of fundamentalists, the Republican party, and the Roman Catholic Church managed to get enough signatures to force a public referendum on the right to marry, and the law was repealed on a 53-47 percent vote.

It was a bitter loss: but I remembered how it had once been in Maine. In the mid-1980s I served the Unitarian Church of Bangor, having been called there by its gutsy congregation just a year after a twenty-three-year-old member named Charlie Howard had been murdered in a clearcut case of gay-bashing—while on his way home from church. He'd moved to the "big city" of Bangor (population 30,000) after being relentlessly harassed in a small Maine town. Here, he thought, he could live openly, and in safety. But in Bangor, too, the harassment and humiliation was unending. He found community and genuine welcome at the Unitarian Church, which had a noble history of opposing slavery and antisemitism. But one day, walking home, he was spotted by three

13 Nicholas Confessore and Michael Barbaro, "Gay marriage approved by N.Y. Senate. *New York Times*, 24 June 2011.

Bangor High School students. They jumped out of their car, chased him down, yelling *"Faggot!"* and *"Queer!,"* and threw him down the high bulkheads into the Kenduskeag Stream, which runs through the downtown. The rapid tide carried his body away. When we scheduled a memorial service for Charlie one year after his death, the *Bangor Daily News* responded with an editorial titled "Not a Martyr." In sum: we all know it's wrong to kill somebody but he did bring it on himself by his effeminate manner. I steamed to the office of the editor and thrust a response into his hand.

So consider: twenty-four years later, the same *Bangor Daily News* editorialized *in favor* of same-sex marriage, and the city of Bangor voted to retain same-sex marriage. Portland voted by something like two and a half to one to keep same-sex marriage. True, the small inland towns and a few working-class coastal communities weren't quite there yet, but it will come. Looked at from a longer perspective, the forward movement had been breathtaking.

In the first year of the Massachusetts law, the far right and the Boston Roman Catholic archdiocese targeted for electoral defeat those legislators who supported us in the first stage of the struggle to prevent a public referendum on our right to marry. Not one was defeated, and we gained five seats. If the idea was unthinkable to many of our neighbors a year earlier, it wasn't anymore.

What the bishops want to protect is religious rite and doctrine. But those are not endangered. No religious body will be compelled to open its sacrament of marriage to any couple whose relationship they don't approve. They can exclude anybody they want to and the law can't do anything about it, just as they can exclude women from religious leadership. But it's wrong to shut out all same-sex couples from *civil* marriage, and worse still to do so on the basis of tired arguments long invoked to support segregation.

Just what is it, anyway, that the professed marriage "protectors" are trying to protect? For many years and still as I write—the state with the very lowest failure rate for marriages in the entire United States is our very Massachusetts! The highest divorce rates and the highest teenage birthrates can be found in the Bible belt.

The Court pointed out that marriage has *not* remained "unchanged for 3,000 years," as then-Governor Romney argued (his great and great-great-grandfathers' multiple marriages notwithstanding); that it took the courts to end the ban on marriage between races or to assure a married woman's property rights; and concluded "Marriage has survived all of these transformations, and we have no doubt that marriage will continue to be a vibrant and revered institution." Marriage *has* changed. Once, marriage had to do with male supremacy and property law. This was essential to its definition. Thus, slaves could not precisely marry—how could property own property? (But something like marriage suited their owners because it produced more slaves; though the man and the woman might yet be resold—separately.) And until the Married Womens' Property Acts of the 19th century, all land or property belonging to the woman was signed over to her husband. It took most of that century to pass those reforms in America and Britain because religious people kept arguing that for a woman to own her own property would fundamentally change the nature of marriage and families.

Here's something else that was considered essential to the definition of marriage. The Catholic Church has long held that the *sine qua non* of marriage is procreation. For many centuries the Roman Catholic Church refused to bless remarrying widows and widowers, especially if the woman was too old to bear children.

That is at least far more consistent than the modernday politician or theologian who argues that the *sine qua non* of marriage is procreation, and then acknowledges as legitimate marriages between people who are either unable or unwilling to produce children.

By a 5-4 vote in July 2006, Washington's Supreme Court judges ruled that "limiting marriage to opposite-sex couples furthers procreation, essential to the survival of the human race . . ."

During the demonstrations at one of the Massachusetts Constitutional Conventions on the anti- same-sex-marriage amendment, I noted a large sign, held by an opponent, reading:

$$\text{Adam} + \text{Eve}$$
$$= 6 \text{ billion}$$

$$\text{Adam} + \text{Steve}$$
$$= 0$$

Extraordinary, I thought. Did not the protestor see a problem with this? Six billion plus—no, now it's seven billion. It took all of human history for that number to reach two billion—and then, *in my lifetime*, it has exploded, and is likely to reach *ten* billion by 2050. A quarter of these can't get decent potable water. This many of us are ravaging the earth and depleting its resources. Six or seven or ten billion is too many. Zero is too few. Shouldn't the figure be somewhere in between? That is why we're not all supposed to be alike. Some must reproduce (and some of these are gay); but please, not all. To expect everyone to reproduce is, in the current predicament, deeply immoral.

The Washington court didn't stop there. The phrase continued "and furthers the well-being of children by encouraging families where children are reared in homes headed by the children's biological parents." Children, the decision continues, "tend to thrive in families consisting of a father, mother and their biological children." A concurring opinion added that "binary biological nature of marriage" meant that only opposite-sex couples are capable of "responsible child rearing." Thus ignoring the rights of the many *children* of gay couples. Don't they have a right to have *married* parents, with the protections and benefits marriage provides? What sort of mind occupies the benches of high courts?

Finally, on August 4, 2010, a fine shaft of judicial light. But first, some background: In 2004, San Francisco filed a challenge to California's exclusion of same-sex couples from marriage. That provoked a court review, which produced a 2008 ruling that the state's prohibition of same-sex marriage violated the equal protection guarantee in the California Constitution. The ruling invalidated a law passed in 2000 by public referendum (Proposition 22). All California counties were now required to issue marriage licenses to gay couples. In reaction, a campaign heavily funded by the Mormons (the LDS) put Proposition 8—a constitutional ban—on the ballot. The same night Californians learned Obama had won the election, they learned that "Prop 8" had passed.

In May 2009 an extraordinary legal team headed by the two opposing lawyers in the 2000 election imbroglio—Theodore B. Olson and David Boies—filed what seemed a risky suit arguing that in passing Prop 8, California voters violated the United States Constitution. Olson had argued—successfully—on behalf of George W. Bush in the contested Florida election of 2000, and is held in high regard by conservative Republicans.

The August 4, 2010 ruling came from the Chief Judge of the U.S. District Court for Northern California, Vaughn Walker, a conservative Republican appointed by President George H.W. Bush. In eighty carefully reasoned points spanning 138 pages, Walker demolished the case behind Prop 8 and declared it unconstitutional. "Proposition 8 fails to advance any rational basis for singling out gay men and lesbians for denial of a marriage license," he wrote, adding "proponents, amici and the court, despite ample opportunity and a full trial, have failed to identify any rational basis Proposition 8 could conceivably advance." More: "The evidence at trial regarding the campaign to pass Proposition 8," he wrote, "uncloaks the most likely explanation for its passage: a desire to advance the belief that opposite-sex couples are morally superior to same-sex couples." He cited much of the campaign message and media promoting Prop 8—evidence replete with examples of vile defamation.

He found the "expert witnesses" defending Prop 8 unqualified to make the judgments they were touting, and said they made no sense. "In the absence of a rational basis, what remains of proponents' case is an inference, amply supported by evidence in the record, that Proposition 8 was premised on the belief that same-sex couples simply are not as good as opposite-sex couples. Whether that belief is based on moral disapproval of homosexuality, animus towards gays and lesbians or simply a belief that a relationship between a man and a woman is inherently better than a relationship between two men or two women, this belief is not a proper basis on which to legislate."

Especially significant was his analysis of the function of evolving gender roles: "The evidence shows that the movement of marriage away from a gendered institution and toward an institution free from state-mandated gender roles reflects an evolution in the understanding of gender rather than a change in marriage. The evidence did not show any historical purpose for excluding same-sex couples from marriage, as states have never required spouses to have an ability or willingness to procreate in order to marry."

He denied that an end to the ban on same-sex marriage in any way threatens heterosexual marriage or the civil rights of those who have moral objections to same-sex marriage. He was particularly severe on the appeals to fear, especially when some "inchoate" threat to children was invoked. Prop 8's defenders didn't have the goods—not, at least, when facing an intelligent, informed judge—who hoisted them on their own antiquated moralistic and gender-role petard.

As it happens, Judge Walker happens also to be gay. That fact might fuel the faith-based hate, but it creates a splendid object lesson. Do those who object wish to argue that only heterosexuals may determine the rights and dignity of the gay minority—as they have long done? Do they wish to argue that Thurgood Marshall should have recused himself from civil rights cases? That female justices should withdraw from cases involving the rights of women and just let the men decide? I found the scene delicious. But there was plenty to turn the stomach: a storm of faith-based vilification of Judge Walker and a fresh yet deeply rancid wave of anti-gay defamation coming from Tea Party Republicans and talkshow hosts including Rush Limbaugh. In fact, when Judge Walker was appointed, it was over the protests of liberals and gay-rights activists, who had previously experienced him as adversary.

The Supreme Court finally ruled on both DOMA and Proposition 8 on June 26, 2013, striking down DOMA and undercutting Prop 8 by leaving Judge Walker's ruling, and a subsequent one by the U.S. Court of Appeals for the 9th Circuit, intact.

The end of DOMA came in a ruling on *United States v. Windsor*, which concerned Edith Windsor, who was widowed when her wife Thea

Spyer died in 2009. Windsor and Spyer were married in 2007 in Canada after being partners for 40 years. Windsor was forced to pay $363,053 in estate tax on Spyer's estate, which she argues she would not have to pay if she had been Spyer's husband. The Defense of Marriage Act prevented her from being considered Spyer's spouse for the purposes of federal taxes. She got her $363,053 back. And millions got the right to marry.

In 2003, far-right Supreme Court Justice Antonin Scalia had complained that the Court's landmark gay rights case, *Lawrence v. Texas*, which decriminalized consensual sodomy, had "largely signed onto the so-called homosexual agenda" and warned that the decision placed "on pretty shaky grounds" state laws limiting marriage to opposite-sex couples. To his displeasure, his prophecy has proven true. Because since the last days of 2013, courts in an astonishing array of states (Utah, Ohio, Oklahoma, Texas, Virginia, Michigan, Utah, Arkansas, Pennsylvania, Oregon, and Wisconsin as of this writing) have ruled that same-sex marriages must be recognized. Every one of these courts drew the same application from the Supreme Court's rulings. It's hard to see how any American state can resist this groundwave.

A SEA-CHANGE, long building, made its appearance in the 2012 election. As it was becoming clear that President Obama had won reëlection, something that had never before happened also emerged: in three states in which GLBT advocates themselves had put marriage equality on the ballot, they won. Maryland, Washington, and finally Maine would recognize same-sex marriage. A ballot question in Minnesota intended to amend the state constitution to bar same-sex marriage failed and, in May 2013, the legislature made Minnesota the first midwestern state to legalize same-sex marriage via legislative vote. Also in 2013, Rhode Island, Delaware, New Jersey (ordered by its courts), Illinois, and Hawaii brought the list to sixteen. Democratic attorneys general in at least seven states—Virginia, Pennsylvania, California, Illinois, Oregon, Kentucky and Nevada—have declined to defend same-sex-marriage bans that have been challenged in court by gay couples. In May 2014, judges in

Arkansas, Idaho, and Oregon ruled those states' marriage bans uncon-stitutional, without issuing stays—making same-sex marriage legal immediately (though Arkansas officials were seeking a stay). Later that month, a G.W. Bush-appointed federal judge in Pennsylvania declared the state's ban (the last standing in the Northeast) unconstitutional, saying "We are a better people than what these laws represent, and it is time to discard them into the ash heap of history." Without issuing a stay, he wrote "By virtue of this ruling, same-sex couples who seek to marry in Pennsylvania may do so, and already married same-sex couples will be recognized as such in the Commonwealth."[14]

If CHURCH DOGMA IS GOING to determine policy—well, *which church?* Is it right to base laws and constitutions on Catholic or evangelical dogma, even while other religious bodies including my own Unitarian Univer-salist Association, now joined by Reform and Reconstructionist Judaism, the Quakers, the Metropolitan Community Churches, and the United Church of Christ, hold the right of same-sex couples to marry essential to the recognition of the intrinsic rights and dignity of every person?[15]

But *civil* marriage—what Massachusetts, and Connecticut, Vermont, New Hampshire, Maine, Iowa, New York, Washington, Maryland, Minnesota, Rhode Island, Delaware, New Jersey, Illinois, Hawaii, Idaho, Oregon, Pennsylvania, Wisconsin and the District of Columbia (some with a hot of help from the courts); and Belgium, the Netherlands, Norway, Iceland, Spain, Portugal, South Africa, and Canada, and the United Kingdom, as well as (with limitations) other European Union and some South American countries have addressed—has to do with advantages taken for granted by heterosexual couples and considered

---

14 Angela Couloumbis and Amy Worden. "U.S. judge strikes down same-sex marriage ban in Pa." *Philadelphia Inquirer,* May 20, 2014.

15 In June 20014 the Presbyterian Church (USA) voted at its General Assembly in Detroit to change its constitution's language from "a man and a woman" to "two people" to accommodate same-sex marriage, reversing previous votes. Thre change must still be approved by a majority of the denomination's 72 regional presbyteries. About 350 congregations left the denomination after its 2010 vote to ordain GLBT ministers, and many more are currently organizing a breakaway denomination— including the Presbyterian Church of Toms River, where I grew up.

essential by them. It means access to the intensive care unit of a hospital or, in the event of death, the right to determine the disposition of one's partner's remains. It means permanent residency or citizenship—not deportation—for a partner when a committed relationship forms across national boundaries. There are social security benefits, pensions, tax and property issues. (Civil *union* provides only certain *state* benefits and nothing more.)

Under the old regime, I could sign a marriage license, easily obtainable by a heterosexual couple, and my signature entitled them to recognition and safeguards for their relationship, and somewhere near 1,400 special rights and privileges; yet no one could sign a document that would (if I had a partner) do that for me, a gay man. That is, for me, a supreme irony that comes with the marriage of church and state.

Along with many of my colleagues—Unitarian Universalist as well as Jewish and Protestant—I stopped signing marriage licenses and serving as an operative of a discriminatory state function (we would do the religious ceremony and send the couple to a justice of the peace who, for $75, would sign the license). I'll sign them now, but prefer *not* to, and so serve as an operative of the state. Civil marriage licenses should be signed by a representative of the state (a notary can do it), not clergy.

HERE IS AN IMPORTANT ETHICAL PRINCIPLE: *it's wrong to deny to others that which you find essential for yourself.* Our opponents tell us, with no evidence, that marriage itself, and possibly their own marriages, are threatened by the prospect of same-sex couples getting married. Now weigh this extremely dubious claim against this one: suppose some legislature or court ruled that as of tomorrow heterosexual spouses wouldn't be able to collect their spouses' social security benefits or pensions, or keep the house—that their right to these things meant nothing next to the imagined threat their being married posed to other peoples' marriages?

I WENT TO CANTERBURY, ENGLAND TO CONDUCT the religious part of two dear friends' wedding, under the new British law providing the same benefits and protections to same-sex couples that heterosexual marriage affords. The language was different—this was called a Registered Partnership, because the Anglican Church blocked the use of the word marriage—but unlike civil unions in America, it actually came with all the protections and benefits. (Full same-sex marriage equality went into effect in England and Wales March 29, 2014; the CoE banned its clergy from officiating.) The next Sunday I attended the morning service at Canterbury Cathedral. I hadn't particularly wanted to go because of what, just a few days before, the Anglican worldwide communion, and the Archbishop of Canterbury, had done. The archbishop, Dr. Rowan Williams, had once been considered a progressive, pro-gay, had gay friends. But under pressure from conservative and evangelical Anglicans and particularly the right-wing Bishop of Nigeria, Archbishop Akinola, he'd caved. The issue had been the consecrating in 2003 of a bishop by the American Episcopal Church—the out gay bishop Gene Robinson of New Hampshire—and then the Episcopal Church's choice in 2006 of a woman to be Presiding Bishop. The evangelicals and conservatives were out to punish the progressives. Archbishop Akinola had already announced his support for a law in his native Nigeria, proposed by the administration of President Olusegun Obasanjo, that would impose a four or five year prison sentence on anyone who even advocated equality or civil rights protections for gay people. It's called the "Act to Make Provisions for the Prohibition of Relationship Between Persons of the Same Sex, Celebration of Marriage by Them, and for Other Matters Connected Therewith."

And what was the response of the Archbishop of Canterbury? To punish the already embattled American Episcopal Church with a demand for an apology for consecrating a gay man as bishop and promise not to do it ever again, and a proposal of a second-class status in the Anglican communion. The bigots were rewarded; those who had the guts to do the right thing would be punished. And Dr. Williams took two days even to acknowledge the new female Presiding Bishop of the Episcopal Church, Rev. Dr. Katherine Jefferts Schori; he never did congratulate her. Then in 2008 came the once-in-ten-years major conference of Anglican bishops at Lambeth, the London headquarters.

Bishop Robinson wasn't invited, but there was no disinvite for the anti-gay contingent including Akinola.

From a good and progressive man, a betrayal. And here I was in Canterbury Cathedral. I considered how to be at a service at Canterbury Cathedral. Would I be morally obligated to disrupt the service and make a speech about hypocrisy and bigotry? Happily for everyone, I was saved from the dilemma when the visiting preacher, the vicar from Putney, delivered a fine pro-gay sermon.

This allowed the Anglicans to speak out of both sides of their mouth—progressive civilized talk for the progressive domestic audience and bigotry for the larger Anglican communion. Nice trick. But moral? As in many instances of churchly sell-out, ecclesiastical unity and institutional calm becomes the highest value. Here the magic of myth allows those inhabiting two different universes—the premodern and postmodern—to use the same shared god-talk without seeming to notice that their language signifies two vastly different things; and to be deluded by the shared god-words to think they have much in common.

I won't forget the wedding. Many loyal friends descended on Kent from afar. The couple appeared with elegant Victorian top-hats and walking sticks and, at the appropriate moment in the ceremony, spoke unforgettable vows to each other. After the sister of one of the grooms made the wonderful day more memorable with her performance of "Zippity Do Da" and we proceeded inside where the County Clerk conducted the civil ceremony.

Did I mention that the United States government declined to recognize the marriage and change the names on their visa? Or that the Anglican Communion went on, in February 2007, to give the American church until September 30 to promise never to authorize celebration of same-sex relationships, or consecrate gay bishops. For the reactionaries, Archbishop Akinola was allowed to consecrate a conservative evangelical vicar in Virginia as a Nigerian bishop to oversee a rival network of American parishes wishing to opt out of the Episcopal church. The actions were taken by a fraught five-day meeting in Tanzania of the primates—archbishops and presiding bishops of Anglicanism's thirty-eight provinces around the world—and the irony goes deeper. The meetings were held in Zanzibar, just as it was commemorating the 100th anniversary of the last slave sold here and the 200th anniversary of the end of the slave trade in the British empire. Worship services (where Akinola led seven conservative archbishops in refusing to share the eucharist with Bishop Schori) were held in Christ Church, which was built in the 1870s on the site of Zanzibar's biggest slave market and has an altar where a whipping post once stood. All justified by quoting the Bible. Archbishop Akinola is unlikely to cite the biblical sanctions for slavery. But he doesn't mind invoking the biblical sanctions for oppression of women and gay people.

And the anti-gay law in Nigeria? Signed into law in January 2014 by President Goodluck Jonathan, it criminalizes homosexuality, imposing a fourteen-year sentence for anyone who "directly or indirectly" makes a "public show" of a same-sex relationship. It also punishes anyone who participates in a gay club or organization, or who simply supports them. Roman Catholic Archbishop Ignatius Kaigama of Jos congratulated President Jonathan: "We commend you for this courageous and wise decision and pray that God will continue to bless, guide and protect you and your administration against the conspiracy of the developed world to make our country and continent, the dumping ground for the promotion of all immoral practices, that have continued to debase the purpose of God for man in the area of creation and morality, in their own countries." Many Nigerians want the penalty prescribed by local Islamic law to be imposed: death by stoning. Police in Nigeria were accused of using torture and entrapment to compile lists of men assumed to be gay, leading to dozens of arrests.

It coincided with a draconian Ugandan law, finally passed in December 2013 and, after he initially refused, signed by President Yoweri Museveni in February 2014. Predictably, both laws legitimized bigotry, and antigay violence spiked in both countries.

Scott Lively, the American head of the right-wing Abiding Truth Ministries, based in Springfield, Mass., is alleged to have played a major role in crafting the anti-gay legislation in Uganda. As of this writing, he is being sued in U.S. federal court by Sexual Minorities Uganda (SMUG), the leading LGBT rights group in that nation, through the

Center for Constitutional Rights in US federal court.

And, as of this writing, more than 2.7 billion people live in countries where being gay is a crime.[16]

WHERE THEY EXIST, THE NEW legal and economic protections for same-sex couples will prevent a lot of heartache and suffering. When the peace activist James Loney was taken hostage while serving as a member of a Christian Peacemaker Team in Baghdad in 2006, his longtime partner Dan Hunt found he had no legal standing as Loney's partner to be kept informed by authorities during the four months of captivity. And for Loney, there was the constant fear that his religious fundamentalist fanatic captors would discover that he is gay—particularly after one of his three co-hostages, Tom Fox, was executed. In less dramatic ways, heterosexual couples rely on a multitude of assumed forms of respect.

Beyond this, there's something sublime after all these years, all these legislative struggles and battles for hearts and minds—to feel a palpable sense of equality and normalcy. Now, love can be simply *love*; and marriage, *marriage*. If some families include children and some don't, that distinction doesn't correlate with sexual orientation. We're all simply human beings with a whole lot more in common than what separates us. When it dawned on a middle-school student in the Northamapton congregation that same-sex couples couldn't marry, she was genuinely shocked. Bigotry isn't a necessary human condition.

And so we sense a new dispensation. We have seen its first manifestations. Narrowness of soul, and the citadels that maintain it, are shaken. I have thought often of long years spent arguing for the really simple things—like protection from discrimination in employment and housing—and of the defamatory rhetoric, and the faith-based hate, we have faced. I recall the firebomb that struck my car in Hartford during the Anita Bryant anti-gay crusade in the 70s. I remember the first Pride march in Worcester, Mass., when maybe thirty of us faced flying cans and stones and a preacher with a very large Bible and a very long,

16 James Ball. "More than 2.7 billion people live in countries where being gay is a crime," *The Guardian*, 16 May 2014.

pointed finger. Now, as I write, four separate polls—including CNN and ABC/*Washington Post,* have shown a (thin) majority of the American public *supporting* same-sex marriage.

MY OWN UNITARIAN AND UNIVERSALIST forebears agonized, searched their souls, over the meaning of love and hate and their faith. Even the best can betray the demands of love. Unitarian's own American "founder," the great William Ellery Channing, remained silent about slavery until 1835, and it took a confrontation from the heroic Rev. Samuel J. May, who revered Channing, yet dared interrupt one of Channing's discussions about the reasons he wouldn't join the call for immediate abolition of slavery—by letting loose an indictment that stunned both of them. He heard himself suddenly saying:

> Dr. Channing, I am tired of these complaints. . . .The cry of millions, suffering the most cruel bondage in our land, had been heard for half a century and disregarded. 'The wise and prudent' saw the terrible wrong, but thought it not wise and prudent to lift a finger for its correction. . . .
>
> Dr. Channing, . . . We are not to blame, sir, that you, who, more perhaps than any other man, might have so raised the voice of remonstrance that it should have been heard throughout the length and breadth of the land,—we are not to blame, sir, that you have not so spoken. . . . Why, sir, have you not taken this matter in hand yourself? Why have you not spoken to the nation long ago, as you, better than any other one, could have spoken?[17]

And at this the great man sat silent, and then he said, *Brother May, I acknowledge the justice of your reproof. I have been silent too long.* And he spent the remaining seven years of his life speaking boldly what his gut had known all along.

Before the year was out, in the name of love, William Ellery Channing had published his daring book against slavery[18], and from that day forward, the attorney general of the Commonwealth, a member of his congregation, would cross the street to avoid looking at him, but that

17 Samuel J. May. *Some Recollections of Our Antislavery Conflict.* Boston: Fields, Osgood & Co., 1869, 170ff.

18 *Slavery.* Boston: James Munroe and Company, 1835.

attorney general is long forgotten, and the name of William Ellery Channing hallows the Unitarian faith.

Once, at a Unitarian Universalist General Assembly, Kurt Vonnegut delivered an address on right-wing religion. His title: *Love Is Too Strong a Word*. Religious people ought to be a little careful before we apply the word to our utterances and stances. The pathways of love are sometimes lonely.

AS OF MARCH 2014:

The states that have passed legislation against legal recognition of same-sex marriage or broader anti-gay family measures are listed below. Those that have even amended their constitutions are indicated by an asterisk.

Alabama*
Alaska*
Arizona
Arkansas*
California*
Colorado*
Delaware
Florida*
Georgia*
Hawaii
Idaho*
Illinois
Indiana
Kansas*
Louisiana*
Kentucky*
Maine (the prohibition was reversed by the Legislature which, in May 2009, approved same-sex marriage pending a public referendum, where same-sex marriage was defeated)
Michigan*
Minnesota
Mississippi*
Missouri*
Montana*
Nebraska*
New Hampshire (reversed by the Legislature which, in April 2009, approved same-sex marriage)
Nevada*

North Carolina*
North Dakota*
Ohio*
Oklahoma*
Oregon*
Pennsylvania
South Carolina*
South Dakota*
Tennessee*
Texas*
Utah*
West Virginia
Virginia*
Wisconsin*

In the United States, same-sex marriage is recognized in:
Massachusetts, since 2004
Connecticut, since 2008
Vermont, since 2009
New Hampshire, since 2009
Iowa, since 2009
District of Columbia, since 2010
New York, since 2011
Washington, since 2012
Maine, since 2012
Maryland, since 2012
Washington, since 2012
Minnesota, since 2013
Rhode Island, since 2013
Delaware, since 2013
New Jersey, since 2013
Illinois, since 2013
Hawaii, since 2013
Idaho, 2014, per ruling by U.S. magistrate judge
Oregon, 2014
Pennsylvaniaa, 2014
Wisconsin, 2014, per ruling by federal judge

States recognizing civil unions:
Nevada

States where status is uncertain pending resolution of 2014 court action:
Utah
Ohio
Oklahoma
Virgina

Texas
Michigan
Arkansas

OF SEX AND SIN

But first, a story.

William Blake, 1793
From *The Marriage of Heaven and Hell*

An Angel came to me and said: "O pitiable foolish young man! O horrible! O dreadful state! Consider the hot burning dungeon thou art preparing for thyself to all eternity, to which thou art going in such a career."

I said: "Perhaps you will be willing to shew me my eternal lot. We will contemplate together upon it, and see whether your lot or mine is most desirable."

So he took me thro' a stable and thro' a church and down into the church vault, at the end of which was a mill: thro' the mill we went, and came to a cave: down the winding cavern we groped our tedious way, till a void boundless as a nether sky appear'd beneath us, and we held by the roots of trees and hung over this immensity; but I said, "If you please, we will commit ourselves to this void, and see whether providence is here also: if you will not, I will;" but he answer'd: "Do not presume, O young man, but as we here remain, behold thy lot which will soon appear."

By degrees we beheld the infinite Abyss, fiery as the smoke of a burning city; beneath us, at an immense distance, was the sun, black but shining; round it were fiery tracks on which revolv'd vast spiders, crawling after their prey, which flew, or rather swum, in the infinite deep, in the most terrific shapes of animals sprung from corruption; and the air was full of them, and seem'd composed of them: these are Devils. I now asked my companion which was my eternal lot: he said: "between the black and white spiders."

But now, from between the black and white spider, a cloud of fire burst and rolled thro' the deep, black'ning all beneath, so that the nether deep grew dark as a sea, and rolled with a terrible noise; beneath us was nothing now to be seen but a dark tempest, till looking east between the clouds and the waves, we saw a cataract of blood mixed with fire, and not many stones' throw from us appear'd and sunk again the scaly fold of a monstrous serpent; at last, appear'd a fiery crest above the waves; slowly it reared like two globes of crimson fire, from which the sea fled away in clouds of smoke; and now we saw it was the head of Leviathan; his forehead was divided into streaks of green and purple: soon we saw his mouth and red gills hang just above the raging foam, tinging the dark deep with beams of blood, advancing toward us with all the fury of a spiritual existence.

My friend the Angel climb'd up from his station into the mill: I remain'd alone; and then this appearance was no more, but I found myself sitting on a pleasant banks beside a river by moonlight, hearing a harper, who sung to the harp; and his theme was: "The one who never alters his opinion is like standing water, and breeds reptiles of the mind."

*But I arose and sought for the mill, and there I
found my Angel, who, surprised, asked me how I escaped?*

*I answered: "All that we saw was owing to your
metaphysics; for when you ran away, I found myself on a
bank by moonlight hearing a harper. But now we have
seen my eternal lot, shall I show you yours?"*

THERE IS, PERMEATING this culture, a powerful force of fear and loathing that frequently turns to hate and violence, a fear and loathing both
fed and cherished by our religious traditions.

It is the same primitive fear and loathing, whether it's seen in the
Massachusetts Bay Colony promulgating its famous "Body of Laws
and Liberties" in 1641, which made lovemaking between men a crime
punishable by death;—or whether it's seen in three high school boys,
carefully taught it at home, who are throwing a gay man off a bridge in
Bangor, Maine, in July of 1984—or in the death Matthew Shepard;—

Or whether it's a majority of the Supreme Court Justices in June
1986 handing down a ruling declaring that the right of privacy protects
heterosexuals but does not extend to gay and lesbian people, not even
in the privacy of their bedrooms—a ruling that upheld a Georgia law
that quotes the Bible;—I mean, of course, the 1986 ruling in *Hardwick
v. Bowers* to send the state into the bedrooms of America to find and
root out the object of their fear and loathing, in the words of dissenting
Justice Blackmun, "invad[ing] the houses, hearts and minds of citizens
who choose to live their lives differently."[1]

And on that Fourth of July weekend when the Court announced its
decision, the promise of liberty and justice for all was declared a fraud.
For the ensuring seventeen years, gay and lesbian Americans would
have to question all preachments about patience, working within the

---

1 *New York Times,* July 1, 1986, p.A18.

system, and pursuing only nonviolent courses. The *Hardwick* decision was reversed by the high court in the 6-3 June 2003 *Lawrence v. Texas* decision, ending sodomy laws in thirteen states. That prompted Justice Antonin Scalia, who voted to uphold the ban, to declare in his dissent:

> If moral disapprobation of homosexual conduct is 'no legitimate state interest' for purposes of proscribing that conduct; and if, as the Court coos (casting aside all pretense at neutrality) 'when sexuality finds overt expression in intimate conduct with another person, the conduct can be but one element in a personal bond that is more enduring'; what justification could there possibly be for denying the benefits of marriage to homosexual couples exercising 'the liberty protected under the Constitution'?

IT WAS THE SAME PRIMITIVE fear and loathing when the Congress of the United States, in 1996, followed by several state legislatures, voted laws and amendments declaring same-sex love invalid and illegitimate; and when eighteen states (as of this writing—Texas being the most recent, in November 2005) amended their state constitutions to ban same-sex marriage. The Republican-Fundamentalist theocratic alliance (to whom the words "sex" and "sin" are pretty much interchangeable) had mobilized its troops.

It was the same primitive fear and loathing when one Protestant denomination after another reënforced their denial of gay and lesbian clergy (until, at last, a discernible turnabout among mainline Protestant denominations), or when the Roman Catholic bishops of Massachusetts promoted the Defense of Marriage Amendment with its bigotry and then denied that it was anti-gay; and there have been pronouncements about us bearing phrases like "objectively disordered," and there was Pope John Paul II in January 2003 saying that families headed by same-sex couples are "inauthentic," and Joseph Ratzinger—the current Pope—calling same-sex marriage and lesbians wanting to have children "the eclipse of God."

The same fear and loathing costs gay people their lives in nations where homosexuality brings the death penalty: Iran, the United Arab Emirates, Saudi Arabia, Sudan, Somalia, Nigeria, and Yemen; and, thanks to the work of American evangelicals, life in prison in Uganda and Nigeria. It upholds laws calling for imprisonment for homosexuality in no less than eighty-two countries.

What is this fear and loathing in the heart of this society? What was it that had me believing that what I am is an abomination in the eyes of God?

The religions and society of the past have taught us to believe that.

The fear and loathing that I am talking about is a fear and loathing of the body and of sexuality, which our religious culture still profoundly believes, even if unconsciously, are evils—as St. Augustine put it—evils forgivable only if they can be justified in the begetting of offspring, within marriage ("because it makes good use of the evil of lust. . . . but the action is not performed without evil"). If a married couple has sex and prevents conception, the act is equivalent to fornication.[2] Every child is tainted with original sin, which is transmitted through the sexual act.

SOME TODAY WOULD MAKE "good use of the evil of lust." In the world of far-right fundamentalist ideology and its megachurches, there's a bit more to this. There's a line that increasingly pervades the movement, and it's explicitly laid out by the "Quiverfull" movement. *Quiverfull* as in Psalm 127: "Like arrows in the hands of a warrior are sons born in one's youth. Blessed is the man whose quiver is full of them. They will not be put to shame when they contend with their enemies in the gate."

The movement is described in some detail by Kathryn Joyce in *The Nation* magazine[3]. The argument: obedience to the commands of God contained in the Bible requires a return to the patriarchal family structure. The divine role for women is to produce children who, properly reared (home schooled or in fundamentalist schools if possible) will become God's warriors in the struggle to establish a proper worldly theocracy and defeat the dark forces of—well, the usual list of

---

2 Augustine. *De Grat. Ch. et de Pecca Orig.* II.41; *De Nuptiis et Concupiscentia* I.4, 6-7, 21, 33; *C. Jul.* III.7.15

3 Kathryn Joyce. "The Quiverfull Conviction: Christian Mothers Breed "Arrows for the War." *The Nation*, Nov. 27, 2006.

foes including homosexuals, contraception, liberals, and feminists. Michelle Bachmann is a believer, and though she wouldn't admit it during a presidential campaign, she studied tax law —an idea she hated—in wifely submission to her husband Marcus who told her to go to law school.

But aren't they worried about the ecological consequences of burgeoning population? Not at all. Which is why throughout the right-wing Christian movement there's a consistent line of attack against the *environmental* movement. If God says "be fruitful and multiply," who are we to worry about the consequences? The Second Coming is at hand, after all.

Joyce describes a number of women who have taken up the duty to multiply (and submit to their husbands). If God gives you fifteen children, it isn't for you to decide you want fewer—as if where babies come from is purely about God. Can't afford more children? Where's your faith? Doesn't God promise to provide? God's army needs those kids, in numbers that can overwhelm the heathen tribes!

In this way, religion defies both logic and morality. Meanwhile, the seas go on absorbing two billion tons of carbon every year, ineluctably acidifying it, while the concentration of carbon dioxide in the air has reached 392 parts per million, the highest in at least 650,000 years—as multiplying throngs of humans kill off their only home. Science has shown where this leads: a horrific sequence of cataclysms.

IF ALREADY IN AUGUSTINE'S TIME the theology of the church was taking a distinctively negative view of sexuality, that dim view would have severe practical consequences. A half century before Augustine, while the Roman Empire was locked in an intricate power struggle to succeed the Emperor Diocletian, the Synod at Elvira was legislating sexual morality. Diocletian had ordered the termination of Christianity upon the festival of the Terminalia in 303, and there had been edicts requiring that all people sacrifice to the gods of Rome in an attempt to revive Roman religious orthodoxy. But by then the struggle was hapless, and Diocletian abdicated in 305. The yet-unconverted Constantine had become Caesar of the West, and the terminally ill Galerius, Augustus of the East—who had previously urged particularly strong measures against Christians, halted the persecution in 311. The political and social situation had simply made continued persecution impossible. In 311 Constantine converted, finding the Cross an effective means for conquest.

By 309 the church was in a dramatically changing position. Says Samuel Laeuchli, "a first function of the sexual legislation at Elvira was to help the Christian church enhance its inner cohesion at a moment when less and less cohesion could be gained from a vanishing conflict with its traditional imperial foes."[4]

What the bishops and presbyters who traveled Roman roads to the little provincial assembly in a church in southern Spain figured they had to do was somehow to assert their authority over the churches. This they did in eighty-one "canons," thirty-seven of which were about sex. Inner cohesion would be achieved by controlling the sexual behavior of the masses by an exertion of clergy power. That hold would be secured by creating an image for the clergy of purity. This "purer than thou" image was to validate their authority.

The bishops had not come to the synod intending to deliberate sex. That strategic move was spontaneous. And now a bishop could feel the "assurance of the righteous amid the turmoil, multiplicity, and dissent" apparent even in the sanctions they were now approving. Assumed in their voting was the serious moral evil of sexual expression. They voted themselves a life without sex, even if the cleric was married.

> The cleric saw himself in the role of the powerful father, alterna-
> tively punishing and forgiving . . . The faithful looked up, or was
> conditioned to look up to him as his paternal authority figure, his
> "papa," as the major bishops since the third century were called.
> Such a vertical relationship, elsewhere expressed as lord-servant,
> teacher-student, undergirds the entire patristic and medieval au-
> thority structure of Christianity, as one of the two components
> in the mother-father substitute presented to man by the ancient
> church. While the church offered itself to the believer as the spiri-

---

4 Samuel Laeuchli. *Power and Sexuality: The Emergence of Canon Law at the Synod of Elvira.* Philadelphia: Temple University Press, 1972, p. 61.

tual mother who comforts and nourishes her children, the elite of the church acted as the father, distributing wrath and clemency in the gratuitous, manipulative technique of aristocratic power.[5]

It would become an oft-used method for consolidating power over the masses. Sex can be exalted to the status of a god in its importance—or a devil. It can be inflated as a good, inflated as an evil, exalted as the god that divides the realm of good from the realm of evil, the ultimate divider of the *us* from the *them*. In fact, it is none of these things, nothing much at all, in itself. It is a potent *medium* for other things, any and all other things, neutral in itself.

The ecclesiastical habit of regulating sexuality would persevere. In 1641 the Massachusetts Bay Colony would promulgate its famous "Body of Liberties." It became the prototype for a lot of Puritan legislation. Among its twelve capital crimes is lovemaking between men. Language for the purpose could have been found in English law, such as Henry VIII's statute of 1533, but America's first settlers turned instead to the Book of Leviticus and declared, verbatim,

> If any man lyeth with mankinde, as he lyeth with a woeman, both of them have committed abomination, they both shall surely be put to death.[6]

In 1655 the New Haven Colony published its body of laws, including the same text, and adding lovemaking between women.

And all the guilt, and all the fear, and all the shadow side of guilty and fearful souls were laid on those scapegoat classes so long defined and enforced by our social and legal systems. Once, it was women burned as witches. And today, it is the people called Queer. This scapegoat status is maintained through a system of social apartheid.

We are still aliens in our own land. The most liberated, the most liberal-minded of us, has not lived in this world without being scarred by it.

AND MY MIND TRAVELS BACK down the years of my life and all the love

---

5 Laeuchli, 90, 96, 26f, 107, 120f.
6 *The Body of Liberties*, Section 94: Capital Laws, par. viii. *Leviticus* 20:13.

lost to this fear and loathing. And I want you to think of the loss, and the hurt, just for a moment. Because there is something in Nature that draws us to another with a kind of force and passion so that our worlds may be expanded by the world of another, so that we may find in intimate encounter with another something that awakens hidden possibility in each, and opens to us worlds of beauty, delight, growth, and fulfillment.

And what happens in the soul of a young person when every time that force of love is felt, it is a forbidden love, it is a sin and a shame, an unspeakable disgrace? What does that do to the soul?

How much, how very much love lost and dishonored there is —that we must mourn. And what becomes of neighborly love when a whole denomination votes its hate, when the governments of your state and nation vote their contempt?

The world of right-wing megachurches has been led by conspicuous homo-haters like Pastor Ted Haggard, at Colorado Springs' 14,000-member apostolic-dominionist New Life Church. An alumnus of Oral Robert University,[7] he professed to be led to build his church, on that precise spot, by God himself. Among his achievements: being a weekly Monday advisor to President Bush; getting an anti-gay-marriage amendment onto the 2006 state ballot; being chosen president of the National Association of Evangelicals. Just before the film *Jesus Camp* hit the screens showing him howling that homosexuality is a sin because God says so in the Bible, his secret long-time monthly rent boy, who'd finally figured out who his client was because he saw him denouncing homosexuality on television, went to public, and the hypocritical preacher was brought down. This is from his letter to the giant congregation:

> I am a deceiver and a liar. There's a part of my life that is so repulsive and dark that I have been warring with it all of my adult life.

That is the bitter account of a life made false to itself under the terrible force of the fear and loathing. It is the account of uncounted millions of lives.

---

7 Another alumnus of Oral Roberts University: Michelle Bachmann, who was among the last to be graduated from ORU's Coburn School of Law, which was closed in 1986. What remained, including its library, became part of Pat Robertson's Regent University School of Law in Virginia.

WILLIAM BLAKE RELATED A DREAM of his in 1793. He had a friend, a righteous angel, who wanted to show him his eternal fate on account of his impious life. So the angel, sure of his own righteousness, took him down a treacherous route to the edge of an immense horror, and they hung over it by the roots of trees looking down at a dark tempest hell and smoke and cataracts of blood and fire and vast swimming spiders and the scaly folds of a monstrous serpent whose eyes appeared as two globes of crimson fire, from which the sea fled away in clouds of smoke. Pretty awful. The angel got scared and fled. But Blake (in his dream) stayed down in that forbidden place for awhile—just curious—to see if divinity might dwell here also. He found himself in a place of beauty and delight.

After awhile he climbed back up to where his frightened angel waited. The angel was stunned—couldn't understand how Blake had managed to survive the blood and fire and serpents and all. So Blake told him.

He said: All that you saw was owing to your metaphysics, your *religion.* When you ran away and took your scary metaphysics with you, I found myself on a pleasant river bank by moonlight hearing a harpist play.

Our religion—or as Blake said it in 1793, our metaphysics—has led us, with his righteous angel, to look at beauty and to see instead a hellish prospect of brimstone, and monstrous serpents.

And the righteous angels of the world have set out to slay the monstrous serpent, and they have slain in the name of righteousness those who represent the hated passion and sexuality, in another time uncounted women called witches, and in our time they have slain Charlie Howard, slain Harvey Milk, slain a group of men gunned down on a city street in New York by a crazy minister's son, a police officer, who said god told him to kill the queers. And Hitler's raiding of gay bars beginning in 1933, and his legal code Paragraph 175 barring all physical contact between men, and his 1936 Federal Security Department for Combating Abortion and Homosexuality, and the transporting of gay men to concentration camps from 1936 onward, and the particularly horrific treatment in concentration camps of those wearing the pink triangle—were carried out without protest from a self-righteous world that stood silent.

AT THE SOUL OF THIS SOCIETY and its religion is the righteous angel who looks at gay and lesbian people and sees the monstrous specter of hated passion, vile body, despised sexuality, a metaphysic that carries us far, far backward. And the righteous angels of the world have set out to slay what appears to them as the monstrous serpents.

Shall we return to a world created by the outworn visions of past ages?

It would mean a return to a narrower view of humanity, the chosen against the heathen. We may as well prepare for religious wars and theocratic rule. And right now there are those who are doing everything they can to impose such a rule.

And how is it that this fear and loathing so permeates the soul of America in the twenty-first century?

Suppose the real and urgent point of religion is not that it function as a lock on the past, but as an engine of the evolution of consciousness.

THERE IS AN EVOLUTIONARY force of nature that has been called *eros*. It began as the imperative to procreate, and its force is great. It has brought a kind of madness into the lives of some of the most respected and apparently mature.

The force has itself evolved. On a smallish planet whose human population has reached 6.77 billion and that number is rising by 78 million every year, where 1.7 billion of them can't get clean water, a planet that is warming dangerously as a consequence of the heat-trapping byproducts of those 6.77 billion lives, nature is smart enough to realize that it is neither necessary nor desirable that *everyone* procreate. Though the urge to procreate still drives some, at some times and to some extent, for most of us by now, the drive is now more to do with penetrating the mystery of another, and of communion. Our "procreative" urge has evolved, too, achieving a far wider meaning. But do not underestimate its commanding power. At the gross physical level, it's the sexual drive; at a more highly evolved level, it's a broader creative drive. In its finest manifestation it drives the profoundest boundary-crossing spiritual quest.

It helps to know what we're grappling with. Related to wisely, from an enlightened vantage point, it is an engine of evolution. It's something holy. But massive stores of outmoded cultural mythology envelop this elemental drive, and misunderstood, mis-handled, it can lead to the profound embarrassment well known to hypocritical politicians and clergy. The sexual impulse can drive us off the rails, as daily news (and your unpublished memories) might confirm. It can drive behavior that is utterly and disastrously mindless, leaving the surrounding landscape strewn with appalling ruin. One can lose all comprehension of the possibility of choice: one was *driven*. For a moment (or, in the case of recent governors of New York or South Carolina or California, for a span of months), nothing else mattered.

That fact doesn't make the force of eros evil. The evil or goodness is determined by the comprehension and the moral vision we bring to it.

SPEAKING OF DREAMS, WALT Whitman had one, too. He wrote:

> I dream'd in a dream I saw a city invincible to the attacks of the whole of the rest of the earth.
> I dream'd that was the new city of Friends,
> Nothing was greater there than the quality of robust love . . .
> It was seen every hour in the actions of the men [and women] of that city,
> And in all their looks and words.[8]

And another dreamer: Ezekiel was a Jewish priest and prophet who was among those taken into exile when the First Temple was destroyed. Israel had been living under the Babylonian-Persian captivity for now maybe 25 years. In the loss of that temple, so much was lost to the spirits and lives of the people. And Ezekiel responded to his situation of captivity by dreaming the dimensions for a great temple.

---

8 "I dream'd in a dream," *Leaves of Grass* Book V, "Calamus."

SOMETIMES WHEN YOU FEEL like an alien in a strange land, you turn inward, you create visions and scenarios. And you just may develop the capacity to See around corners. And dream. Draw deeply from the sacred well of our souls and dream.

But we have not been beyond this point, and we hesitate, wondering what next. Tony Kushner writes:

> The world howls without; it is at this moment a very terrible world.
> . . . Together we organize the world for ourselves, or at least we
> organize our understanding of it; we reflect it, refract it, criticize it,
> grieve over its savagery; and we help each other to discern, amidst
> the gathering dark, paths of resistance, pockets of peace, and places
> from whence hope may be plausibly expected . . .[9]

IT TAKES A WELL-DEVELOPED SPIRITUAL orientation to get what is going on, what world is dying, what world is coming into being.

SO MY QUESTION IS TODAY, Who has a dream? Where is Vision?

I believe a dream is gathering clarity in the hearts and minds of many in our time, even if in our fear and discouragement we have buried it so deeply within our hearts that we cannot at the moment find it. But I say the dream is potent enough to engage our creativity and our courage to find ways to make it real in this reactionary time.

I HAD MENTIONED EZEKIEL. Ezekiel and his vision.

His was a powerful vision but it was not a perfect vision—it was an exclusive one where no foreigners or outsiders were allowed in. He dreamed of a reconstruction and restoration of something that once was, not modified at all by an expanded consciousness. So his was no final or perfect vision and ours won't be either. But we must go on dreaming.

Sometimes it seems that all religion is capable of doing is returning

---

9 Tony Kushner. Afterword, *Angels In America*, Part II: "Perestroika." New York: Theatre Communications Group, 1994, p. 158.

to ancient dreams as if they were the final vision. Make doctrines out of the dreams of others long ago and far away.

But the religious act consists not in returning to ancient dreams,
but in the dreaming.

And religion has served either as a lock on the past, or as an engine of evolution.

It remains for us to dream dreams and make them real—make a world large enough for love.

THE FUTURE, IF THERE IS to be one, belongs to the dreamers. It doesn't belong to the outworn pronouncements of the bishops or the evangelists of the new right.

It belongs to those who are now remaking the world on the strength of a vision of life as one whole that cannot be divided asunder by hatred and fear.

Let there be Vision. Let there be those who, quite aware of the world that howls without, dare to live the Vision.

In the name of love.

I HAVE THE PROOF THAT human community can be built on higher ground. In my own spiritual tradition, there are the early pioneers who had so much to do with making it possible: there was Rev. Robert P. Wheatly, my long-time predecessor as Director of the UUA Office of Lesbian and Gay Concerns, who took up the job in 1977. There was Rev. Richard Nash, who led the move to establish the Office in 1973. There was Rev. James Stoll, a Unitarian Universalist minister who came out in 1969 in an address to a conference when he said he'd been doing a lot of hard thinking and he could no longer live a lie—now, *that* took guts!—an action that led to a UUA General Assembly resolution condemning anti-gay discrimination. There were Revs. Barbara Pescan and Ann Tyndall, the first out lesbian parish ministers serving Illinois congregations as co-ministers as early as 1984. There were the search committees that chose them and the congregations that elected them and supported them. Or —talk about pioneers—there was Rev. Phoebe Hanaford, the feminist-abolitionist Unitarian minister in Jersey City, N.J. in the 1870s who shared her life with an Ellen Miles, known as the "minister's wife." Of course, all this required a faith community that had already declared itself free from the presumptive authority of premodern myth and superstition. Other religious movements have had their pioneers and heroes, who sometimes had to apply an enlightened interpretation to a body of myth.

I THINK OF THOSE WHO FOUGHT this fight and never lived to see victory. I think of those in the nineteen states that have voted bigotry into their constitutions, rendering impossible, in those states, what is now possible in Massachusets alone among these United States. I think of a bold Court and brave Chief Justice Margaret Marshall. It is a long road that we have travelled, and there is far, far more of it ahead.

But sometime, somewhere, there have to be victories. There has to be a place where what you dream can happen and the world can see it. There's plenty of ignorance and bigotry in Massachusetts, as there is in every state. But despite all of it, several thousand couples are—so far as this state is concerned—as honored and protected as all the rest. Outmoded metaphysics have scared the masses enough.

BEING DUST
- or -, A world without guilt?

Every autumn come the High Holy Days, culminating in Yom Kippur, calling us to repent. In the early spring comes Lent and the holy day with which it begins, Ash Wednesday, reminding us that we are dust. For many postmodern folks, Yom Kippur and Ash Wednesday are a little too—well, *grovelly* for us. Yet they remind us of an uneasiness that is hardly just seasonal.

We can feel guilty about the dumbest things. I used to feel guilty when I skipped Boy Scouts, which is particularly ironic because today I might feel guilty if I did participate in that discriminatory organization, but anyway. My guilt *then* was particularly silly if you know that going to Boy Scouts meant putting on your uniform and going to the Methodist Church where Mr. Strang, who was the minister and the Boy Scout Leader, would take attendance, using your last name so it would feel like the real grown-up Army, then have us recite some Boy Scout Pledge or salute the flag or something, do a couple of push-ups, and then, if Mr. Strang was feeling ambitious, tie a couple of knots. All this was done slowly, so as to give the impression of having been a full evening's worth of program, and we would go home. Deciding whether or not to go hardly ranked with the great moral dilemmas of our time; and yet when I'd stay home instead of engaging in this foolishness, I'd feel GUILTY.

Well, that's guilt. I'll call it *habituated guilt,* which we feel for lack of any real moral vision. If you haven't learned any sharper moral sense than habit and routine, which I hadn't as a kid of boy scout age, then you haven't got anything more worthwhile to feel guilty about than breaking the habit and routine.

There are other equally specious guilt trips endured by humans. Take sex. In some forms of religion, sin and sex are precisely the same thing. I have a little book with gold edges, leather cover that looks like a pocket New Testament, but it isn't—it's called *The Catholic Girl's Guide,* and was published in 1906. Want guilt? It assaulted a multitude of young minds with fusillades of it.

And then there's *The Directorium Asceticum; or, Guide to the Spiritual Life,* published at the beginning of the twentieth century in several languages, the English edition bearing the imprimatur of the Archbishop of Baltimore:

> The first remedy against the depraved tendencies of the sense of touch is an extreme care never to lay hands on any one, especially of the opposite sex. A Christian should never allow himself to be led to do this on any conceivable pretence, whether of affability, friendliness, pleasantry, play, or politeness; because such liberties, though devoid of any evil intent, are an incitement to this frail sense, and always turn out fatal to the soul.[1]

There's a heroic example of one who held herself pure:

> But I must own that I am most impressed by the heroic resolve of a young girl of twelve years of age in defence of her virginal purity. She was a native of Alexandria, and was pursued by the amorous looks, smiles, and enticements of a dissolute youth. The more the innocent maiden avoided him, the more did he seek her company. . . . Being anxious, however, not to be robbed of the priceless gem of her virginity, she took the most extraordinary step that can be imagined. She went and hid herself in an old tomb, and there concealed for twelve years those charms that had kindled the love of the shameless youth—receiving through a small hole . . . the food necessary to support life.[2]

---

1 John Baptiste Scaramelli. *The Directorium Asceticum; or, Guide to the Spiritual Life.* 6th ed., 4 vols. London: R & T Washbourne Ltd., 1908, II:10

2 *Directorium,* II:298.

And advice on how to keep from falling into sin and shame:

> Modesty must be practiced by the custody of the eyes, which
> should usually be kept downcast, to avoid the inconveniences to
> which we have alluded . . . Above all, in conversing with persons
> of the opposite sex, we should avoid looking them full in the face,
> but rather fix our eyes somewhat lower.[3]

HERE'S ANOTHER NEUROTIC guilt. It's artistic guilt, creative guilt. If
you create some new artwork—of whatever kind—if you've created
something, you may feel artistic guilt. Such gall we have, to lay our own
creation next to some older established works of great artists. What
have I done, who do I think I am, does my painting imply that Monet
isn't good enough for this world that I should paint something else.
Pretty silly, isn't it?

SO THEN. WE'VE DONE AWAY with guilt. Congratulations.

BUT WAIT—THERE IS TRUTH HERE which we can ignore to the impov-
erishing of our souls.

Once, in his *Markings*[4], Dag Hammarskjöld wrote

> Uneasy, uneasy, uneasy —
> Why?
> Because—when opportunity gives you the obligation to create,
> you are content to meet the demands of the moment . . .
> Because—anxious for the good opinion of others, and jealous
> of the possibility that they may become "famous," you have low-
> ered yourself to wondering what will happen in the end to what
> you have done and been. How dead can a man be behind a façade
> of great ability, loyalty—and ambition! Bless your uneasiness as a
> sign that there is still life in you.

Surely you've felt *uneasy*. The question is, what to make of this uneasi-

---

3 *Directorium*, IV:103.
4 *Markings*. Ballantine Books, 1982, p. 137.

ness? Does it mean, as the old theology says, we are fallen, and mean and small and miserable—or does it mean that, when we feel it, we're actually undergoing something that might exalt us?

Uneasy. To be human is to have this anxiety, to live with it. We ask (though not very loudly, muffling the question so we ourselves won't hear it): *do I have enough value to keep living? To justify my being here?*

WE HUMANS COME EQUIPPED WITH moral capacities—which have to do with the values we share or have learned in our cultural context, emotional reactions like empathy and disgust, long-outworn hard-wired attitudinal habits, our neurobiology, an instinctual human capacity for morality comparable to human linguistic capacities—and the conclusions of our more recently evolved capacity for rational ethical deliberation. Current thinkers like Roy Baumeister, Peter Singer, Paul Bloom, Richard Joyce, Joshua Greene, Jonathan Haidt, Sam Harris, Marc Hauser, Joshua Knobe, Elizabeth Phelps, and David Pizarro are expanding our understanding of the human as moral creature.[5] Their work is valuable—and advanced far beyond the revelation-based absolutes many of us were taught. It seems to me that evolving spiritual communities will have to struggle with a new moral compass.

THERE IS A WORD THAT LIES AT the heart of the High Holy Days. It means "to turn," as in "Turn back, turn back, forswear thy foolish ways." In the Hebrew Bible it's the word *t'shuv*. Turn. Or the noun: *t'shuvah*, turning, sometimes translated repentance.

This is a stupendously hopeful idea. The hope at the heart of the Jewish faith is that we humans are not helplessly depraved and fallen creatures but are instead the crown of creation, a stupendous achievement of the evolution of life—even if, at times, we crash and burn. And in this, the Unitarian Universalist tradition has more in common with the Jewish than the Christian.

It's not the presence of the worst, most perverted, most barbaric

---

5 Notably Hauser's *Moral Minds* (Ecco, 2006); Joyce's *The Evolution of Morality* (MIT Press, 2007); and Harris' *The Moral Landscape* (Free Press, 2010).

elements that should surprise us; no. Rather than these, what ought to astonish us is the appearance of the highest and best and finest human magnificence: because there is at work in this world—gradual as it is, imperiled as it is—the inexorable evolutionary advance of consciousness—or, we might say, the realization of the Spirit hidden in all nature.

The call of these days is to turn—to turn to our highest, finest selves, our most godlike capacities.

T'shuv, to turn.

THINK, NOW, ABOUT ANOTHER word because it's something that, in the human process that leads to our *turning*, we may experience first. It's *guilt*.

Maybe a funny topic for a liberal-minded postmodern person, in the case of the writer, a Unitarian Universalist!—isn't guilt the specialty of the more traditional religions? Aren't we beyond it? Aren't we godlike? Someone will remind me, *You said so yourself.*

Guilt has held a prominent place in the history of religions. To get rid of it, Moslems make pilgrimages to Mecca so they can return home guiltless as a newborn child. Look in a synagogue at Yom Kippur. Such a crowd you will see, standing room only.

Catholicism seems to specialize in guilt, and confession, and absolution of guilt.

Protestantism is built on guilt, and its meeting-houses are built like courtrooms, and its theology built on the thought of St. Paul, not of Jesus, but of St Paul , who asks one central question before all others: what is your legal status before God? Have you been justified by Christ's sacrificial atonement on your behalf to pay your fine to a wrathful righteous God?

Howard Moody, longtime minister of Judson Memorial Church in New York, recounted a story about a friend he met in college after the second World War. This friend fought, as Howard did, in the war. It's a war story—his friend told him about a terrible day out there lying on an open field in France. And there were German soldiers all over on one side of the field pinned down by the mortar fire and he had a rifle with telescopic site. And he picked off fourteen Germans that day, looked through the telescopic sight right into their magnified faces and shot them. After it was over he couldn't sleep for days. There were nightmares and cold sweat. So he went to the chaplain. Who said, patting him on the head,

"There, there, son, you've done nothing wrong, this is war!"

He said after that he gave up on religion.

Howard calls that chaplain a "hired absolver" paid by the government to absolve the guilt about war so it wouldn't constitute a morale problem.

This human being didn't want to be told he shouldn't feel guilty. There is an inner wisdom in people that won't accept so easy and false an answer. There are things worth lying awake over and having cold sweats over.

And there's a splendid humanity in us that protests against the violence and barbarity.

So THINK AGAIN ABOUT *GUILT*. In the human process that leads to our *turning*, we may experience, first, guilt.

When the experience of guilt strikes, we can usually benefit by imagining a courtroom and looking to see who is the judge and who is the accuser.

Is it a nagging, moralistic parent who has become a part of you and whose judgments are as irrelevant to any real offense as the actual parent's were? Is it a fire and brimstone preacher out of the past who was only yelling out of his own neurosis and unresolved conflicts? Or was it a distorted and oppressive society that accuses you? Is it some false expectation of someone who expects of you things that are simply not yours to give?

Or is it something more authentic and vital—some voice within you that represents dimensions of your life that have been shortchanged, neglected—or contradicted by what you are doing? Is it your most human and divine striving and aspiration—is it your destiny calling to you?

If I'm being accused by a Self larger than the egoic self that has so far evolved, then I think I want to listen. *That* guilt reveals the chasm between what potentially we are and what actually we dare to be in our living. It has to do with the fact that we are responsible for our own evolution. It is our own inner way of knowing that we are missing the mark and that we are capable of more. Sin, in New Testament Greek *hamartia*—means, literally, missing the mark. It's not really about violating somebody's rules, but about the violation of something far more essential about ourselves.

And that something more essential is What We Are. Manifestations of the very Life of the Universe. Magnificent, full of splendid possibility.

In Yom Kippur there is a very important parallel between my own Unitarian Universalist tradition and Judaism, a common thread. Yom Kippur is not built on the idea of original sin, of essential human depravity. That's a Christian idea. It is not a Jewish one and it is one of those supremely bad ideas that Unitarians have always instinctively rejected.

If you're coming at this with the idea—maybe conscious, maybe something you assume without thinking—but the idea that human beings start off with "original sin" and are fallen creatures, depraved in our essence and incapable of good—then when you look at the disastrous greed that is running our economic life you will say "Well, of course, what did you expect?" and you will live out of low-quality expectations—and you will look at yourself as locked into your past, stuck in a loop, trapped in a round and round rut out of which you cannot get.

No, Yom Kippur looks on our humanity as sacred, magnificent, good.

Humanity is the magnificent achievement of Nature, and the lesson of our recent history and of centuries and millennia before, is that our humanity can be compromised, distorted.

Now, we know that a person can, under extreme conditions, be robbed of a sense of worth. A child relentlessly bullied at school. Someone who's simply different in some way, humiliated, violated, and alone with no one to believe in them. It takes extraordinary strength to survive emotionally in those circumstances.

And we know we need a community that believes in us. What if that bullied child has not a nurturing, faith-giving home and the loving arms of parents where they can find solace; what if the person who, because she's different, and so has been humiliated and faced contempt—has no community in whose welcoming arms she finds again her pride and courage?

But in even the best of circumstances, there is an essential *unease* with which we live, and it cannot be relieved from the outside of us, and the answer to that unease can come only from the heart and soul of each of us.

Unease. A hole in the ego.

Sam Keen's[6] phrase, from his little book *Beginnings Without End:* —

> The hole in the ego
> is where the holy
> flows in and out . . .

Poor, poor ego. Punctured daily. Why have we always to doubt ourselves?

On one of my trips to the UK I heard a BBC report about the work of some social scientists showing that popular assumptions about "self esteem" might be misguided. In a February 2002 *New York Times Magazine* picked up on the story, running a piece[7] by Lauren Slater questioning of Americans' faith in the doctrine that we must promote self-esteem. He described the ways we do it, such as school self-esteem programs that "dole out huge heapings of praise, regardless of actual accomplishment." His conclusion: "It didn't work." Instead, research found a positive correlation between high self-esteem scores and poor social skills, and poor academic performance. One researcher reported no evidence whatever that low self-esteem is harmful, and concluded that it may lead to higher achievement. A research collaborator went further, saying that high self-regard can maim and even kill.

And there were three withering studies of self-esteem in the United

6 Sam Keen. *Beginnings Without End.* New York: Harper & Row, 1975, p.56.
7 Lauren Slater, "The Trouble With Self-Esteem," *New York Times Magazine,* February 3, 2002.

States. The news? People with high self-esteem pose a *greater* threat to those around them than people with low self-esteem and feeling bad about yourself is not the cause of our country's biggest, most expensive social problems!

Huh!? To our ears, that sounds all wrong . . .

OH. IN THE BACKGROUND, I'm listening to the BBC again, and as I write, they're discussing—*again!*—how it happened that the whole nation was led into a war somebody wanted enough that they cooked the intelligence to make it happen. Meanwhile, the supremely self-confident architects and deciders of this war, who dreamed it and planned it and executed it—show no unease, *no lack of confidence.*

So we ought to ask just *what* self we are talking about as the object of this esteem. If by self all you mean is *ego*, the esteem is misplaced.

There is a mass-egocentricity of nationalism—as if we had no part in the rest of the world except as its masters. That ought to cause *us* some uneasiness. The uneasiness begins in the heart of us, in our own want of humility.

This nation, and its leadership—it would seem—had gone to some extreme of self-deception to _ease the unease_, and in public life, *truth* seems the rarest thing, and to admit a mistake flies in the face of the image of the self-assured successful person. Or, as Stephen Colbert said, when corrected by a guest whose name he'd gotten wrong: "Okay, but I'm going to continue to call you that because if I admit I'm wrong, then I lose the argument."

Once, many years ago, I was thunderstruck by a phrase from M.K. Gandhi. "The seeker after truth," he wrote—"The seeker after truth must be humble as the dust." *Dust.*

I DON'T WISH TO DISOWN OR DISHONOR the ego. If you mean the organizing principle in the psyche, we'd be in dire shape without it. No, I want to befriend it. It gives us the sense of being an individual "I", not just a cipher embedded in a tribe or clan. Without it, we'd have no capacity for interiority. In Jungian terms, you can't *individuate* without an ego. There wouldn't be a "self." It's a gift of evolution, and it's taken us through adverse winds and tides as a self gifted with personality and fairly astonishing capacities.

And along the way, it's developed survival techniques, defenses, pretenses, fears, and wants. It turns up with neuroses and narcissism. Spiritual development is, in large part, about transcending these limitations—and encountering a deeper, higher essence, a pure subjectivity that is never an object, but always the subject, witnessing the egoic self, observing it in a way that can see through the ego's sometimes desperate defenses and pretenses. That Self (here I'll capitalize the "S") is Emerson's Over-Soul. It's pretty much what Hindus mean by Atman, and senses itself to be one with absolute Spirit, the Hindu Brahman. But you don't need to embrace Hinduism or Buddhism to embrace that perspective. It's shared by (admittedly a small minority of) Christians, Jews, Muslims, as well as people like me who reach beyond historic religious traditions. It knows itself as the manifestations of the very Ground of Being, or what the great Jean Gebser called the "ever-present Origin." And if that applies to everything that is, we're a bit different in that we, *homo sapien sapiens*, are conscious and, indeed, self-conscious, aware of ourselves, aware that we are conscious. And in that apparently unique sense, we are the Universe *aware of itself.*

There is something that implicates us in its creative work and accuses us when we live as less than we are—when we bring this ego-self, with its capacities and uniqueness, to the service of low-quality intentions. Our highest future possibilities flow from that deeper, higher essence, that evolutionary impulse, which is an expression of what some will call God. As we have seen, no language is quite adequate to the job *that* word attempts.

SOMETIMES WE DISAPPOINT OURSELVES. Sometimes we observe ourselves falling prey to mechanical instinct and to the desperate moves and maneuvers and hungers and self-delusions of the ego. Sometimes we *need* that unease that reminds us that we are "earth to earth, ashes to ashes, dust to dust;" that reminds us that sometimes we are wrong, that our precious personal dramas are specks of dust in this great living Universe. That we are not the center of the Universe and we aren't separate from it, and we have not forever to live, though this world of life lives on.

Sometimes our unease is just about unbearable, and when it is, we might do almost anything to drown out the voice of our unease. We know the ways we do it. It's the story of our time. T.S. Eliot captured it in his "Ash-Wednesday":

> *Where shall the word be found, where will the word*
> *Resound? Not here, there is not enough silence.*

SOMETIMES, TO RELIEVE THE UNEASE, people are driven to what they assume to be good works, doing the will of their god, maybe in the form of righteous judgmental scrupulosity, maybe a crusade of faith-based bigotry, sometimes even in the form of genuine cruelty and violence. A little bit of pious self-righteousness can feel so darn good!

They say that Ivan the Terrible would go down periodically and *personally* torture his prisoners, and he always returned feeling pretty good, feeling righteous and *empowered.*

THERE IS AN ANCIENT STORY associated with the High Holy Days—the story of the prophet Jonah, whom God sends to wicked Ninevah to preach repentance. But Jonah doesn't want to go. God has to send him there in the belly of a whale because he won't get on the plane and go. He doesn't want Ninevah to repent and here's why.

Jonah seems to think that not only he, individually, but his people, as well, his nation—are beyond sin, beyond fault. But *Ninevah*—Ninevah is the lynch-pin of the great Axis of Evil. The right thing to do with Ninevah is to obliterate it. The last thing Jonah wants to do is to allow Ninevah the space to turn. Jonah was so sure that he and his people were always right, that God was always on their side because they were the special chosen people, that the world would be just fine if his own people simply maintained overwhelming military might. He couldn't see how everyone else felt bullied; how this brought out the worst in others.

To him, evil was something "out there"—so when he looked at the disorder and suffering in the world, the violence and the injustice, he could only say *"not me!"*—because he lacked the capacity to see the other in himself and himself in the other, all one humanity, with god-like potentialities for good or for ill. And he lacked the capacity to see himself within that larger context as a contributing factor.

He could acknowledge no wisdom, no moral vision, out there. Consequently he couldn't have wanted his people to have any part in an international court of justice, or climate treaties, or missile treaties. Poor Jonah. He felt no guilt. He could not ask: what am *I* contributing to this disorder, this injustice, this cycle of destruction?

ONE SEPTEMBER MORNING, AMERICAN EYES witnessed horror on a scale, and of a kind, that no human eye ought ever to see, and that no human psyche is quite prepared to handle. New York became Serajevo and Srebrenica and Stalingrad and Fallujah and Ramallah.

The British newspaper *The Guardian*, in a leader, or editorial, on September 12, 2001, wrote:

> The hurt that all Americans must feel today cannot be under-estimated. Two immediate dangers arise. One is that, wounded, bewildered, and convinced that the world is its enemy, America will draw back into itself. Too often in recent months, the US has seemed at odds with its friends and partners on a range of issues, big and small. But an even greater unilateralism, even a growing siege mentality, is to be avoided at all costs. It would be a victory for the terrorists.
>
> Likewise, American over-reaction, especially of the military variety, must be guarded against. The temptation right now is to make somebody pay. And pay . . . and pay . . . and pay. Take a deep breath, America. Keep cool. And keep control.

But America didn't keep cool, not in Falluja, not at Guantanámo or abu Graib, not in the manufacture of fictitious claims about weapons of mass destruction or Iraqi involvement in 9/11.

We look at the other and we say *Not me!* We're not like that. If we do it, it isn't terror.

We have come to a crossroads in human history. It can be a moment of dramatic advance or of dramatic retrogression.

THERE'S A BOILING SEA OF RAGE out there, and it's directed at us. Moral people, people who want to be more and better than they have been, will want to know why there are people who hate us so much they'll kill themselves to hurt us.

We all know the difference between where our primitive rage might go, and where the best energies of our intellect, love, and spiritual vision might take us. And we know these are starkly different places.

To some greater or lesser degree, we have practice in this choice most days of our lives.

There must be greater men and women, because today this planet, through whose life-process we ourselves came to be, is threatened by its human inhabitants, who now have the power to extinguish life on earth.

Yet we are expressions, perhaps the latest and highest expressions, of the great Life of the Universe. We are an unfolding of the genius and an artistry at the heart of all things. Surely there is more yet to unfold.

Our continued evolution requires that we learn new and finer ways of being in the world. And our best friends require that we be true to our best selves. "What is it we heartily wish of each other?" Emerson asked.

> Is it to be pleased and flattered? No, but to be convicted and exposed, to be shamed out of our nonsense of all kinds, and made [humans] of, instead of ghosts and phantoms. We are weary of gliding ghostlike through the world . . . . We crave a sense of reality, though it come in strokes of pain.[8]

Our Yom Kippur moments come to us as a friend, to ask hard questions.

---

8 Essay "New England Reformers."

THE TRANSFORMATION OF OUR PUBLIC life must be a flowing-out of an inner transformation in the minds and hearts of individual persons in our time; and a new era will be the work of new people.

That implies a new and vital role for a transformed religion. In past ages, and still today, religion has been, more than anything else, a backward-looking force fixated on an imaginary perfection that once existed, long ago, and from which we have fallen. Therefore it cannot imagine higher laws than those that once seemed adequate, but which cannot serve us now.

Yes, some of the worst atrocities of history have been committed in the name of religion. It was not, after all, Adolf Hitler who invented the yellow badge that stripped Jews of their rights, but the church, for six hundred years. And then there was the joint statement from Falwell and Robertson, declaring that the September 11 attacks on America were God's punishment for tolerating feminists, gay people, and certain federal judges.

That is religion looking backward, fixing ancient fears and ignorance as divine law. I'm interested in religion looking forward.

In this and coming ages religion must be visionary, prophetic, bold.

It will not be afraid of the sting of an elevated conscience that creates for us that space, hinged between worlds, that precedes change and allows it.

Yom Kippur reminds us to be grateful for the sting of guilt we feel when we betray our highest possibilities. That our ethical sensibilities are alive and well is a tribute to our humanity. We can receive from the heart of life itself and from our own hearts the full measure of forgiveness, and go on, try again, pick up the work of making our lives, and this world, magnificent artworks.

These days call us to a spiritual life that is direct and real and your own, unfettered by outworn dogma, undiminished by obedience to the false authority of those who claim to be God's spokespeople and brokers in the world, undistorted by conformity to the limited understanding of past ages, transcending primitive laws demanding retribution and blood.

A spirituality of soul that insists on living out of our highest and best selves—that alone—will have the potency to lift us above the worst, the most primitive of human capacities and crown the new day when, as John Greenleaf Whittier put it, "all speech [shall] flow to music, all hearts beat as one."

IF YOU CARE ABOUT YOUR INNER LIFE—how can you hold this unease you feel? how can you hold it within a vital, an authentic—*spirituality?*

Maybe you grew up with Ash Wednesday in a Roman Catholic, or Anglican, or Lutheran church, with the blessing of ashes, and they're placed on the foreheads of the worshipers, and you remember those words that come from Genesis, "for dust thou art, and unto dust shalt thou return." It goes back to a time when penitents would bestrew themselves with ashes and clothe their bodies with sackcloth on account of their sins.

"Human life," says Sam Keen, "comes from the humus, that 'brown or black complex and varying material formed by the partial decomposition of vegetable or animal matter; the organic portion of soil.' To be human is to remain humble . . ." [9]

We are a strange amalgam of god and dust.

God and dust. Nature's highest achievement, crowned with consciousness, capable of the insight and art that created Shakespeare's plays and Handel's music and Dr. King's moral vision. The human mind has penetrated deeply enough into the powers of nature to threaten the very continuance of life on Earth . . . godlike and demonic all at once. Alone among the inhabitants of the known Universe, we have the power to reflect, to choose, to make moral choices. No other creature can do that. It took the Universe, and the evolutionary impulse at the heart of the Universe, fourteen billion years to come up with the achievement that we are.

And so our humility cannot be a "grovelling," the definition of which is, "to creep with the face to the ground, to lie or creep with the body prostrate in token of subservience or abasement."

As I've mentioned, our Unitarian forebears were enlightened enough

---

9 Keen. *Beginnings Without End*, p.5.

to dismiss the old Calvinist doctrine of human depravity, the conviction that you and I are pretty much a mess incapable of any good whatever. The wisest and best part of our religious traditions have forever returned to the theme of the seed of divine life that is in us, have said that the final aim of all our efforts, the deepest longing of our hearts, can only be the freeing and full unfolding of this divine potential. At Yom Kippur, the call is for a return to our truest selves. Beyond our ego there's an authentic human-divine self.

In 1828, in a daring sermon called "Likeness to God," William Ellery Channing, the founding figure of American Unitarianism, dared to declare—these are his words —

> The idea of God, sublime and awful as it is, is the idea of our own spiritual nature, purified and enlarged to infinity. In ourselves are the elements of the Divinity. . . .

And he said that beneath and beyond the dust that we are—we have to be able to see:

> the greatness of the human soul—that faith which looks beneath [the false veneer of ego, the failure, and all the worst that we are capable of, looks beneath that], and discerns in the depths of the soul a divine principle, a ray of the Infinite Light, which may yet break forth and shine as the sun.

WE ARE NOT *fallen, broken wretches.* We are a very grand work—*in progress.*

We are, so far as we know, the dominant life-form in the universe, we, the product of many billions of years of kosmic evolution, possessed of consciousness. We are part and parcel of a larger Whole, expressions of it; we share the struggle of Life Itself. And now we are the creators of what is to be.

In us, and in perhaps *no other* way—the universe is aware of itself. If we awaken from our stupor, it's the universe that awakens.

Our little dustlike egos only enclose and obscure and distort—*something more,* this big Self, this bigger identity.

And here is the heart of what is good and true about Yom Kippur and Ash Wednesday. Beyond all the gloomy guilt-ridden theology you may remember from your past—is this call to humble silence, to contemplation, to wonder. It's nothing more or less than the call of the soul, the call of our highest and most genuine selves, something that exists beyond the egos we present to the world, something that shares the One Life of this Universe and is not separate from the energy and intelligence that made it, and makes it still.

You are that.

In that light,—everything, even our failures, become steps on the path. We begin to see those mis-steps as what we do under the delusional influence of the ego, but at the very same time something from which we can learn that our small, bumbling, confused egos are not the final word about who we are.

And it's in the *silence beyond the noise and tumult and pretension* that our creative, godlike possibility turns up.

EMERSON ASKED:[10]

> What is the ground of this uneasiness of ours; of this old discontent?

Here's his answer:

> What is the universal sense of want and ignorance, but the fine innuendo by which the soul makes its enormous claim? . . . Man is a stream whose source is hidden. . . .
>
> The Supreme Critic on the errors of the past and the present, and the only prophet of that which must be, is that great nature in which we rest, as the earth lies in the soft arms of the atmosphere; that Unity, that Over-soul, within which every [one]'s particular being is contained and made one with all other; that common heart, of which all sincere conversation is the worship, to which all right action is **submission**; that overpowering reality which confutes our tricks and talents, . . . and which evermore tends to pass into our thought and hand, and become wisdom, and virtue, and power, and beauty.

And there it is. *Critic.* The *Supreme Critic.* It isn't somebody out there who disapproves of you. The Supreme Critic in here, in the heart of you.

---

10 Essay "The Over-Soul."

It's Hammarskjöld's "uneasiness" that he has decided to bless. It's to *that* that we must answer. Answering to *that* is something that no other person or entity or force can do for us. For that, you need silence, and in the silence, a reckoning, and a commitment to what in us demands the highest and best in us, a commitment to a rising, deepening human consciousness.

That supreme Critic on the quality of our lives is in us, and we in it—a Self bigger than our little egos.

It's not enough to be supremely confident, not enough to affirm our human drives and passions, not enough to recognize the fallacy in the old theology's dim view of human beings.

Not enough without the Supreme Critic on the errors of the past and the present, and the only prophet of that which must be.

We all can know this higher consciousness in moments. To be enlightened is to live in that consciousness. We can know it in moments, and those moments make all the difference.

A strange amalgam of god and dust. So we'll have to find our way to that bigger Self that spills out into the whole Kosmos. We'll have to be conscious and maintain consciousness of both the god that we are and the dust that we are, and while giving the dust its due, at the end of the day, it is the dust that must bow to the god; it is the god that will fill the dust with glory.

DON'T BELIEVE
EVERYTHING YOU THINK

DON'T BELIEVE everything you think.

No, really.

Thinking is a quite good thing. Really, the problem is *thought*, not *thinking*. *Thinking* is something you're doing right now, fresh, new, with the possibility of being creative.

Thought is stored reheated leftover memories of previous thinkage, if I may invent a word. Left over from previous thinking, stuck in your memory so that when it's triggered, it pops up so fast you don't realize it. And it runs, like a little app in your head, and distorts your perception with its stale content. Or, as the late, great theoretical physicist David Bohm put it, messes up your head with electrochemical smog.

And it sticks us with a rigid, inflexible identity that we think we are, when actually we are much more than we realize.

I mean, we might think we're free because there isn't somebody else who's controlling us. But a far greater freedom is when your actions are not predetermined by your habitual ways of thinking and acting in reaction to circumstances, not controlled by reflex reactions that set off that electrochemical smog in your head.

SO LET ME TELL you how this works.

You're an infant and everybody adores you, and then you get a little older and everybody isn't charmed and they yell at you. You feel awful.

And then one day, about 40 years later, somebody yells at you.

There's a part of you that you call *I* that is always the subject, in control, that's a bit godlike. And there's a part of you that you call *me* that is always the *object*. Things happen to *me*, are done to *me*. The victim. That part of you gets told you don't amount to much and gets yelled at. The old thought-apps run. You feel unvalued and worthless. And you feel angry—you've been assaulted, attacked. Victimized.

Oh, did I mention the *felts*[1] that kick in. A *felt* is an old feeling that got stored in memory and is now dragged out, so fast you don't see it happening. So you feel what you felt when you got yelled at as a little kid. And you feel the anger you felt on various now-unspecified previous occasions. Your adrenalin starts flowing, your muscles tense, your heart beats rapidly. *Electrochemical smog.* And now you've got into a situation where you've got to act with mature intelligence, and how are you going to do that, in this smog? It involves your whole body. That's what thought does. And then you're quite surprised to find that what you do isn't coherent with your intentions. Your actions are arising out of the pollution of your thought.

I BELIEVE THAT IN EACH of our lives, individually and communally, and in our life as the human presence on this Earth, something new is always trying to emerge, to come into being. That's what an evolutionary view of the world means. And religiously, spiritually, we find the meaning of our lives, the sense of authenticity and purpose, when we make ourselves available to that higher purpose, to be vehicles of the future that wants to emerge. There's something inherently creative going on. And you and I are expressions of that.

But there's stuff that seems to get in our way, keeps us stuck in old habits. It's got a lot to do with how *thought* works.

Thinking implies the present tense, you're doing it right now, and it's capable of something new. *Thought* is the past participle of think. Thinking doesn't just disappear. It goes into the brain and leaves a trace—a *thought*. Which then runs like a little app in your head, automatically. And our thought sets off a sequence of reflexes, so fast we don't see it

---

1   Another Bohmism.

coming.

Maybe you think the activity of the mind is something separate from the body. Or from emotions. *It's all one.* Feelings and thoughts affect each other. You can see it in the structure of the brain. There's an intellectual center in the cortex, the outer layers of your brain. And deeper down there's the more ancient emotional center, and between them there is a very thick bundle of nerves connecting them. There's an entire soap opera waiting to play out in your head the instant something pushes your buttons!

How CAN WE GET FREE of this system that pervades everything we do? How can we get free of the reheated past that keeps us numb to the present and unavailable to the future?

Is there an intelligence, a quality of *perception*, that's fresh and live and not just reheated memory?

So think about this. Where does our Being come from? What is that Emptiness that spiritual teachers are always talking about, from which the possible future might emerge, from which anything fresh and vital might come? What is that emptiness?

One OF THOSE HABITUAL stored-up *thoughts* is this idea that I know what I am. This is my identity. And I'm going to maintain it at all costs. *But I don't know what I am.* What I am is unknown, but constantly revealing itself.

If there is something which is infinite—the universe, or some dimension beyond it, that Emptiness from which everything flows—I am somehow grounded in that. So *that* must be the source of whatever I am. It's unknown—but it reveals itself.

So maybe we make way too much of this idea of an identity, of an all-important identity onto which we are going to hold, because that gets in the way of discovering that unknown, keeps us from changing those reflexes. Because once we identify with something, our reflexes kick in. And all those memories and those reflexes can tell us is *the past.*

They know nothing new, only the past. They want to preserve that identity even if it's kind of false.

But what if you understand yourself as a creative being rather than an identified being, whose identity is all wrapped up and determined? What if you are instead a fresh, living expression of something Beyond rather than something fixed and unchanging? Part of an eternal flow and movement that is creative?

David Bohm used to say that the ground of any person is really unknown. It's really in the whole universe.

And in modern physics, one of the things they say is that empty space is full of energy, a vast amount of energy. Each wave in empty space has a certain minimum energy, even when it's empty, and if you add up all the waves it would be infinite. Space is mostly full, and matter is a little ripple on it.

Whatever is behind the mind—consciousness itself, whatever you want to call it—is an unbounded stream; and thought is just ripples on the surface of that stream. You can look out into the night sky tonight and you won't see titanic stores of energy because matter and light go right through it without deflecting. So you think what you see is empty space. But even though you cannot see it you are looking into the fullness of space, the ground of all existence. The matter you are made of is a little variation, a ripple, on this ground.

Maybe mind is another "side" of that same thing. Dr Bohm asked if maybe—his words—"that which we call energy on one side is mind on the other side. Energy is pervaded with a kind of intelligence, out of which perhaps insight comes, or deeper perceptions of truth." [2]

DR CHANNING SAID—well, he really *insisted*—that the human bears a likeness to God. Here's what he said:

> The divinity is stirring within the human breast. . . . Let [us] hold fast . . . a faith in the greatness of the human soul, that . . . discerns in the depths of the soul a divine principle, a ray of the Infinite Light, which may yet break forth and shine as the sun. . . .

2 David Bohm. *Thought as a System*. London & New York: Routledge, 1992 , p. 172. It's the source of some concepts in this chapter.

The idea of God, sublime and {awesome} as it is, is the idea of our own spiritual nature, purified and enlarged to infinity. In ourselves are the elements of the Divinity. . . .

That unbounded spiritual energy which we call God, is conceived by us only through consciousness, through the knowledge of ourselves. . . . The Infinite Light would be for ever hidden from us, did not kindred rays dawn and brighten within us.[3]

But we have all sorts of representations of ourselves which are really pretty superficial. And we identify with those superficial representations.

It's sort of like the rainbow. We see a rainbow, but that's not exactly what's really there. What we really have we have is drops of rain and light—a process, creating a representation in our minds.

Well, so what we "see" is a self; but what we actually have is a tremendous creative process that involves a whole lot of thoughts going on in consciousness. And some of those thoughts aren't very creative at all—just rehashed memories. Against the backdrop of consciousness we are projecting a self, rather than a rainbow.

I was driving home toward the pair of bridges to Rhode Island's Aquidneck Island. Beyond the first was Conanicut Island (Jamestown), and as I approached it, I saw it: the most perfect arc of a rainbow over the island. The thing about a rainbow is, if you try to drive to it, or walk to it, you'll never find it because it isn't there. There are no arcs of colored bands floating above Conanicut Island. Physics says there's a bunch of raindrops falling and there is light reflecting off the water and it reaches your eye in a certain way. The light reaches everybody's eye in a rather similar way, so everybody agrees there's a rainbow. That doesn't mean that what is there is what you think you see. What's there is falling rain and light refracting. As I drove, I looked forward to seeing it from the Newport Pell Bridge, over Aquidneck Island, but it vanished.

No harm in that. We can use a little beauty, even if it's a bit illusory.

You can be watching a movie or the tellie and getting lost in the characters and feel that one of the characters is actually you. If you look at it carefully you see nothing but flashing lights on an LED or LCD screen. But *you* see people, trees, characters; you see emotional

---

3 Sermon, "Likeness to God," 1828.

conflicts and danger; you see anger, fear, pleasure. And feel it. But it's all yourself. It's all the imagination being infused onto the flashing dots on the screen.

Kind of like a rainbow, really.

Its nature is the same as the rainbow. A representation. You're infusing your imagination, your past, your knowledge into the flashing dots. Thought is doing it all by itself.

There are plenty of contexts in life where that's necessary. You couldn't get through the day if you had to think through everything you did. Reflexes can help us. But when you fail to see that this is what's happening, and think it's real, then you're in danger.

We have a self-image that's a lot like a television program going on inside. There are other kinds of illusions, too, and they can mislead us. Have you ever seen somebody who seemed very attractive to you, and now you're quite interested, and then he opens his mouth. And you hear what he says, maybe a little bit of Glenn Beck he's been listening to. You've entirely lost your interest. Well, *I* have, anyway.

IF YOU WALK TOWARD THE rainbow you will never get there. If you try to touch the *self*, it'll work out just about as well. It's ephemeral. The attempt to treat the self as an object is just not going to mean anything.

So instead, suppose we say that this self is unknown. Its origin, its ground is unknown. And it is constantly revealing itself, through each person or through nature and through everything that is.

The basic meaning of the word "self," is the "quintessence"—the essence of the essence. The fifth essence, it was called in ancient times, the essence of the whole thing. So what you mean by the "self" is your very essence. It's something bigger than the *I-identity* you think you are, and the victimized *me* that you think you are. Those are just representations, which we are liable to mistake for actuality.

SO IF WE WANT TO BE FREE from the tired reflexes of thought and tightly contained identity, here is what I think we have to do: pay attention to thought. Notice how it runs, kind of mechanically, pulling up the old thoughts and *felts* and projecting them onto the present, distorting your perception. Notice how it happens instantly, faster than you can do anything about it. Your thoughts are running you, not you running your thoughts.

Get used to noticing. It's hard to do this when it happens because it happens at lightning speed. But you can evoke the same electrochemical smog on your own, at your leisure, when you *can* observe it. Get hold of the words that set off the smog in your head, and say them. Get the right words that produce the effect. The anger, the feeling like crap, the rapid heartbeat, whatever. Do it until you really get it, you really recognize how mechanical it is, how it doesn't really mean anything at all. When you see how infallibly it works, it will be a revelation. It won't stop the electrochemical smog from ever happening again, but it will be an insight, a perception, that will, over time, weaken its grip, liberate you.

When I learned Greek, I learned the word for *truth—alethia—*and it's stuck in my mind. What it means, literally, is "out of lethargy," "out of sleep." Being *awake.* Truth.

And once awakened—you have to be conscious. You can't be lured by feed-good thoughts alone. There is awareness that is not comfortable, that sets off the chemistry of uncertainty, anxiety, discomfort. It takes courage to just be with it. Many in our time refuse to think about our current climate crisis, for instance. They just won't go there because it doesn't feel good. But a person who is awake and has roused from their stupor knows our lives cannot be all about chasing pleasant feelings. Such a person is nourished from deeper wells than just their feelings in the moment, has found a deeper joy that isn't shattered by discomfort. An awakened person has committed their life to truth, the pursuit of truth, which is a state of *awakened* consciousness. To be awake is no longer to be looking at the world through automatic reflexes that have been built up for the purpose of never allowing an unpleasant awareness to make you feel bad. That's a pursuit that never leads to real joy. It's flawed thinking, and you can't believe everything you think! That flawed thinking is completely disconnected from why we are here.

And those auto-run reflex apps in your head can run on ideology, too, to filter out truth. Like American "national exceptionalism" or the widespread refusal to believe that we face a massive climate emergency. Our culture is loaded with them. That culture creates us. The potential good news is that *we* get to create that *culture.*

Cultivating the capacities for attention, perception, and insight—and not being run by mere *feelings*—is what spiritual practices like meditation can give you.

REAL INSIGHT, PROFOUND PERCEPTION, comes in an instant, without time, beyond time. It comes fresh from that vast stream behind the mind, beyond the brain, the energy and intelligence that is the source of your very being, and everything that is. It can alter the synapses in our brains. It can open the doors of our perception to a new vision of life, driven by meaning and purpose that flood into you from some deep place. We can experience its creative imagination, showing us possibilities that never were, but that we can bring into being. We can touch a profound source of *truth*, which is "being awake," "out of lethargy."

And then we can be available to what calls to us to do and to be, to be vehicles for something larger than ourselves to emerge.

THE BIRTH OF GOD?

EVERY WINTER I'VE HAD to contend with Christmas and its strange mythology. Congregations expect it. Oddly, the idea of God being born as a baby has become so familiar that it strikes almost no one as a startling idea. What, indeed, might we mean by using the word God at all in these times?

Truth is, we know very little of the actual Jesus of Nazareth, who seems to have been a kind of street-philosopher living, not in Judaea where Matthew put his birth so he could be the Bethlehem-born Son of David, to suit the myth he was making, but in the cosmopolitan Hellenisticly-inclined land to the north. He sure wouldn't have recognized the stuff churches say about him at Christmas. And if he was a pretty fine mystic, he didn't say he was God, at least not anymore than he said you and I are. Lots of Gospels were written about him by later followers, as they formed a new religion. But only four—those that, conveniently enough, reënforced the emerging churchly empire's apostolic authority scheme—made it through the churchly filters. And myths weren't first meant as metaphors, but as real events in real history with real characters and venues. That's how they're still taken by most people even in this allegedly postmodern era. Funnily, religion is the *one* arena where it is common to find educated professionals still teaching people to believe myths more or less *literally*.

Alright then. I contemplate the Christmas myth, as each year I must.

Maybe a fresh look will reveal—within the symbolic language of the Christmas story—an astonishing possibility. Consider the hope woven through it:

For, lo! the days are hast'ning on by prophet bards foretold,
When peace shall over the earth its ancient splendors fling.

The prophets longed, yearned, anticipated something that was not yet. They were taking part in the making of the human story, and when you do that, there's anguish and longing. All the universe shares the anguish and longing.

The former era was ruled by the eternal Parent-Father-God whose once-and-for-all creation was finished. From there, everything was pretty much downhill. But something more was already at work, laboring to come to birth. The prophets knew an unsatisfied anguish of longing. They lived in a world that was too narrow and they reached out for space and room to be more than they were.

The hold of the old order was strong. Its God is changeless. So are his followers.

So it is that I was reading the *New York Times* at Christmas in 1981 and came across a headline you could have found this year, too. I kept the story. It read, (now get this headline:)

IN RURAL ARKANSAS, EVOLUTION BETOKENS BALEFUL WORLDLINESS

The people they interviewed were cutting the references to evolution out of school textbooks with scissors. It seems Arkansas had passed a new law that required that Creationism be taught in public schools and the judge had ruled it unconstitutional, but still they're at it. *That* fight rages on still today.

THE STORY OF CHRISTMAS, THOUGH. Doesn't the story of Christmas, the birth of God, ever make you wonder?

You have to admit, the birth of an infant God is a startling idea. What will it do to the foreverness of God? the eternity of God? the changeless One who stood before the beginning of time and cannot, experience any change or growth because God is already perfect?

Parents in giving birth become more than themselves, transcend themselves. So may we.

The Angry Old Man in the Sky, and with him
All superstition that cannot be squared with knowledge,

And all enslavement of pariahs and outcasts,
And all exile of people who don't fit in,
And all pre-determined answers and all pre-formed worlds,
And all suppression of creativity and all timidity about New
Thoughts and New Visions
    gave way on that silent night to a Child-God
But I speak not of one birth in the Bethlehem stable or Nazareth
or wherever, just one birth long ago, far away.

Rilke asks:

> Why do you not think of him as the coming one, imminent from
> all eternity, the future one, the final fruit of a tree whose leaves
> we are? What keeps you from projecting this birth into times that
> are in process of becoming, and living your life like a painful and
> beautiful day in the history of a great gestation? For do you not
> see how everything that happens keeps on being a beginning, and
> could it not be *his* beginning?[1]

You want a religion of changeless forever standing still stagnation
halted stunted creation? Finished. What you see is all you ever get. You
want a religion of one singular savior sent down from heaven to redeem
miserable fallen humans?

No, for the Christmas story to have any meaning for me, it has to
be the story of a God who is born as a child, born in our compassion
and courage and creativity, born vulnerable into uncertainty.

Now maybe that's an audacious claim for any human to claim, that
we are divine enough to give birth to God and to create God and bring
this child up. But inasmuch as it's no more funny than telling the peas-
ant woman Mary of Nazareth that she is the Mother of God, we may
as well try it out.

Mary of Nazareth. She and her carpenter friend, to whom she is
betrothed, are journeying to Bethlehem. She is pregnant, won't say how,
it wasn't Joseph the carpenter. And they get there for this big census
and she gives birth in the side of a hill, stable in a cave smelling of cows,
no rooms left, didn't phone ahead, feel the clammy cold air
    unto you this day . . . God is born

---

1 Rainer Maria Rilke, *Letters to a Young Poet*. New York: W.W. Norton, 1934. Letter
   Six (23 Dec., 1903), 49.

God is a child born. And where's Joseph? He's not around for most of the rest of the story. Some holy family. Look. So are *you*, so are we. The holy family giving birth to God. Nurturing God, bring God up.

And her son, the son of this poverty and humility in a cave.

His claims are *very* audacious. Are not his claims a bit out of proportion, jut a human child, child of Mary in a cave? But he persists in making the bold audacious claim of divinity, and parts of the world around him get transformed. Other divinities are born.

And it happens that in their compassion
     their courage
there are more births of God.

And it is given to us to be creators.

A baby God. One born in our living, because not one of us lives without consequence, leaves nothing behind. We in our living give birth to God, we implant particles[2] of the Divine where we go, whether that divinity be noble or mean, whether we enrich the world with grace, compassion, and possibility or whether our contribution is smallness, meanness.

And this—to which we give birth—continues to evolve, carrying within it all that has ever been, while expressing also the new—unfolding entirely new possibilities.

What we are creating may be magnificent or it may be mean, but what is to be, we are creating. Let it express our grandest, our noblest possibility, the gathering divinity of the struggle of life.

On a summer evening in 1838, Mr. Emerson stunned the graduation exercise audience that crowded the Divinity School chapel at Cambridge when he told the graduating class (among the stunning things he had to say that day):

> Jesus Christ belonged to the true race of prophets. He saw with open eye the mystery of the soul. Alone in all history he estimated the greatness of man. One man was true to what is in you and me.

2 The visionary architect Paolo Soleri distinguishes between the traditional "Alpha God" at the beginning of time and an "Omega God" who is the fulfilment of human courage, creativity, and compassion, drawing human evolution forward as realized individuals become "particles of God"—in his *The Omega Seed: An Eschatological Hypothesis* (Garden City, N.Y.: Anchor/Doubleday, 1981).

He said, in this jubilee of sublime emotion, "Would you see God, see me; or see thee, when thou also thinkest as I now think." But what a distortion did his doctrine and memory suffer in the same, in the next, and the following ages!

Too much of a claim for humanity? If you were around forty years ago, maybe you noticed this at the front of Stewart Brand's *Whole Earth Catalog*, echoing Buckminister Fuller: "We are as gods and we might as well get good at it." He's revised it: "We are as gods and *have* to get good at it."[3]

What we are giving birth to

is contained within us as a seed

containing all of the past, all that has ever been,

but is not yet complete, will be more than all the past.

We must make of the universe a home for compassion, justice, peace, and luminous creativity. We must fill it with particles of God.

---

3 In *Whole Earth Discipline*, Viking, 2009.

F I R S T   F I R E
The Earth, the human presence, and the future

ONCE, MARGARET FULLER—Emerson's friend and, for awhile, editor of his journal *The Dial*—took a trip to Niagara Falls, a trip she described thus:

> Just as I had seated myself [at Table Rock, close to the great fall], a man came to take his first look. He walked close up to the fall, and, after looking at it a moment, with an air as if thinking how he could best appropriate it to his own use, he spat into it.

"This trait," she went on, "seemed wholly worthy of an age whose love of utility" is so extreme.[1]

By JUNE 2010, CONCENTRATION of atmospheric carbon dioxide (CO_2) had reached 392 parts per million. That is 5.5 percent over what it was in 2000 and 10.1 percent over 1990. The quantity of CO_2 thrown into the atmosphere in 2010—30.6 billion metric tons—exceeded all previous years, despite the faltering economy.[2] In May 2011 it hit 394.97 ppm.[3]

THOMAS BERRY WAS ONCE A ROMAN CATHOLIC priest, but came to call himself a Geologian. He was a prophetic voice whose impact on me is matched by his impact on an awful lot of others who have come to

---

1 *Summer on the Lakes*, Ch. 1 (entry for Niagara, June 10, 1843). In *The Portable Margaret Fuller*, ed. Mary Kelley. New York: Penguin, 1994, pp. 71f.

2 Andrew C. Revkin, "Tracking economy, CO_2 emissions hit new high." *New York Times* Dot Earth blog, 30 May, 2011.

3 John Vidal, "Carbon levels hit new peak, research shows." *The Guardian*, 31 May 2011. You can track the latest readings at http://esrl.noaa.gov/gmd/ccgg/trends/.

an edge where the exhausted thinking of previous eras collapses. For decades Thomas Berry had been telling us that the planet as a whole is in a traumatized state. These are his words: "We are in a situation beyond anything ever experienced before in the course of human or earth history."

Never has there been anything like the first years of the new millennium, when the ink on one urgent scientific report is barely dry when another, more ominous, more appalling, is issued.

We would be right to tremble.

IN JANUARY 2005, A MAJOR international report called *Meeting the Climate Challenge* became only one more in a succession of reports coming from thousands of scientists around the world—one of them even commissioned by the Pentagon but then suppressed by the Bush administration—to warn of apocalyptic consequences of climate change that are already beginning to show up. And extremely comprehensive computer analysis done on supercomputers at the Commerce Department's lab in Princeton, New Jersey warned in September 2004 that hurricanes would become stronger, wetter, and more frequent because of global warming.

The week before Katrina, the then U.N. Ambassador, John Bolton, demanded that all references to the battle against global warming be removed from the new statement of the ideals and purposes of the United Nations. America's senior climate change scientists were being investigated and bullied by the chair, then, of the House Committee on Energy and Commerce—Joe Barton of Texas, who has long ties with the fossil-fuel industry.[4]

IF YOU GET YOUR NEWS FROM the European press and not the American—or you follow the alternative press in the U.S.—you may have learned about a stunning Pentagon report issued in November 2003 and suppressed by the Bush White House for four months until the

---

4 Paul Brown. "Republicans accused of witch-hunt against climate change scientists." *The Guardian*, August 30, 2005.

Observer [5] of London and, of all things, *Fortune* Magazine got hold of it. A *Pentagon* report! And it calls climate change during the next twenty years a greater threat to national security than terrorism.

It says the worst advances of climate change will come abruptly, not gradually, finally inundating London, New York, Boston, Miami, Bombay, Calcutta, Sydney, Shanghai, Lagos and Tokyo, and submerging them under rising seas. And this report says it would leave six billion people on an overburdened planet in a state of perpetual war contending for vanishing supplies of energy, water, and food as catastrophic shortages would also mean mass migrations, famine, and disease. It's especially astounding because it was commissioned by the revered defense advisor who was the mastermind behind some of Donald Rumsfeld's favorite schemes. Oops.

And it wasn't the only warning. Similar reports have come from the German government, whose scientists came to almost exactly the same conclusions, and by British scientists, and by the Intergovernmental Panel on Climate Change, and by many American scientists.

A quarter of all land species, maybe a lot more, will go extinct in the process.

At an international conference of 114 governments, in January 2005, the then chair of the Intergovernmental Panel on Climate Change, Dr Rajendra Pachauri—said he personally believes that the world has "already reached the level of dangerous concentrations of carbon dioxide in the atmosphere" and he said there must be immediate and "very deep" cuts in the pollution if humanity is to "survive." That's his word. The American government was shocked.

This is why the Administration was shocked. The White House had gotten the previous chair, Dr. Robert Watson, *removed*—at the request of ExxonMobil, because he persisted in calling for urgent action. They wanted him replaced by Dr. Pachauri—and so the Bush Administration lobbied other countries to vote Watson out and Pachauri in.

So here's the new guy, the one Exxon and the Bush White House wanted, and he tells the delegates: "Climate change is for real. We have

5 *The Observer*, London, Sunday February 22, 2004.

just a small window of opportunity and it is closing rather rapidly. There is not a moment to lose."[6] Later he said that the danger point the IPCC had been set up to prevent us reaching—*had already been reached*.

In February 2005, Tony Blair convened two hundred of the world's leading climate scientists at Exeter, in the south of England. They issued the most urgent warning to date.

Writing in *The Independent* of London, environment editor Geoffrey Lean mused:

> Future historians, looking back from a much less hospitable world, will certainly pay special attention to the first few weeks of 2005. They will puzzle over how a whole generation could have sleep-walked into disaster—destroying the climate that has allowed human civilisation to flourish over the past 11,000 years—and they may well identify the first weeks of this year as the time when the last alarms sounded.[7]

IT ALL CAME TOGETHER AT EXETER. The conference had been called by the Prime Minister to advise him on the urgent steps that would have to be taken. He needed help persuading the world to act.

It opened with his Secretary of State for the Environment, Margaret Beckett, saying that "a significant impact" from global warming "is already inevitable." [8]

There were presentations from top scientists and economists from every continent showing that dangerous climate change is already happening and that catastrophic events that were once thought *highly improbable* were now seen as *likely*. Avoiding the worst would be technically simple, and cheap, they said, provided that governments could be persuaded to take immediate action.

As Lean reports, the conference learned that glaciers are shrinking. Arctic sea ice has lost almost half its thickness and will disappear

---

6 "Pachauri: Climate approaching point of 'no return.'" *The Independent*, 23 January 2005.

7 Geoffrey Lean. "Sleepwalking toward apocalypse now." *The Independent*, 6 February 2005

8 Geoffrey Lean, *op cit.*

altogether by 2070. By 2075, most of the glaciers on the Swiss Alps will be gone. The director of the British *Antarctic* Survey showed that the West Antarctic ice sheet is beginning to melt, which could mean a rise in sea levels of fifteen feet: which is something when you consider that 90 percent of the world's people live near sea level.

They learned more things:

There are now far more natural disasters caused by violent weather.

The bird populations in the North Sea has collapsed. Maybe a quarter of the world's coral reefs are already gone.

There is powerful evidence that the oceans are slowly turning acidic.

There is a new scientific consensus—that the warming *must be kept below an average increase of two degrees celsius (3.6F) if catastrophe is to be avoided.* Some are convinced that a single degree celsius is all the planet can bear; others argue that processes already in motion render that small an increase impossible. Concentrations of carbon dioxide, the main cause of climate change, must be gotten below 350 parts per million and kept there. But we've already reached 394.97 ppm.

In October 2006, the British Government issued The Stern Report—authored by former World Bank chief economist Sir Nicholas Stern. It paints an apocalyptic picture over 700 pages of where global warming could lead economically, arguing that, unless we act, it will cost more than two world wars and the Great Depression of the Thirties and render swaths of the planet uninhabitable. Even if the world stopped all pollution tomorrow, the slow-growing effects of carbon already pumped into the atmosphere would mean continued climate change for another thirty years and sea levels rising for a century. (More recent science says much longer, like a 2009 NOAA (the federal National Oceanic and Atmospheric Administration) study directed by scientist Susan Solomon that says sea rise, changes in precipitation, and surface temperature will continue for *a thousand years.*[9]) Nor, wrote Dr. Stern, is unilateral action by one country enough: if Britain closed all its power stations tomorrow, within thirteen months China would

---

9 "New Study Shows Climate Change Largely Irreversible," press release from National Oceanic and Atmospheric Administration, 26 January 2009, at www. noaanews.noaa.gov/stories2009/20090126_climate.html.

fill the gap left in global emissions. Given that the effects will be felt around the world—from the collapse of the Amazonian rainforest to the melting of Greenland's ice sheet and changes in the Indian monsoon—the response must be global, too. But in April 2008, Lord Stern had to tell the *Financial Times* "We underestimated the risks . . . we underestimated the damage associated with temperature increases . . . and we underestimated the probabilities of temperature increases." In retrospect, he said, he would have taken a much stronger view in the report on the drastic changes that would come about if greenhouse gas emissions were not abated.

THE BIG QUESTION IS WHETHER governments will act. Or will our children and grandchildren wonder—"how could they have been so blind?"

I WAS STRUCK BY WHAT the *Independent* correspondent Lean, who reported the Exeter conference, wrote about his experience:

> I am willing to bet there were few in the room who did not sense their children or grandchildren standing invisibly at their shoulders. . . . The cautious scientific language scarcely does justice to the sense of the meeting.[10]

Then the biggest study of climate change ever made, based at Oxford University, said that what we're headed for will be twice as catastrophic as the IPCC's worst predictions. Then an international task force reported that we could reach "the point of no return" in a decade.

And then, just before *Shell Oil* reported record profits mainly achieved by selling oil, the head of Shell in the UK, Lord Oxburgh, warned that without urgent action by the governments of the world, there "will be a disaster."[11]

What could happen?

Wars could break out over diminishing water resources as popula-

---

10 Geoffrey Lean, *op cit.*

11 Saeed Shah. "Shell boss warns of global warming 'disaster.' *The Independent*, 26 January 2005.

tions grow and rains fail. Not today's seven billion, but more than 10 billion, will be competing for water, and food, and habitable space by 2050 (and 9.3 billion by 2100), according to United Nations Population Division.[12]

What could happen? London, New York, Tokyo, Bombay, many other cities and vast areas of countries from Britain to Bangladesh disappear under many feet of water as seas rise. The EPA says that by century's end it will only take a storm to flood Boston—and all the way to Duxbury would be under water.

How likely is it? Inevitable. Even if global warming stopped today, the seas would continue to rise for centuries.

Even the United States Energy Information Administration during the Bush years said that world demand for all forms of energy will rise 54 percent in the next 20 years.[13] We can hope that a combination of subsequent conservation and technology progress will mean a smaller increase, because if the tide isn't turned, by 2025, the world will use twice as much electricity and 50 percent more oil.

But—here is what we're letting our corporations get away with.

Carbon dioxide is one of the principal greenhouse gases that cause all this. An unusually candid executive at ExxonMobil says his company expects CO_2 levels to rise 50 percent by 2020.

But there was a handy solution. In 2003 the Bush Administration's EPA proclaimed that CO_2 and those other greenhouse gases—are *not pollutants* and so they don't have to be regulated.

The greenhouse gases *aren't pollutants?!* Handy. So the major carmakers—Ford, GM, Toyota, BMW, Porsche, Volkswagen, DaimlerChrysler, Mazda, Mitsubishi, and Nissan and Honda—in order to defeat a new set of regulations in California—launched a TV and print ad campaign declaring their vehicles "virtually emission-free." The auto makers' alliance explained that the term "virtually emission-free" should be understood to refer only to emissions classified as pollutants

---

12 Justin Gillis and Celia W. Duggar, "U.N. forecasts 10.1 billion people by century's end." *New York Times*, 3 May 2011.

13 "EIA: Global oil use seen soaring." Reuters, April 15, 2004.

by the Environmental Protection Agency.[14] Finally, at the end of 2009, the Obama Environmental Protection Agency ruled CO_2 a "dangerous" threat to public health, giving the agency regulatory power of emitters. Or maybe not "finally": on April 7, 2011, the House of Representatives—since the 2010 election under the control of the Republican Party now driven by the far-right "Tea Party" movement—voted to bar the EPA from regulating CO_2 and industrial emissions. Fortunately, there weren't enough votes in the Senate, which would have to override a presidential veto.

NO WONDER DR PACHAURI concluded: "We are risking the ability of the human race to survive."

The American Geophysical Union added its voice to the chorus in January 2008, saying "Earth's climate is now clearly out of balance and is warming." Then on February 1 the Scripps Institute of Oceanography published, in *Science*, its conclusion that the persistent and dramatic decline in mountain snowpack in the American West comes down to the amount of carbon we're putting in the atmosphere, producing an even drier, more arid West. In the same issue, a group of fifty scientists predicted a series of sudden shifts:

- Melting of Arctic sea-ice (about 10 years)
- Decay of the Greenland ice sheet (about 300 years)
- Collapse of the West Antarctic ice sheet (about 300 years)
- Collapse of the Atlantic thermohaline circulation (about 100 years)
- Increase in the El Nino Southern Oscillation (about 100 years)
- Collapse of the Indian summer monsoon (about 1 year)
- Greening of the Sahara/Sahel and disruption of the West African monsoon (about 10 years)
- Dieback of the Amazon rainforest (about 50 years)
- Dieback of the Boreal Forest (about 50 years)

Subsequent science has produced only starkly more alarming projections. As I write, AMAP—the international Arctic Monitoring and Assessment Program—is reporting the Arctic ice sheets melting three

14 Danny Hakim, "An auto industry ad leaves critics choking." *New York Times*, March 22, 2005.

times faster than previously thought—so much faster that a three to five foot sea level rise will result from this factor alone by 2100. Meanwhile we're learning that some mountain glaciers are melting a hundred times faster than at any time in the past 350 years. In Patagonia in South America the lost ice is already equivalent to 120 percent of the contents of Lake Erie. Most of the loss has happened within thirty years. Around the world, mountain glaciers are the source of water that billions of people rely on for crop irrigation and water supplies. As the melting deprives the planet's farmlands and thirsty inhabitants of water, it has begun raising sea levels.[15]

The prediction of ice sheet melting and resultant effect on ocean circulation was borne out by scientists' discovery in 2011 of a massive volume of freshwater floating on the Arctic Ocean like a cap. If this result of melting sea ice flows into the North Atlantic, it could affect the complex "thermohaline" ocean circulation that keeps the warm Gulf Stream flowing toward Britain and keeps Britain temperate.

The warnings from the Geophysical Union and the Scripps Institute in early 2008 were followed immediately by a warning from an international scientific team from the National Academy of Sciences, the Potsdam Institute for Climate Impact Research in Germany, the University of East Anglia, and Oxford University's Environmental Change Institute, ranking the most vulnerable regions on the planet and warning of sudden and catastrophic collapse before the end of the century. They warn of thresholds beyond which ecosystems will enter abrupt decline. There's already a fifty percent chance that the Greenland ice sheet will begin melting irreversibly, which alone would lead eventually to a 23-foot rise in sea levels. The warming would bring droughts and floods first.

In March 2008 James Hansen, head of NASA's Goddard Institute for Space Studies, said the EU target of 550 parts per million of CO_2— then the most stringent in the world—must be slashed to 350 ppm if

---

15 Charles J. Hanley and Karl Ritter, "As Greenland melts faster into sea, researchers forecast up to 5-foot rise in ocean levels." Associated Press, 3 May 2011; Lewis Smith, "Glaciers melting at fastest rate in 350 years, study finds." *The Independent*, 4 April 2011.

"humanity wishes to preserve a planet similar to that on which civilisation developed." Hansen is one of the genuine heroes in the climate emergency. That's the same Hansen whom the Bush Administration had sought to silence when, studying the data, he connected the dots. He knew how the Bush Administration was manipulating (and squelching) scientific data. He tried to go public, citing as grounds for doing so the first line of NASA's mission statement: "to understand and protect our home planet." The statement had come out of an extensive, participatory process at NASA. In 2006, Hansen discovered that the statement had disappeared from the NASA web site and had somehow been revoked.[16] Simultaneously, the budget for earth sciences was mysteriously slashed.

But conference after scientific conference, study after study, warns of a situation more appalling than the last conference or study. The Intergovernmental Panel on Climate Change regularly draws together thousands of scientists representing most nations on earth, organized by the United Nations. Its landmark report in February 2007 contained stark warnings that even now seem mild. We know a lot more now.

In it, there is a list of tipping points that we're approaching at breathtaking speed. We know that the Arctic sea ice and the Greenland ice sheet are in danger of sudden catastrophic collapse and it may already be too late to save them and prevent the catastrophic rise in sea levels that would result.

In March 2009, something happened that you may not have noticed because the American media chose to ignore it. At Copenhagen, an Emergency Climate Summit, in preparation for the international climate conference there the following December ended with desperate pleas from the scientists.

Two thousand five hundred scientists from eighty countries came to reveal more terrifyingly stark facts and projections than even the worst previously made public. You wouldn't have read about it in the *Chicago Tribune* or the *Orlando Sentinel* or even the *New York Times*. You *could* find it on the front pages of the better British newspapers not owned by

---

16 James Hansen, *Storms of My Grandchildren: The Truth About the Coming Climate Catastrophe and Our Last Chance to Save Humanity.* New York, Berlin, London: Bloomsbury, 2009, pp. 124-135.

Murdoch's News International, or on the BBC,[17] but Americans remain uncomprehending, thanks, inexplicably, to our media.

Sir Nicholas Stern, the economist commissioned by the British government to analyze the economic impact of climate change, told the summit that politicians have failed to take on board the severe consequences of failing to cut carbon emissions, and that the consequences will be "devastating." His words: "Do the politicians understand just how difficult it could be? Just how devastating four, five, six degrees centigrade would be? I think not yet."

Why the urgency? Back in the 1990s, carbon emissions were rising by 0.9 percent—less than one percent—a year (averaging about 1.5 percent per year between 1973 and 2000). That represented real progress, since the growth rate of emissions from 1950 to 1973 was 4.5 percent. But the growth rate is again approaching that of the pre-environmental 1950-1973 era. It now stands at about *3.5 percent every year.* Rapidly increasing regression to burning *coal* has a lot to do with that. So much for the optimistic projections that greenhouse gas emissions would be dropping by now.

The scientists at Copenhagen in March 2009 said carbon emissions have risen more in recent years than *anyone thought possible,* and the earth seems to be losing the ability to soak it up. And they said that failure to agree strong carbon reduction targets at political negotiations this year could bring "abrupt or irreversible" shifts in climate that would render parts of China, India and the eastern United States uninhabitably hot.

---

17 Indeed, *The Guardian* and *The Independent* are a major source for most of this section: David Adam, "Stern attacks politicians over climate 'devastation.'" *The Guardian,* 13 March 2009; Michael McCarthy, "Lord Stern on global warming: It's even worse than I thought," *The Independent,* 13 March 2009; Randolph E. Schmid, "Global warming increasing faster than predicted." *Huffington Post,* 14 February 2009; David Adam, "Severe global warming will render half of world's inhabited areas unlivable, expert warns," *The Guardian,* 12 March 2009; David Adam, "Global warming may trigger carbon 'time bomb', scientist warns," *The Guardian,* 10 March 2009; Michael McCarthy, "Fate of the rain forest is 'irreversible,'" *The Independent,* 12 March 2009; David Adam, "Amazon could shrink by 85% due to climate change, scientists say," *The Guardian,* 11 March 2009; Katherine Richardson, "A kick-start in Copenhagen: The picture scientists laid out at our climate summit is bleak, but the research paves the way for action," *The Guardian,* 13 March 2009; Robin McKie, "President 'has four years to save earth'; US must take the lead to avert eco-disaster," *The Observer* (Sunday edition of *The Guardian*), 18 January 2009.

Uninhabitably hot.

• Sea levels will rise twice as fast as official predictions we have now.

• Even modest warming could unleash a carbon "time bomb" coming from the Arctic soils. In fact, permafrost in the Arctic—and elsewhere—holds massive, frozen stores of methane, billions of tons of it, in boggy soils which, when they melt, release this most potent of greenhouse gases, twenty-five times more potent than CO_2 over a time horizon of a century, and as much as seventy-two times more potent over twenty years. In the Arctic, warming is proceeding twice as fast as anywhere else. Methane emissions have risen by almost one-third in five years' time. The problem is particularly severe under the East Siberian portion of the Arctic Ocean seafloor. The permafrost there, long thought to be an impermeable barrier sealing the methane in, is perforated by melting and leaking large amounts of methane into the atmosphere—in fact, as much methane is coming from the East Siberian Arctic seafloor as is coming from all the rest of the world's oceans.[18]

• The rising temperatures will almost certainly kill off half of the Amazon rainforest— it's too late to reverse that—and could kill off 85 percent of it.

• It turns out that ocean temperature is rising about 50 percent faster than anybody predicted.

It had been pretty well agreed that we cannot allow temperatures to rise more than 2° C—which is 3.6° F. But the experts at Copenhagen warned that temperatures are probably going to soar beyond that 2° C target. One of them said what they're now thinking: "The 2° C target is gone . . . I think we're heading for 4° C at least." Not a few scientists think it's going to 7° C. Four degrees celsius is 7.2° F. Seven is 12.6° F. What will that mean?

If things go poorly, scientists now think a 4° C rise could come as

---

18 David Adam, "Arctic permafrost leaking methane at record levels, figures show," *The Guardian*, 14 January 2010. National Science Foundation press release "Methane releases from Arctic shelf may be much larger and faster than anticipated," 4 March 2010, at http://www.nsf.gov/news/news_summ.jsp?cntn_id=116532&org=NSF&from=news. Judith Burns, "Methane seeps from Arctic sea bed," BBC News, 4 March 2010. Cornelia Dean, "Study says undersea release of methane is under way," *New York Times*, 4 March 2010.

soon as 2060.[19]

• A 4° C rise could turn swaths of southern Europe to desert.

• And that other stunner: it could render half of the world so hot as to be uninhabitable. That includes the Eastern United States.

All the messages coming in are telling us that the climate system is operating on the worst-case scenario.

Scientists usually avoid commenting directly on policy, but the scientists at Copenhagen had had enough of silence. They insisted politicians have got to stand up to "vested interests that increase emissions" and "build on a growing public desire for governments to act." They called for a "shift from ineffective governance and weak institutions to innovative leadership in government, the private sector and civil society."

Rob Bailey, the senior climate adviser for Oxfam said: "The verdict of the world's top scientists is clear. The big question now is whether the world's richest countries, who created the climate crisis, will act before it's too late. Our climate is changing fast and if left unchecked its impacts, particularly on the world's poorest people, will be devastating."

Another of the scientists, Kevin Anderson, who's the research director at the Tyndall Centre for Climate Change Research in the UK, said: "The scientists have lost patience with our carefully constructed messages being lost in the political noise. And we are now prepared to stand up and say enough is enough."

When President Obama took office, he got a message from James Hansen. His message: We now have only four years to save the earth, or the processes already set in motion will be unstoppable. Two years later, in 2010, a "Tea Party" -driven right wing surge put Republicans decisively in control of the House of Representatives and left Democrats with a thin hold on the Senate. This brought new influence to Darrell Isa, a California Republican who got the chair of the House Oversight Committee. He was planning investigations of—*climate scientists*. His

---

19 Richard A. Betts, Matthew Collins, Deborah L. Hemming, Chris D. Jones, Jason A. Lowe, Michael G. Sanderson, "When could global warming reach 4°C?" *Philosophical Transactions of The Royal Society* (London: Royal Society Publishing, 2 June 2011), at http://rsta.royalsocietypublishing.org/content/369/1934/67.full.

perspective is reflected in nearly every Republican in Congress. Illinois' John Shimkus, one of the contenders to chair the House Committee on Energy and Commerce, rejected scientists' warnings about climate change by simply quoting *Genesis* 8:22 —

> As long as the earth endures, seedtime and harvest, cold and heat, summer and winter, day and night will never cease.

"I believe that's the infallible Word of God," he said. Discussion closed. And then there was good old Joe Barton, famous for his rejection of humanity's contribution to warming, who hoped to regain that Energy Committee post, explaining that if the earth gets hot, people will just adapt and find shade.[20]

In 2011, while his state was literally on fire—the result of the worst droughts ever recorded for Texas and the highest temperatures ever recorded for any American state led to wildfires that consumed the equivalent, in square miles, of Connecticut—Republican governor and presidential aspirant Rick Perry repeated his rejection of the science of global warming.

In her work of "space fiction" *Shikasta*, Doris Lessing writes as though from the perspective of a far future time, reflecting on the history of the Earth, describing a "Century of Destruction:"

> These were maddened creatures, and the small voices that rose in protest were not enough to halt the processes that had been set in motion and were sustained by greed. By the lack of substance-of-we-feeling.[21]

Indeed. Today the scientists issue their increasingly urgent warnings, and the small voices that rise in protest are not yet enough to halt the processes that have been set in motion and are sustained by greed.

In December 2009, representatives of the 192 nations returned to Copenhagen to negotiate. European news media and alternative media in America covered the event closely; major U.S. media barely mentioned it. Largely because the United States Senate had failed to approve a serious proposal for international agreement and resistance

---

20 Elizabeth Kolbert, "Uncomfortable Climate." *The New Yorker*, 22 November 2010.
21 Doris Lessing, *Re: Colonised Planet 5, Shikasta*. New York: Alfred A. Knopf, 1979, p. 90.

from Russia and China, the conference ended in fetid failure. President Obama went with a fake promise of a seventeen percent cut—fake because all other nations based their comparisons on 1990 emission levels. The American "seventeen percent" was a scam based on a comparison with *2005*. When based on the same 1990 standard, America was really proposing a pathetic *four* percent cut. Europe's intention of a 2050 fifty percent emissions cut commitment (Germany's Merkel wanted eighty percent) that would be legally binding was shot down by the refusal of China and India to agree. Subterfuge, drama, and hard bargaining drew in President Obama, British Prime Minister Gordon Brown, France's Sarkozy and Germany's Merkel. Chinese president Jiabao contemptuously sent lower-level representatives in his place. That any agreement at all came out of Copenhagen owed to a heroic last-minute intervention by Ed Miliband, then the British environment minister and now leader of the Labour Party. All that remained was a vaguely worded two and a half page political agreement with no binding force and very little content. In sum, more than 100 heads of state agreed to limit the rise in global temperatures to 1.5°C – 2°C (2.7°F – 3.6°F) above the long-term average before the industrial revolution which set in motion the massive rise in greenhouse gases.[22]

But six months later came the analysis of a major international effort led by the UN Secretariat to monitor the emissions reduction targets of over sixty countries, the Climate Interactive Scoreboard. Its conclusion: even if the agreed "promises" are kept, global temperatures will rise a catastrophic 3°C (5.4° F). And analysts at Climate Analytics, at the Potsdam Institute for Climate Impacts Research in Germany, concluded that whatever pledges were made at Copenhagen will fail to hold global warming below 2°C, and that, instead, 2020 will bring 3.5°C (6.3° F), and catastrophe. They expect to see global emissions rise between 10 and 20 percent by then. Further, even the specific promises aren't being matched by real reductions.[23]

---

22 John Vidal and Jonathan Watts, "Copenhagen: The Last-Ditch Drama That Saved the Deal from Collapse." *Guardian*, 20 December 2009.

23 Survey of 1,546 adults, April 21-26 2010, reported in *The Smithsonian*, July-August 2010.

Meanwhile there are signs that the simultaneous corporate and fundamentalist propaganda campaign to undermine climate science is having an effect. In 2008, a Pew poll found more Americans believing in angels than in anthropogenic (human-caused) climate change. Only 30 percent of American voters saw climate change as a top national priority. Pew Research polls for the *Smithsonian* magazine showed 76 percent of Americans believing in 1999 that the earth will get warmer, but by 2010, that percentage had been reduced to a mere 66. And 47 percent actually believed that "the quality of the earth's environment will improve" by 2050, damning evidence that major media had failed miserably to convey the bitter facts.[24]

As I wrote a draft of this chapter, the mid-Atlantic region was deep in snow after a blizzard of historic proportions—actually two, all within a few days' time. The Capital was shut down for days. For some, that's proof enough that climate change is a liberal lie. The Oklahoma Republican climate change denier Sen. James Inhofe built an igloo on Capitol Hill with a cardboard sign reading "Al Gore's New Home."

But local weather—whether it's snowing or sunny in your garden or what the weather's been like this year in your state—establishes nothing. Although it must be noted that climate scientists had actually predicted more snowstorms in the Northeast as climate change brings more violent weather and more moisture in the atmosphere brings more precipitation.

Note, please, the distinction. *Weather* is not the same as *climate*. *Climate* is average weather conditions over time, and climate change refers to those conditions globally, not just in your state or your garden. Even as Washington and Baltimore and New York dug out, most of the world was hotter than it has ever been. By the time of this writing in 2010, seventeen nations have experienced the highest temperatures

---

24 Richard Black, "'Paltry' carbon curbs point to 3C," *BBC News*, 21 April 2010. Potsdam Institute analysis published as "Copenhagen Accord pledges are paltry," *Nature*, 22 April 2010. Article by Joeri Rogelj, Julia Nabel, Claudine Chen, William Hare, Kathleen Markmann, Malte Meinshausen, Michiel Schaeffer, Kirsten Macey & Niklas Höhne. Online at: http://www.nature.com/nature/journal/v464/n7292/full/4641126a.html. Juliette Jowit and Christine Ottery, "Studies predict major extinctions and collapse of Greenland ice sheet with temperatures rising well above UN targets," *The Guardian*, 5 July 2010.

ever recorded.

Consider, then, the massive irresponsibility shown by political leaders who can't be bothered with the science. How would they explain the idiocy to future generations who must live—if they can—with the consequences?

PAST THE POINT OF NO RETURN?

The British scientist and Fellow of the Royal Society James Lovelock proposed his "Gaia hypothesis" in the early 1970s—asserting that Earth is a single living system that self-regulates so as to maintain conditions favorable to life, that human activity is altering it, that it's a complex system difficult to predict, that it holds "critical thresholds and abrupt changes," and that it's now in trouble. For his efforts (along with colleague Lynn Margulis) he was awarded the Geological Society's very prestigious Wollaston Medal.

Now, a "hypothesis" is an untested idea proposed to explain the facts—not quite yet a "theory," something that's been tested and found true. But his insistence that Earth is a living system, and is sick, is supported by mounting evidence. It's come to be known as "Gaia" or "Earth System" Science.

In January 2006, James Lovelock announced his conclusion that we have passed the point of no return, that the damage is now irreparable, and that we must now act to limit the scale of the coming catastrophe.[25]

In *The Independent,* he wrote:

> This article is the most difficult I have written . . . The climate centres around the world, which are the equivalent of the pathology lab of a hospital, have reported the Earth's physical condition, and the climate specialists see it as seriously ill, and soon to pass into a morbid fever that may last as long as 100,000 years. I have to tell you, as members of the Earth's family and an intimate part of it, that you and especially civilisation are in grave danger.

Before the industrial revolution, the concentration of carbon dioxide in the atmosphere stood at about 280 parts per million; now it's above

25 James Lovelock, "The Earth is about to catch a morbid fever that may last as long as 100,000 years" *The Independent on Sunday,* January 16, 2006; and *The Revenge of Gaia* (London & New York: Allen Lane/Penguin, 2006).

394 ppm, and there's already enough CO_2 out there to raise the official concentration to the vicinity of 430 ppm. And that implies that a fairly sudden and very fatal jump could happen at any time. Now we know that a concentration exceeding about 350 ppm will lead to disaster, in part because the last time CO_2 reached that level, 125,000 years ago, the sea level was 4 to 6 meters higher than today (5 meters is 17 feet). That leaves Florida, Bangladesh, the European lowlands, and count-less coastal cities—*under water.*[26] Earlier scientific complacency about sea-level rise was shattered by the stunning rate of ice sheet melting, especially in Greenland and Antarctica.

The IPCC had predicted that once that concentration surpasses 400, a rise would result in global temperature of about 2 to 3 degrees celsius (that's 3.6 to 5.4 degrees fahrenheit). But that was based on older data, and, more importantly, doesn't factor in the precipitous, difficult-to-calculate jumps that come when "tipping points" are passed. Lovelock predicts a jump of 9 degrees celsius (16° fahrenheit), within the next few years or decades, probably following a temporary period of cooling.

Lovelock is convinced that humanity isn't up for facing reality and changing its suicidal behavior. It's still possible to avert the worst, though too late to avert the very bad. What we have to do, he says, is adapt to the horror we've made.

If Lovelock's climate science is right, his negativity about human capacity to take hold of the emergency and create a viable future is merely understandable given the experiences of his life and work, and given the response of the United States of America.

I prefer to believe in human possibility—in the highest sense. But between our current deadly predicament and that higher possibility must lie a spiritual revolution. We have the facts; we have the technology nec-essary to halt this slide into hell. But we continue the slide, deliberately ignoring the truth that cries out from scientific studies, measurements, and models. Leaders won't lead; not if offered the alternative of self-aggrandizement and popularity. Too many leading voices of the right wing seem to enjoy playing bully to science.

It's time for another leap in consciousness: not just for the sake of

26 Hansen, p. 142.

survival now; but for the sake of unimagined future possibility.

THERE IS SOME GOOD NEWS. California has worked seriously at improving the energy efficiency of its power plants and buildings, and insisted on more fuel-efficient vehicles. And noting that ten percent of home electrical use involves television sets, and the (surely foolish) federal action pushing people to buy more energy-hungry sets, the state has set the first energy standards for television sets.

The greatest achievements to reduce global warming are happening now in Europe. A popular movement may well have forced an end to coal burning in the United Kingdom by 2025. Britain has agreed to cut carbon emissions by 60 percent over 50 years, Holland by 80 percent in 40 years, and Germany by 50 percent in 50 years. Russia has ratified Kyoto. And even China—whose intention to burn huge quantities of dirty coal has everyone scared—*China* has established fuel economy standards for its cars and trucks that are much tougher than ours in the U.S. Faced with a combination of the scientific facts, and of notoriously serious air pollution, and with a government free from political restraints, China is investing heavily in alternative energy. On December 25, 2009 its National People's Congress passed a law requiring China's energy companies to buy a fixed percentage of energy generated through renewable sources—wind, solar power, hydropower, biomass, geothermal and ocean energy; the government will set the percentage every year and the power companies will have to do it. If that's more expensive, they'll have to buy it anyway or pay twice its cost in fines. Inadequacy of the power grid won't work as an excuse—they'll just have to upgrade the grid. China, meanwhile, outstripped the U.S. as the biggest emitter of CO_2—nevertheless leaving the United States as the biggest *cumulative* emitter of CO_2 since 1751, and by a wide margin (27.2% to 9.1%).

The Kyoto Protocol (relatively ineffectual as it is) is now in force, at least until 2012—signed by 142 nations—most recently Australia, in 2007, whose new Labour Prime Minister Kevin Rudd immediately signed on. But it was still resisted by the Bush Administration in the

United States, leaving it the only major industrialized nation to refuse. Meanwhile, the Bush Administration had been blocking a coalition of eighteen states led by California to impose more stringent economy and emissions standards. The Bush EPA Administrator overruled his own staff scientists and lawyers.

Germany has shown real commitment to making the transition to 100 percent renewable energy sources. The German government accepts the proposition that it is possible and they believe that everything depends on what we do between right now and 2020. Their accomplishments so far have been simply astonishing. In wind, in solar electricity, in solar water heating. Germany is the single fastest-growing market for photovoltaic power. The German government's planning and commitment runs through 2050. All this happened within ten years. But Germany's record is marred by a sharp reduction in 2009 in subsidies for alternative energy conversion resulting from the global recession, and, incomprehensibly, by plans to build new coal-fired plants to replace nuclear ones which are being shut down.

Britain, with 3,400 wind turbines in over 300 wind farms in operation so far, is spending $117 billion to build more offshore wind farms—and the government believes they could generate three times Britain's electricity needs that way.

Already wind farms provide more than a fifth of Denmark's total power. While the affluent folks of Cape Cod were blocking the first serious windfarm in America because they don't want to look at it, the Danes think they're beautiful.

Will this be enough? James Lovelock thinks it won't be; that we must turn to nuclear energy—a view he shares with Hansen, who proposes a renewal of development of fourth-generation "fast" fourth-generation reactors that use 99 percent of the uranium as well as the very dangerous transuranic actinides that remain dangerous for 10,000 years. They leave far less waste, waste that can't be turned into weapons of mass destruction. By 1994 the Argonne National Laboratory had completed all the essential tests, and "fast" reactors might have become a reality, but in the wake of anti-nuclear sentiment following Three Mile Island and Chernobyl, the Clinton Administration killed the program entirely.

Better, safer nuclear reactors may be the only way to halt the mining and burning of coal. But that new generation of reactors doesn't yet exist.

THE OBVIOUS ALTERNATIVE, MISSED

But, to many of us, it appears that America and the world have repeatedly missed the chance to develop what would seem to be the obvious alternative. The molten salt reactor (MSR); specifically, the type of MSR known as the liquid fluoride thorium reactor (LFTR).

Oak Ridge National Laboratories first developed the concept in the 1970s. So a half century ago, and at several subsequent points, this safe, inexpensive, and unlimited alternative energy source was passed over. One of the reasons was the military's interest in the uranium-235 and plutonium reactor: you can make bombs with it. Another is the sheer momentum of what you're already doing. Westinghouse and General Electric developed the reactors that were built instead, and those are the reactors we're all familiar with—pressurized water reactors (PWRs) with solid nuclear fuel cooled with water under great pressure and controlled by control rods.

We know the problems. Quantities of nuclear waste. The possibility of meltdown and release of radioactive clouds. We witnessed Three Mile Island, Chernobyl, and Fukushima.

Somehow the fact that our daily use of fossil fuels creates massively more death and devastation than even the worst mishaps involving these outmoded reactors ever did—seems to escape us. The nuclear panic persists, especially among environmentalists, ironically enough.

So whatever is a molten salt reactor? What is a liquid fluoride thorium reactor, anyway?

Well, to jump backward a bit in time. Maybe five billion years ago some star in the vicinity of our Sun burned up its hydrogen and collapsed, as stars are wont to do, creating elements that included uranium and thorium—clouds of elements that coalesced into planets.

There's energy in those heavy metals. At the core of our Earth, it's thorium whose heat keeps the iron core molten and creates the magnetic field which, in turn, divert the solar wind which would otherwise strip the plant of its atmosphere and water.

Nice benefits of thorium, to be sure, but here's what counts for our discussion of energy. Thorium is cheap and abundant all across the planet. And as fuel in an LFTR, it's dissolved into molten salt, becoming a liquid fuel that can circulate continuously through the reactor until it's burned completely. No waste.

Fluoride salts are the most chemically stable elements on Earth. They prevent dangerous radioactive materials from being released, even in the event of a serious accident. They stay liquid at the high temperatures necessary for the reactor's operation without having to operate at high pressure. They don't require an external energy source to cool them.

A thorium reactor is safe. It operates at high temperature but the fuel cannot melt down—it's already molten. And if the radioactive salt *leaks*, it solidifies in place. The reactors are compact and efficient, inexpensive to build and to operate.

Thorium is the nuclear fuel we should have been using. It's abundant, tremendously energy-dense, and safe. Thorium as a liquid fuel would be one thousandth as hazardous as uranium. And there's no out-of-control chain reaction because fission happens only as long as the thorium is bombarded with neutrons. Switch it off and it stops.

There are other variations of MSR, by the way. Some could burn the spent fuel from conventional water-cooled nuclear reactors, creatively getting rid of that dreaded nuclear waste we don't know what to do with.

So. Liquid fluoride thorium reactors offer the solution to global warming, and the world's energy poverty, and resource depletion and ensuing conflict.

A growing chorus is advocating thorium as the fuel of choice, and the development of LFTRs. The technology would be cheap, inexhaustible, secure, virtually waste-free, and safe.

LFTR can end developing nations' reliance on coal. Thorium can fuel small, modular reactors that could be mass produced and be affordable for poorer and developing nations. They could even produce hydrogen that could replace petroleum fuels for our vehicles.

And—no small consideration—this boundless energy source can address the dramatic uptake in energy demand in developing nations, and that, it seems to me, is a necessary component for uplifting the world's poorest.

Another vital consideration. A reactor is a continuous, non-intermittent energy source. Solar and wind are both very intermittent. And when the wind stops and there's no sun (this regularly happens at night, if you hadn't noticed), the gas- and coal- and oil-fueled generators crank up. And this cranking-up process is a big piece of the problem because it produces enormous quantities of emissions, rivalling the cost of just running them all the time. When you factor in this consequence of backup from conventional sources, solar and wind may not ultimately do much to reduce CO_2 emissions.

I'd rather leave a fuller, better explication of all this to a physicist and expert, Robert Hargraves, whose book *Thorium—Energy Cheaper Than Coal*, you should read.[27]

There is a problem, of course. I have spoken as if LFTRs actually exist. They don't. Hargraves thinks that a prototype LFTR could be operational in five years, and that another five years could see mass production. But U.S. R&D funding is nonexistent except for small projects at MIT, UC Berkeley, and the University of Wisconsin. France, the Czech Republic, Japan, Russia, the Netherlands—and now China—are investing in MSR research.

The great irony is that it was the United States that was developing thorium technology—a program that was quite advanced when Chernobyl-and-Three-Mile-Island panic scared the bejeezus out of the public. Doubling the irony, it was the Clinton-*Gore* Administration that halted the development of thorium-fueled reactors. It was finally President Obama's Energy Secretary Stephen Chu who, despairing of acceptance of anything nuclear in the U.S., and apparently understanding the urgency of developing thorium reactors, turned over the technology to China.

27 Hanover, NH: Robert Hargraves, 2012. More at www.thoriumenergycheaperthancoal.com.

In 2011, a 9.0-scale earthquake and resultant tsunami catastrophically destroyed the first-generation 1960s-era Fukushima Daiichi six-reactor plant on the northeast coast of Japan. The weeks of uncontrolled radioactive emissions shattered the recovery of faith in nuclear power. The fear was intensified by a new compendium of studies published by the *Annals of the New York Academy of Sciences*, that had concluded that the 1986 meltdown at Chernobyl in then-Soviet Ukraine had killed nearly a million people (though the official death toll is fifty-four). Its publication moved China to cancel thirty-five new reactors, with the likely consequence that China will replace them with coal-burning plants—coal, the one fuel unquestionably, and infinitely, more destructive than nuclear. We must hope their LFTR development proceeds apace.

Before Chu provided China with America's thorium technology, China approved the pebble-bed reactor, less prone to overheating and meltdown, cooled not by water but by nonexplosive helium gas. Pebble-bed and thorium-based reactor systems are among six classes of Generation IV reactors.[28]

The Fukushima plant was a copy of the General Electric Mark 1 boiling water design, one so flawed that a safety official with the Atomic Energy Commission recommended in 1972 that the Mark 1 system be discontinued, one so flawed that three members of the design team resigned in 1976 in disgust, particularly because of what they knew would happen if the plant lost the capacity to cool both the active and spent fuel rods. And this one was built in a geologically unsafe fault zone on a tsunami-prone coast. Thirty-two of them are currently operating, twenty-three in the United States. One is located down Barnegat Bay from the town where I grew up; another one, Vermont Yankee, lies about 45 miles north of my former home in western Massachusetts,

---

28 Ambrose Evans-Pritchard, "The reactor that saves itself: safe nuclear does exist and China leads the way with thorium," London: *The Telegraph*, 23 March 2011. Keith Bradsher, "A radical kind of reactor," *New York Times*, 24 March 2011; Tuan C. Nguyen, "China to develop a greener nuclear reactor," *Smart Planet*, 4 Feb. 2011 (http://www.smartplanet.com/technology/blog/thinking-tech/china-to-develop-a-greener-nuclear-reactor/6205/). Bryony Worthington, Peer, "Why thorium nuclear power shouldn't be written off," *The Guardian*, 4 July 2011.

just over the state line. Vermont's Senate voted in 2010 to overrule the Nuclear Regulatory Commission and refused to relicense it to operate another twenty years. The NRC overruled Vermont.

Halting the planet's quickening warming will require nuclear power. It needn't come from outmoded and discredited technology.

It will take every effort to counter the continuing slide into disaster.

In December 2007 came the Bali Conference (there was another one at Bali in 2009), where the goal was to arrive at an international agreement on binding greenhouse gas emissions targets. As the nations of the world gathered, it was becoming clear that the situation is worse than previously thought; the IPCC's figures weren't up to date and its conclusions too conservative. Scientists were stunned by the progress of Arctic melting.

And what was at stake at Bali? United Nations Secretary General Ban Ki-moon opened the conference with this:

> The situation is so desperately serious that any delay could push us past the tipping point, beyond which the ecological, financial and human costs would increase dramatically. . . . Succeeding generations depend on us. We cannot rob our children of their future. . . . The science is clear, climate change is happening, the impact is real, the time to act is now

adding that the price of inaction would include floods, famine, rising sea levels and loss of biodiversity, and that the choice is between a comprehensive agreement and "oblivion." [29]

Philip Clapp, head of the National Environment Trust, said:

> The scientists are telling us that this is the world's last shot at avoiding the worst consequences of global warming.[30]

And speaking of the biggest polluters, the United States and China, Al Gore said

29 Thomas Fuller, "Global Climate Talks Divided on Emissions Targets." *New York Times,* Dec. 12, 2007; and "Crunch Time for Climate Change." BBC News, Dec. 12, 2007.

30 Geoffrey Lean, Environment Editor, "Rich countries blamed as greenhouse gas emissions hit record. Bali conference is the world's last chance to avoid 'catastrophic' global warming, experts warn." *The Independent on Sunday.* Dec. 2, 2007.

They will need to make the boldest moves, or stand accountable before history for their failure to act.[31]

The Bush Administration blocked the agreement on binding emissions cuts of 25 to 40 percent. Never mind that scientists have been warning that something more like a 90 percent cut will be necessary, and soon. It blocked technical and financial assistance to poorer nations to cut their emissions and to protect against rising seas and other devastating effects of climate change. It capitulated only in acknowledging the need for a new agreement to replace Kyoto. At various points the United States was booed and chastised by other nations.

"If you cannot lead, leave it to the rest of us. Get out of the way," said Kevin Conrad, Papua New Guinea's ambassador for climate change.[32]

AND WHAT WOULD IT MEAN to *lead?* For political leadership, it would mean putting ample resources and the best minds to the twin tasks of *mitigating* the causes of global warming and *adapting* to the now-inexorable consequences of the warming that has already been set in motion. It would mean investing an agency of government with sweeping powers to implement the measures the science requires. It would do what is necessary to halt, as rapidly as possible, the burning of fossil fuels, putting human brilliance and labor to the transformation of transportation, infrastructure, and the lived environment of towns and cities. It would effectively curb the appetites of the wealthiest corporate powers on behalf of the good of the whole. It would clean up the scummy political process that now turns a very deliberately deaf ear to science, reason, and morality.

Instead, by a vote of 240-184, the United States House of Representatives, dominated by the Tea-Republican Party, rejected a resolution that said, simply, "Congress accepts the scientific findings . . .that climate change is occurring, is caused largely by human activities, and

31 Sarah Lyall, "Gore Urges Bold Moves in Nobel Speech." *New York Times*, Dec. 11, 2007.

32 Juliet Eilperin, "Nations Forge Pact on Global Warming, Climate Change." *Washington Post*, Dec. 15, 2007.

poses significant risks for public health and welfare."[33] The statement
was an amendment proposed by Rep. Henry Waxman to a Republican
bill to strip from the EPA the power to regulate greenhouse gases,
which passed. The House went on to slash NOAA's budget for satellite
hurricane tracking and weather forecasting. The prevailing votes were
cast, mostly, by Republicans, but the disgraceful festival of idiocy was
joined by a few Democrats, too.

Nearly everywhere, mitigation and adaptation projects already voted
are being delayed, compromised, and curtailed to "save money." That
means delay, and delay is expensive. "We add $1 trillion to the cost
[of tackling climate change] with every year of delay," said Christiana
Figueres, executive secretary of the UN Framework Convention on
Climate Change speaking at before the start of more international
climate negotiations at Bonn as summer 2011 cranked up. She'd already
upset several governments with her insistence that the negotiations
need to be about holding the global temperature rise not to 2° C, but
to 1.5° C.[34]

In late summer 2011, Republicans who controlled the U.S. House of
Representatives undertook a barely-noted attack on environmental laws
by including thirty-nine riders to 2012 spending bills for the Interior
Department and the EPA.[35] Among their riders: a one-year restriction
during which "the Administrator of the Environmental Protection
Agency shall not propose or promulgate any regulation regarding the
emissions of greenhouse gases . . . to address climate change." A ban on
funding for the EPA to regulate motor vehicle emissions. Weakening
protections against mountain mining. Allowing uranium mining in the
Grand Canyon, halting a moratorium that is meant to protect Colorado
River aquifer water on which 27,000,000 depend. Blocking the EPA
from strengthening protections for wetlands under the Clean Water
Act, exposing the wetlands to commercial development. Blocking the

33 Ben Geman, "Amendment that says climate change is occurring fails in House."
   The Hill, E² Wire energy and environment blog, 6 April 2011.
34 Fiona Harvey, environment correspondent, "Global warming crisis may mean
   world has to suck greenhouse gases from air." *The Guardian*, 5 June 2011.
35 "Concealed Weapons Against the Environment." *New York Times* editorial page,
   31 July 2011.

EPA from labeling the toxic ash from coal-fired power plants as hazardous waste. Blocking the EPA from limiting runoff of pollutants such as phosphorus and nitrogen into Florida's lakes and river. Defunding any effort by the Interior Secretary to limit oil, gas, and commercial development on public lands that are potential wilderness protection areas. There was more. There will be more. And when they happen, few will notice.

ON THE NIGHT OF APRIL 20, 2010, an offshore oil rig called Deepwater Horizon—so named because it was drilling for oil under 5,000 feet, or nearly a mile, of seawater in the Gulf of Mexico—exploded. The rig had drilled a further 13,000 feet—altogether, three miles—pushing the limits of both technology and safety. Water at 5,000 feet is under tremendous pressure. Oil and gas from even deeper surges upward under more extreme pressure, *between four and six tons per square inch.*

A month before the explosion, there'd been a series of accidents. One resulted in the damage (undisclosed by its operator, British Petroleum) to the blowout preventer, or BOP, a 400-ton device near the seabed. It's used to seal the well shut once it's been drilled so as to test the well's pressure and integrity. In the event of a blowout, it's supposed to seal off the well. The BOP had other malfunctions, and there have been subsequent claims that even with flawless maintenance, the design is flawed, and they simply don't work.[36]) In defiance of law, it hadn't been tested since 2000. Now the well couldn't actually be tested, and there was no working blowout prevention device.

---

36 Mark Clayton, "Gulf oil spill: failure of blowout traced to bent drill pipe," *Christian Science Monitor,* 23 March 2011. Harry R. Weber and Michael Kunzelman, "Gulf probe: blowout prevent was flawed," *Associated Press,* 23 March 2011. *Final Report for United States Department of the Interior, Bureau of Ocean Energy Management Regulation, and Enforcement: Forensic Examination of Deepwater Horizon Blowout Preventer,* prepared by Det Norske Veritas, at http://www.scribd.com/doc/51393879/DNV-Report-EP030842-for-BOEMRE-Volume-I; with appendices at http://www.scribd.com/doc/51393957/DNV-BOP-report-Vol-2-2. Jim Landers, "Offshshore well blowout preventer was supposed to be fail-safe," *Dallas Morning News,* 4 May 2010. Tom Fowler and Jennifer A. Dlouhy, "Blowout prevent report could prompt design changes," *Houston Chronicle,* March 24 2011. David Hammer, "Blowout preventer failure in Gulf of Mexico oil spill traced to bent drill pipe," New Orleans *Times Picayune,* 24 March 2011.

Then it came time to seal the well. Deepwater Horizon would motor off and another rig would be moved into place to pump the oil. And BP, which leased the Horizon from Transocean, had decided the procedure was taking too long, and cut some corners. Two hours before the explosion a pressure test showed "a very large abnormality" and was ignored. A vast cloud of methane—natural gas—rippled up from the bottom and settled over the area around the rig. The methane made the rig's diesel engines rev wildly. There was an almighty explosion and inferno that incinerated eleven men.

So that 2010 incident. For weeks the oil flowed into the Gulf. BP's early public estimate was 1,000 barrels a day, but the number was revised upward: 5,000, 30,000, 80,000, more. Could anyone measure accurately at such great depth? As vast plumes of oil began to flow into the critical Gulf Stream, the public got a revelation about what President Obama would call the "cozy relationship" between the oil companies and the government agencies that were meant to regulate them.

The Bush-appointed head of the Minerals Management Service, Chris Oynes—an old friend of former Vice President Cheney—announced that he was going into "retirement." BP, it turned out, had been given a waiver from having to conduct the required environmental assessments prior to undertaking the project. MMS is a division of the Interior Department. Sixteen months into the Obama Administration, Oynes was still there. The corruption-plagued Interior Department was now led by Ken Salazar, whose career to date had demonstrated a pronounced fondness for offshore drilling. There were employees at Salazar's Interior Department who describe their experience there as "the third Bush term." Salazar had put fifty-three million new Gulf offshore acres up for lease, more than had ever been opened to drilling in a single year.[37] President Obama had just announced his support for offshore oil drilling, insisting that America needs the oil. The Tea-Republican Party had already distinguished itself with the phrase "Drill, Baby, Drill," and now the GOP blocked efforts to raise limits on oil

---

37 See Tim Dickinson, "The Spill, the Scandal and the President" in *Rolling Stone*, June 8, 2010 for a damning chronicle of a President who seemed to half-believe the scientists, whose initiatives seemed like half-measures, and who seemed over his head and short on wisdom.

companies' liabilities for oil spills, while mustering not a single sponsor for climate legislation (like the severely anemic Kerry-Lieberman bill, then under debate).

It came out that an MMS scientist had complained to his bosses of catastrophic safety and environmental violations, but MMS had already granted at least five final approval permits for new Gulf drilling as recently as the time of the Deepwater explosion.

To mitigate the mess, both BP and the government had deployed two types of a "dispersant" brand called Corexit. After 1.84 million gallons of Corexit were sprayed on the surface and hundreds of thousands of gallons more injected directly over the hemorrhaging wellhead, warnings were sounded that the substances could prove more lethal to life in the gulf than the oil itself.

Some degree of effectiveness can be claimed for the strategy. Microorganisms and bacteria seem to have consumed more of the dispersed oil than in the worst-case scenarios. But scientists wonder what effects these products, banned in nineteen countries, will prove to have had with the passing of time.

Some Corexit ingredients remained suspended deep in the Gulf, and some of the sea floor is covered with a layer of petroleum-related chemicals. A year after the incident, in the Bay Jimmy area south of New Orleans, scientists found a layer of glistening oil, the consistency of peanut butter, six inches under matted marsh grass, where the elements cannot break it down. No effective method had yet been found for cleaning those marshes, on which so many life-forms depend.[38] There were masses of casualties among birds, oysters, and tuna larvae. Hundreds of corpses of dolphins and their newborn have washed up on gulf shores. The Center for Biological Diversity estimated casualties at 26,000 dolphins and whales, and 6,000 sea turtles, and 82,000 birds, and countless fish and invertebrates.[39] A count of recovered carcasses cannot tell the real story, since most will have sunk without being spot-

38 Raffi Khatchadourian. "Gulf Wars." *The New Yorker*, March 14, 2011; Dahr Jamail, "BP's Criminal negligence exposed," Al Jazeera, 20 April 2011 (at http://english. aljazeera.net/indepth/features/2011/04/2011420104533120290.html).

39 Elizabeth Shogren, "In cleaning oiled marshfields, a sea of unknowns," *National Public Radio*, 20 April 2011 (http://www.npr.org/2011/04/20/135571426/in-cleaning-oiled-marshlands-a-sea-of-unknowns).

ted. Oiled wildlife are still washing up dead. And NOAA has done no tissue sampling. But Nature seems to have shown a remarkable capacity for renewing itself from an assault by what seems to have been 4.9 million barrels (or 205 million gallons) of crude, and the accompanying 200,000 metric tons of methane. So far. It still isn't known what the consequences will be that the gulf floor is covered with the oily remains of oil-eating bacteria, or that miles of marsh are now fouled with heavy oil, or the death of so much fan coral. Meanwhile, doctors were seeing frightening symptoms in Gulf patients.[40]

As of this writing, the full extent of the damage can't be known. Meanwhile, many scientists warn that any declaration of recovery would be premature because too much research has been either delayed, or kept secret. And while some of the secrecy is defended as necessary to the integrity of federal legal action against BP, it's hampering the science. And the delays, some political, mean the loss of the best data.[41]

The new Bureau of Ocean Energy Management (BOEMRE), part of the Department of the Interior, resumed permitting of new deepwater drilling at the end of February 2011. The first was for a site 6,500 feet down, 70 miles southeast of Venice, Louisiana, to be drilled by Noble Energy. Said BOEMRE Director Michael R. Bromwich: "the operator successfully demonstrated that it can drill its deepwater well safely and that it is capable of containing a subsea blowout if it were to occur." Faced with the unconvincing effectiveness of those blowout preventers, Noble contracted with Helix Well Containment Group for a "capping stack" device. Royal Dutch Shell, ExxonMobil, and Chevron already had permits; BP was requesting permission to resume drilling.

At least, more than eighteen months after the incident, the reëlected Obama administration temporarily banned BP from new federal contracts. The EPA said it was doing it because of BP's "lack of business integrity" and that it will last until BP can prove it can meet standards.

---

40 Dahr Jamail, "BP anniversary: toxicity, suffering and death," *Al Jazeera*, 16 April 2011 (at: http://english.aljazeera.net/indepth/features/2011/04/20114161153981347. html).

41 Christopher Joyce, "'Quagmire of bureaucracy' stifles gulf spill research," *National Public Radio*, 20 April 2011 (at: http://www.npr.org/2011/04/20/135573152/quagmire-of-bureaucracy-stifles-gulf-spill-research).

Massachusetts Representative (now Senator) Ed Markey, who had called for the contracting ban, said "The wreckage of BP's recklessness is still sitting at the bottom of the ocean, and this kind of time out is an appropriate element of the suite of criminal, civil and economic punishments that BP should pay for their disaster." But it didn't affect existing contracts or oil and gas production.[42]

Oh, and in the *Times*, did I mention? Here it is, in the May 16, 2010 Auto section: a rave review of the Twin-Turbo Ford Flex SUV, "blissfully turbocharged, 355-horsepower EcoBoost V-6." Reviewer Lawrence Ulrich gushes that the "federal mileage rating of the Flex with EcoBoost, 16 miles per gallon in town and 22 on the highway," allows Ford to boast that "the power lunch is free, at least at the pump." *EcoBoost? The lunch is free?*

A year and a month after the disaster, President Obama announced steps to *accelerate* oil and gas drilling on public lands and in public waters.[43]

It could happen that in the near future, the struggle for required energy resources—whether the remaining petroleum or lithium for batteries or whatever—could give rise to literal war.

Michael Klare calls the contest for dominance among tomorrow's possible energy sources a war. It engages what are apparently the most powerful entities on earth, the very corporations that already dictate policy to our governments.[44] Doesn't promise to be pretty. In the summer of 2011, the five biggest oil companies reported combined profits of $35 billion—in second-*quarter* profits. ExxonMobil boosted its lobbing budget by 25 percent and paid taxes at a rate far lower than the average American citizen while oil companies get billions of dollars in tax breaks while funding Republican political campaigns.

The Deepwater Horizon disaster, one would have thought, should have provided a fulcrum moment when rare Democratic majorities in

---

42 John M. Broder, "United States suspends BP from new contracts." *New York Times*, 28 November 2012.

43 John M. Broder, "Obama Shifts to Speed Oil and Gas Drilling in U.S. *New York Times*, 14 May 2011.

44 Michael T. Klare, "The New 30-Years' War: Who Will Be the Winners and Losers in the Great Global Energy Struggle to Come?" TomDispatch.com, a blog of the Nation Institute, 26 June, 2011.

both houses of the U.S. Congress could have effected fundamental change, but the moment was pretty much wasted.

THEN CAME THE MONSTER STORM Hurricane Sandy in late October 2012. It was the largest Atlantic hurricane on record, 1,100 miles in diameter. After taking its toll in Jamaica, Haiti, Cuba, and the Bahamas, it devastated the Jersey Shore and portions of Long Island, Staten Island, and Queens. Over the U.S. Sandy sucked in a winter storm that dumped feet of snow on West Virginia. The damage extended to the Great Lakes. I've sometimes found myself haranguing that, on our present course, we could expect the flooding of the New York subways; in this storm, they were severely flooded, particularly in lower Manhattan, and the city learned that its subways, rail, and traffic tunnels have no protection against rising waters. (London and European cities guard their subway and rail tunnels with a series of gates that can be closed against floodwater.) My beloved Jersey Shore was reshaped; the barrier island resorts were rendered inaccessible. For awhile it seemed America had awakened to the fate we have prepared for ourselves. The cost: at least 253 lives and $65 billion. Millions were left without electricity or telephones; many thousands were left homeless. The following month there appeared a scientific report that satellite measurements show sea levels rising sixty percent faster than the IPCC's computer projections. Another study had shown that sea rise due to global warming has already doubled the risk of extreme flood events, noting that half the U.S. population lives less than one meter above the high tide mark.[45]

FROM LONG CENTURIES AND millennia of unchallenged myths and religious certainties about the Universe, we are left with a legal system that's incapable of protecting the very planet that sustains life, recognizes no inherent dignity or rights for the rivers, the forests, the animals, the air; recognizes in them no sacred quality.

But it cannot be enough merely to turn to ancient myth for our answers. Human consciousness must continue its advance, with the

---

45 "Satellite measurements show flooding from storms like Sandy will put low-lying population centres at risk sooner than projected." *Guardian*, 27 November 2012.

help of its science and its rational capacities, knowing that this advance is not inexorable; that our own greed and folly has brought us to the brink of an inconceivable chasm. We have learned astonishing things, and amassed a store of knowledge never before available. Reversion to the beliefs and perspective of an earlier time is not the answer. We need a larger, stronger religious vision of one family of Life. There can be only one planetary citizenship: *that* is the only flag we can now afford to salute. But way beyond that, we need a spirituality that looks with awe to the Kosmos around us and within us and that begins to feel its place in the Kosmos.

You would think from the behavior of the human race today that we still held the beliefs and cosmology of primitive religions, from a pre-scientific age. It's brought us to the edge of a precipice. Here's how that primitive cosmology goes—so different from the universe we have discovered actually to stretch about us:

Above, the shining gods, and below, their obedient subjects, and under *their* feet, the earth, just a bunch of dead rocks and dirt with no life in it, no divinity about it.

And the human part of that hierarchy, the part between the gods above and the dead earth beneath—some of them were the god's special chums, the specially chosen elect. All the others were just heathen.

Under that vision, the earth's human inhabitants have sectioned off the planet into just short of two hundred nation states, and—to quote the eloquent Thomas Berry —

> these nations exist in an abiding sequence of conflicts that have grown especially virulent in more recent years as our scientific and technological skills have given us increasing control over the enormous powers contained in the physical structures of the earth.[46]

BEYOND THE NATIONALIST FERVOR and the greedy despoiling of the earth, we need a larger, stronger religious vision of one family of Life. There can be only one planetary citizenship: *that* is the minimal jurisdiction

---

46 Thomas Berry. *The Dream of the Earth*. San Francisco: Sierra Club Books, 1988, p. 218.

of the only flag we can now afford to salute.

BUT EVEN THIS LARGER HUMAN IDENTITY is not yet large enough. I was struck that Thomas Berry, who was once a priest and now calls himself a geologian, would say this:

> My own view is that any effective response to these issues requires a religious context but that the existing religious traditions are too distant from our new sense of the universe to be adequate to the task that is before us. . . .The traditional religions . . . cannot presently do what needs to be done. We need a new type of religious orientation. This must . . . emerge from our new story of the universe.[47]

And Thomas Berry says this new religious orientation is really a new revelatory experience, one that we can understand as soon as we recognize that the evolutionary process is, from the beginning, not just a physical process but a spiritual one.

WE MUST HAVE A NEW SPIRITUAL VISION that is not accountable to the ancient mythic universe and its gods and scriptures, its bishops and ayatollahs and, I say, its corporate powers. We must hear the new story of the universe and take it to heart. It is true—and extremely fortunate—that many religious people in many faith-traditions have found in their traditions a basis on which to champion the cause of the Earth. But in a time still largely governed by outworn myth—it's time for a life-giving alternative.

THOSE WHO STUDY THE VERY STRUCTURE of the universe are coming at last to understand a universal story, and even though there are still many variations,—for the first time in its history the human community has a single story of its origin. Physicist Brian Swimme[48] sums it up well:

---

47 Berry, *The Dream of the Earth*, p. 87.
48 Brian Swimme. *The Universe is a Green Dragon: A Cosmic Creation Story*. Santa Fe: Bear & Co., 1985, p. 27. Also recommended: his 2011 *Journey of the Universe* with Mary Evelyn Tucker (Yale University Press).

This was a fire that filled the universe—that *was* the universe.
Every point of the cosmos was a point of this explosion of light.
And all the particles of the universe churned in extremes of heat
and pressure, all that we see about us, all that now exists was there
at the beginning, in that great burning explosion of light. . . . We
can see the light from the primeval fireball. Or at least the light
from its edge, for it burned for nearly a million years. We can see
the dawn of the universe because the light from its edge reaches
us only now, after traveling twenty billion years to get here.

That great light is now spread through this universe. You can hear it
on the radiotelescopes; and you can't look up into the night sky without
looking back into our origin. I don't know what that sight evokes in you.
It makes me tremble.

There is not a thing in this wide universe that does not share a
common origin. What does this mean? Swimme:

> The material of your body and the material of my body are in-
> trinsically related because they emerged from and are caught up
> in a single energetic event. Our ancestry stretches back through
> the life forms and into the stars, back to the beginnings of the
> primeval fireball. This universe is a single multiform energetic
> unfolding of matter, mind, intelligence, and life. And all of this
> is new. None of the great figures of human history were aware of
> this. Not Plato, or Aristotle, or the Hebrew Prophets, or Confu-
> cius, or Thomas Aquinas, or Leibniz, or Newton . . . We are the
> first generation to live with an empirical view of the origin of the
> universe. We are the first humans to look into the night sky and
> see the birth of stars, the birth of galaxies, the birth of the cosmos
> as a whole. Our future as a species will be forged within this new
> story of the world.[49]

Albert Einstein was repelled by the implication of his own theories—
that the cosmos originated in a singularity in the distant past—out of
nothing. He tried to find a way to make it not be true, a way to be able
to see the Universe as having some sort of cosmological constant so that
it would not have to have come into being like that, in an instant, from
an inconceivably small, inconceivably dense beginning, in inconceivable
heat, exploding into being. The British astronomer Fred Hoyle tried
to mock the whole idea by calling it the "Big Bang." Seems Einstein's

49 Swimme, *The Universe is a Green Dragon*, p. 28f.

later idea was wrong, and that he'd been right in the first place.

But why is there anything at all, instead of nothing? Consider: apparently, at the heart of all Being, there is a roaring engine of creativity. In his 1927-28 Gifford lectures at Edinburgh published as *Process and Reality: An Essay in Cosmology*, Alfred North Whitehead spoke of "primordial" Being—unmanifest, pure potentiality without any of it realized—and "consequent" Being (or rather, *Becoming*), manifest within the stream of time, evolutionary in its nature. Which is another way of saying: *out of the nothingness and void, Something. The Big Bang.*

It's baffled scientists tremendously that it would all have come off so perfectly as to create a Universe that could evolve and support life.

How is it that every aspect of the evolution of the Universe is dependent on the very precise values of what seem like arbitrary constants of nature—like, for instance, the strength of gravity, not too strong, not too weak?

You'd think I was about to make a case for "Intelligent Design," wouldn't you? I'm not. There's a very basic flaw in "Intelligent Design." It's a decoy to try to force the conclusion that if there is intelligence in the design of the Universe, there had to be a Designer, a God who was clever enough to design it.

Theoretical physics is now in search of a far more sublime way to see this Universe of Life. It hints at a life and intelligence about everything, and about the universe as an intelligent organism. What is this Universe, anyway? What is the nature of—well, of Nature?

The dominant hypothesis (though it still defies experimental proof) is something known as M-Theory or Superstring Theory. At the heart of it all, it says, beyond the subatomic particles, quarks and so on, electrons, photons—are tiny submicroscopic one-dimensional strings of energy—modes of energy vibrating with delicate precision in a very specific way in some eleven-dimensional hyperspace.

Cosmologist James Gardner[50] —along with Stephen Hawking and along with the Astronomer Royal of Britain Martin Rees, and along with others—thinks there's some sort of fundamental intelligence about the Universe itself. It is self-organizing. It is inherently creative and

50 James N. Gardner. *Biocosm: The New Scientific Theory of Evolution: Intelligent Life Is the Architect of the Universe.* Inner Ocean Publishing, 2003.

intelligent. Nobody, no god outside of it, had to design it.

Its inherent intelligence seems to have at its heart a purpose: an unfolding, ever-more complex, evolving Life, higher and higher Life, higher and higher intelligence.

Maybe we are part of some vast and still-undiscovered cosmic community. Maybe we share a common fate with that cosmic community.

What if we are part of an astonishing wave of creation that includes the future as well as the past? What if we're being drawn into a very creative future, but faced with choices about whether or not to participate, about how to participate.

Maybe the future fate and destiny of something far more than the Earth—maybe the future fate and destiny of the Kosmos itself—depends in part on us.

THE UNIVERSE BECOMES AWARE of itself through the humanity it has created. In everything you do, the Universe reveals itself and discovers itself. You are defining what is to come. For we are not merely descended from the first fire; —

We are that first fire after 14 billion years of creative work.

We are the universe aware of itself, reflecting on itself, communicating and reflecting on its own existence, its own possibilities, deciding its future.

SOMETHING IN US RESOUNDS, RESONATES from that first fire, and resonates from the very Heart and Ground of all Being from which that fire ignited, and resounds from the stars that churned out the elements we are made of, and from the implicate genius of this living, this intelligent universe. It is a part of us. You were there.

But that is not the song we hear much of the time, and if you listen carefully some Sunday morning you will not hear very many songs about the interdependent web of all existence. You will hear, "Onward Christian soldiers, marching as to war," and you will hear frothing declamations about the saved and the damned. Outside, you will hear the hum of an economy so insensitive to the earth that the seas, the air and the ground are still receiving fresh poisons.

WE MIGHT FIND OURSELVES YEARNING for an earlier time, to live as long-vanished ancestors lived. *They* didn't bring life on Earth to a precipice, after all. But if the ancients didn't bring us to the brink of ecological cataclysm, it wasn't because they possessed moral superiority or a greater grasp of the interdependent ecology of all things. In fact, there just weren't enough of them, and they hadn't developed the powerful technologies that we now have at our command, for good or for ill. You can't create nuclear winter with bows and arrows. Horses and buggies don't pollute a whole lot (though there is the methane), not unless you're thinking of horse poo in the streets. Let's not romanticize the past. With an awareness never before known, we stand at a threshold.

THERE'S SOMETHING VERY PERSISTENT about the old myths.

When Giordano Bruno, a priest and philosopher who had studied with Copernicus, challenged the prevailing doctrines about the universe, his ideas got him shackled in an ecclesiastical prison for his last seven years and then burned at the stake in Rome in 1600. If today you speak on behalf of the Earth and the interdependent web of all existence of which we are a part—you will have corporations, right-wing media, the Republican Party, and the and popular consumer culture against you.

This is from the *Guardian* of London, by Paul Brown:[51]

> A far-reaching inquiry into the careers of three of the US's most senior climate specialists has been launched by Joe Barton, the chairman of the House of Representatives committee on energy and commerce. He has demanded details of all their sources of funding, methods and everything they have ever published.
>
> Mr Barton, a Texan closely associated with the fossil-fuel lobby, has spent his 11 years as chairman opposing every piece of legislation designed to combat climate change.

The inquiry was directed at Michael Mann, director of the Earth System Science Enter at Pennsylvania State University; Raymond Bradley,

---

51 "Republicans accused of witch-hunt against climate change," August 30, 2005.

director of the Climate System Research Center at the University of Massachusetts; and Malcolm Hughes, former director of the Laboratory of Tree-Ring Research at the University of Arizona. Barton launched his inquiry after the *Wall Street Journal* quoted an economist and a statistician—neither with any background in climate science—claiming methodological flaws and data errors in the scientists' calculations and accusing them of hiding their original material. Nor was he content with the allegedly undisclosed data: he was demanding details of everything they had done since their careers began. *The Guardian* continued:

> The inquiry has sent shockwaves through the US scientific establishment, already under pressure from the Bush administration, which links funding to policy objectives.

Joe Barton no longer chairs the House Energy and Commerce Committee (though when Republicans won back control of the House in 2010, he attempted a return—and when, after he apologized to BP when President Obama secured a twenty billion dollar escrow fund to pay claims for spill-related losses—calling the President's demand a "shakedown"—the party allowed him to retain his membership on the committee). Instead, the chair went to Fred Upton, of Michigan, who proceeded to have his GOP-controlled chamber vote to block EPA regulation of greenhouse gases.

Democrats had barely taken control of Congress in 2006 when the Bush White House intensified its campaign—exposed by Dr. James Hansen, who insistently warns that we have very little time to halt the catastrophic processes now in motion—to thwart and throttle government research on climate change. Public leaders united with public media in communicating the message that there's nothing much to worry about. We've gained a kind of security, or illusion of security, from the idea that we are separate from nature and can control it.

Now the dominant forces in our society are desperately betting everything on the idea that the universe is just dead matter. How could an Alaskan wildlife reserve have a spiritual life? If a mountain has no inner reason, no sacredness unto itself, then to get coal out of the soil you just cut away half the face of the mountain. But all of this is part and parcel of the world of life that has given rise to human consciousness and now sustains it. Never mind that the mountain begins to erode and chemicals enter the streams and trees die, and plants, fish, and animals. And eventually, so do we.

It doesn't really matter how obvious the consequences of the madness are. The madness goes on because it is madness.

There is an intelligence, by which the grass knows how to grow, by which, when we can transcend our own narrow thoughts and identity, we know ourselves to be a part of Nature. There is a unitive force, a love toward all existence. We know that *we are* nature, that *we are* the first fire.

AND WE OURSELVES: WE HAPPEN to be living our lives just at a turning point for life on this threatened planet. We ourselves are becoming part of this change.

The equilibrium is disturbed.

The late physicist Ilya Prigogine wrote that

> we are at a moment of profound change. . . . We know that societies are immensely complex systems involving a potentially enormous number of bifurcations [or turning points]. We know that such systems are highly sensitive to fluctuations. . . . As a result, individual activity is not doomed to insignificance.[52]

We live not in a universe of eternal laws but of implicate intelligence and innovation, a roaring engine of creativity. We are participants. We are this world, this Universe. We are the vehicle by which this Universe becomes conscious.

When you allow the magnitude of all this to settle in, when you contemplate the depth of our existence, and its possibility and its destiny and its unity—then do not words like "worship" and "reverence" take on a whole new meaning?

And does not your life take on dimensions of expansiveness and possibility and beauty you hadn't imagined?

And don't your choices and commitments take on a power and a magnitude you hadn't imagined?

---

52 Ilya Prigogine and Isabelle Stengers. *Order Out of Chaos: Man's New Dialogue with Nature.* New York: Bantam, 1984, p. 312f.

How *then* shall we live these lives of ours? Shall we participate by subjugating higher intelligence and higher human possibilities to the lower interests of greed and domination? What will become of this immense upward journey of Life and intelligence?

The times require those who will commit in some profound way to take our place in this interdependent web, and to *love* this community of life, this first fire, of which we are a part. What we do on behalf of the Earth will not be the skin-deep effort on the part of those whose chief aim is to appear politically correct. Nor will it be a burden or a sacrifice—anymore than the things we do for someone we love feel like a burden or sacrifice. *Love does not worry about doing too much, being too extravagant.* We must now speak and act out of devoted love and not less.

The times require moral leadership, and they require creativity, and above all things, they require the gentle force of love.

And the times require those who know their place in this web of life, know they are bound by an everlasting covenant to a larger life, know they are come from that first fire and share as citizens in a vast community of life. Who believe in the significance of their own words and deeds.

But our vision will be helplessly befogged as long as we insist on cheating on our fundamental covenant with life. For one thing, we will have to curb the thirst for oil that has bent our moral compass, a thirst that is always made more vivid for me when I return to the United Kingdom, with its tiny automobiles and abundant public transit and thousands of giant wind turbines. It may begin with something as simple, in our own household, as figuring out how to replace more of these incandescent bulbs with compact fluorescent ones and LEDs, because that is something that lies within our power to do. But those who care enough to do the simple things must now do the big things: change the laws and revolutionize the popular imagination.

In these times, doesn't sacred imagination take on a new urgency? See how old institutions, blinded by conventional vision, bankrupt of holy imagination, lacking the vision to see that there is far more future than past, far more unfolding for this Universe of Life to do to fulfil its destiny and purpose—see how they fail us. How, then, shall we live? How structure our lives?

We must be a force and a factor, together in communities, and each of us where we are. The changed consciousness and the gentle aware-ness that all of Life is one—will have to replace the cynicism, and the campaign rhetoric, and the official lies and the unofficial denial, soon.

The generation coming of age now—and all of us living—have the potential to bring a new vision to society. Like this, proposed by Andrew Harvey:[53]

> Any spiritual vision that does not ask us to calmly face the appalling facts is, I believe, whether consciously or unconsciously, conspiring in our infantilization and so in our destruction. . . .
>
> The only response that I find honorable in this potentially terminal situation is that of dedicated love.

And this is the important part, and this is where the prophecy comes in. Because if the glaciers continue to melt into the rising seas, and if the oil and coal goes on burning (and the oil and coal industries go on owning and operating the United States Congress), and the carbon and methane and pollutants go on streaming into the seas and rivers and air and ground, and the public carries on its self-delusion, it will be literally the case, as Harvey points out, that it's our own lungs we're burning, our own veins we're pumping with poison, our own bodies that will be engulfed.[54]

WITH THE NEW MILLENNIUM, NEW powers arose and took the reins of government. The scientists began issuing their increasingly urgent warnings, and the small voices that rose in protest were not enough to halt the processes that had been set in motion and were sustained by greed.

But never has there been anything like the last few years, when the ink on one urgent scientific report is barely dry when another, more

---

53 Andrew Harvey. *The Return of the Mother.* Berkeley: Frog Ltd., 1995. 436f.
54 Andrew Harvey with Mark Matousek. *Dialogues with a Modern Mystic.* Wheaton, IL: Quest Books, 1994, 36.

ominous, more appalling, is issued. Among scientists and scientific organizations there is virtual consensus. The only holdout is the American Association of Petroleum Geologists, with its deep ties to the fossil fuel industry. By 2002 fourteen scientific papers on global warming had been published; now there are a thousand. A 2004 *Science* magazine survey of scientific studies on climate change showed that 928 peer-reviewed papers supported the reality of global warming and zero denied it. Yet the American media continue to pretend that the jury is out.

WE WOULD BE RIGHT TO TREMBLE at the thought of what will happen to this world of Life and Nature if we, the human component of the world, fail to do what must be done to save it.

Can we see with holy imagination this radiant world, ourselves participants in its unfolding, sharing, if we will, its magnificent destiny?

The alternative—the consequence of moral blindness and the failure of sacred imagination—the failure to see what we are, and of what we are a part, and the consequences of our choices—is a cosmic tragedy that is just too tragic to contemplate.

Toward the end of his book, *Biocosm*, James Gardner says this:

> The notion that every creature, great and small, plays some indefinable role in an awesome process by which life gains hegemony over inanimate nature implies that every living thing is linked with every other bit of living matter in a joint endeavor—a kind of cosmic "Mission Impossible"—of vast scope and indefinable duration. We soldier on together—bacteria, people, extraterrestrials (if they exist), and hyper-intelligent computers—pressing forward, against all odds and the implacable foe that is entropy, toward a distant future we can only faintly imagine. But it is together—in a spirit of cooperation tempered by conflict—that we journey hopefully toward our distant destination. If, like Sisyphus, we are occasionally pained by the weight of the stone we are pushing uphill and if our task strikes us, at least sporadically, as futile and absurd, we can at least take comfort in the astonishing fact that every creature that ever lived and ever will live shares our existential plight.[55]

If, reading this, you decide to become sad, depressed, discouraged— *that is a choice.* I recite these things so that you can become energized

55 Gardner, *Biocosm*, 216f.

by the knowledge that this Earth that gives us life, this Earth we love, now needs us.—

That our lives need not be lived without meaning or purpose —

That what we do now matters and that we are honored to share in a great work. What an honor to be a part of the generation of humanity to which this work is entrusted!

Who will do what must be done? Whose committed and daring efforts will turn the tide? This is who:

It will be those who love this Earth and love the evolutionary process of which both the Earth and we ourselves are a part, as much as they love their lives, love them more than their possessions, their ambitions, their security; who know the threatened planet as their beloved friend.

There is a stark difference between using this Earth, and loving it. It will be those who, like Annie Dillard, everywhere they look, see fire; and in whose eyes the whole world sparks and flames with glory. It will be those who, like Mary Oliver, in the morning feel themselves held in great hands of light.

Henry Thoreau's Transcendentalist friend Bronson Alcott wrote this in 1840:

> Nature is not separate from me; she is mine alike with my body; and in moments of true life, I feel my identity with her; I breathe, pulsate, feel, think, will, through her members, and know of no duality of being. It is in such moods of soul that prophetic visions are beheld . . . for the joy and hope of mankind.

When you breathe the spectacular Spring air, tell me, is there anything beneath, beyond the surface?

If there is a human capacity to forget, to lose sight, to see only the daily grind and the quest for wealth and advancement —

— there is also a human capacity to feel something else, some universe beyond this surface, a sense of belonging to a bigger drama, a realm beyond the surfaces and appearances of things.

Shelley gave words to this sense:

> The everlasting universe of things
> Flows through the mind, and rolls its rapid waves . . .
> I seem as in a trance sublime and strange

To muse on my own separate fantasy,
My own, my human mind . . . ,
Holding an unremitting interchange
With the clear universe of things around . . .
. . . all seems eternal now.

You and I are part of a larger drama and we can become forces of Nature.

Let us ensure that the youngest among us learn from our deep commitment and passion for this magnificent Earth. We will have to find palpable ways to structure and focus our lives to that end. The work that beckons to us is a work of love.

And, says St. John of the Cross, when we "drink at the very sources of the science of love," we finally see what ordinary consciousness cannot.

Look and see the world radiant with the glory from which it flows. See the radiant and majestic grace in a day, in every leaf and tree;—in the air you breathe feel its life, let it wash you through with music, and let it penetrate to a core of you that can never, never close to it again.

Can we see beyond the rubble and turmoil—this great surging Mystery of Life? this Nature and the Life of the Kosmos, the Intelligence that made of the cosmic dust, stars and planets and rivers and people, and that is not finished its work?

Its work is now our own. A humanity whose imagination has been fired by that understanding can, out of the heart of the crisis itself, answer this climate emergency with brilliant innovation and a new vision of human life on earth that makes real our highest future possibility, living and creating from that coming splendor.

Now: Imagine you are the Universe, since you *are*. It's taken you 14 billion years to achieve *consciousness*, which you've done through your human presence. When you awaken, it's the Universe itself that's waking. Look around you. Your capacities are great, your creative powers almost without limit. What are you going to do?

A HIGHER *'WE'*
To create a new cultural context for the possible human

William Ellery Channing
Founder of Unitarianism in America
"The Union," 1829

[SPEAKING OF GEORGE CABOT:] *He had too much the
wisdom of experience. He wanted what may be called the
wisdom of hope. . . . There are seasons in human affairs,
of inward and outward revolution, when new depths
seem to be broken up in the soul, when new wants are
unfolded in multitudes, and a new and undefined good
is thirsted for. These are periods when the principles of
experience need to be modified, when hope and trust and
instinct claim a share with prudence in the guidance of
affairs, when, in truth, to* dare *is the highest wisdom.*

THERE IS, IN THE ANCIENT Book of Ecclesiastes, a statement whose
banality only underlines its truth. Here it is:

> Two are better than one . . . for if they fall, one will lift up his fel-
> low; but woe to him who is alone when he falls and has not another
> to lift him up. Again, if two lie together, they are warm; but how
> can one be warm alone? [1]

1 Ecclesiastes 4:9-11, Revised Standard Version.

Gee thanks. A piece of drivel almost anybody could have said better. Maybe it's memorable because it states the blindingly obvious—with blinding plainness. But there's a lot more to this than staying warm, or having a hand getting up again after you fall.

WHEN PEOPLE COME TOGETHER, a culture is created. That culture shapes the people who exist within it.

But what *kind* of culture? What kind of people?

We are makers of our culture, of whatever sort it is. When I became aware of the diaries of Victor Klemperer[2], whom we met in Chapter Six, I was riveted. I couldn't put them down, kept reading all night long—Klemperer, a Jewish professor who somehow survived the Nazi era in Dresden, Germany and then lived through the grim rebuilding of Soviet East Germany. He saw people living in a society where the terms and conditions of civilized life were turned on their head. The air was thick with fear, intimidation, and hatred. Those were the terms and conditions. That society was so designed that this was the way it was *supposed* to be.

He saw what that did to people, how personalities and relationships were poisoned—first in Nazi Germany, and then, after the war, to Professor Klemperer's great disillusion, in Walter Ulbricht's Stalinist East Germany. He saw what his neighbors, his former associates, people in positions of responsibility and ordinary people—were capable of becoming: false, monstrous, organizing life around terror and never-ceasing lies, doing despicable things that once they could not have dreamed of doing.

If you think of Nazi Germany, you're contemplating a highly educated European country where people have abandoned their **autonomy**. You didn't think for yourself; you sank into some archaic mentality of the tribe or even a *herd*. Heil Hitler. Whatever he says is true and has to be. *So* some of our neighbors are having to wear those yellow stars

---

2 *The Klemperer Diaries 1933-1945: I Shall Bear Witness, and To the Bitter End.* London: Phoenix Press, 1998, 1999. *The Diaries of Victor Klemperer 1945-59: The Lesser Evil.* London: Phoenix, 2003. Both abridged and translated from the German edition by Martin Chalmers.

or pink triangles or whatever and aren't allowed on the trolleycar and get humiliated everywhere they go. So a few of our neighbors are disappearing. Heil. Goodbye conscience, so long autonomy.

A gathering of postmoderns, Unitarian Universalist or otherwise, is likely to show some expression of personal autonomy. Sometimes verging on the extreme, but let's celebrate the radical independence and authenticity.

Of course, we aren't anywhere nearly as original and unique as we like to think. *We are shaped by the culture*, or the cultures, in which we live, aren't we? For autonomous individuals with some integrity and courage, the challenge is to go a step farther.

To find an authenticity, an autonomy, that flows from the deepest part of ourselves—not just some quirky egos gathered together. No, I'm talking about a kind of unselfconscious creative freedom flowing deeply, powerfully, beyond ego, with each of us bringing our particular individual capacities and gifts into some larger communion.

But usually when an individual experiences autonomy it happens at the expense of **communion** with others. The communion I'm talking about is a dynamic field that's created when the many know also that they are really one. You bring your truest self, you bring your particular gifts, into a larger whole. So in the service of a higher purpose, there's a quality of consciousness that transcends your individuality and yet depends on it.

HISTORY DEMONSTRATES THAT HUMAN QUALITIES and capacities develop most fully and flourish *where they're valued*—in cultures that *prize* them. Consider what the context—a human community—can make of us. What it can make of us when it's founded *not* on some nightmare of lies and violence, not on the rock-rigid dogma of other ages;—but on highly evolved human principles, on faith in each other, faith in the possible; organized on the principles of love and care; guided by a creative vision of hope.

BUT *WHAT HAPPENS* WHEN people are joined together in that way? They begin to feel an evolutionary tension. Something crackles. Something begins to come into being and it requires your care and attention and even your sacrifice. It challenges your own inertia. It overwhelms your sense of inertia with its radiant sense of possibility. There's respect, there's right relationship, because some compelling creative work needs you and commands you, and it's thrilling and it's challenging.

It's not always comfortable. It's transformative. And now it depends on you. It needs you.

There's respect and care and there's moral vision where people come together as a higher kind of *"We."*

That's the kind of context where the most enlightened kind of spiritual inquiry can happen. And not just *inquiry*. You begin to do what can't be done, and say what can't be said, for a purpose that maybe you'd previously known in an intellectual sort of way, but in a deeper sense you couldn't have imagined it, at least until now. Now it's absolutely, palpably real.

It has happened before. Earlier I've spoken of William Ellery Channing. From this one congregation in Boston came:

Horace Mann, the great educational reformer and congressman, who brought us tax-funded free public schools; [if he were just coming up with that idea today—introducing public education for the first time—they'd call it socialism.]

Elizabeth Palmer Peabody, with her lifelong advocacy of early childhood education, who introduced the kindergarten to America.

A hospital for women was founded in that church, and now it's among the best in the world, still with its Channing Laboratory— Brigham and Women's Hospital in Boston.

And indirectly, from the influence of that place, came Emerson himself, and Theodore Parker, whose congregation of 7,000 included escaped slaves, abolitionists, laborers, and thinkers;—Theodore Parker, who formed the "Committee of Vigilance" to rescue slaves captured under the Fugitive Slave Law and set them free; Parker, whose printed sermons inspired Abraham Lincoln.

There were abolitionists and reformers, caregivers and visionaries.

This was a people with a passion potent enough to give them courage to stand up to the powerful institutions everybody assumed couldn't be changed, whose grip they thought couldn't be broken: political and cultural and, yes, religious powers that were crushing, choking the human spirit, snuffing out the light at the heart of an age.

I've often contemplated the community of people who gathered in Emerson's parlor in Concord, Massachusetts, and the culture they created there, people who opened new vistas of spiritual understanding and experience. How could so few people be responsible for so much advancement of human culture and consciousness? There was Margaret Fuller, whose *Woman in the Nineteenth Century* broke ground for modern-day feminism. She was the first literary critic in an American newspaper (Horace Greeley's *New-York Tribune*); and there was Bronson Alcott, who along with Margaret Fuller and Elizabeth Palmer Peabody led a revolution in the education of children; and there was Henry Thoreau, the great naturalist and antislavery activist, the influence of whose *Civil Disobedience* seems to widen with the passing years beyond its well-known impact on Gandhi and King; and there was Moncure Conway, the great radical religious and abolitionist leader whose influence spanned the Atlantic; and Senator Charles Sumner, I think the greatest political leader of the era and the most uncompromising advocate of black Americans; and Theodore Parker himself; and leaders of a generation of religious visionaries who would transform the ossified Unitarian movement into a powerful vanguard.

Why would so many visionaries and great leaders come from one little town? Was it something in the water?

BUT OF COURSE, THESE WERE JUST folks with warts and foibles, such as you might find anywhere. But they were caught up in something greater than themselves, something that implicated and compelled them, something that challenged the terms and conditions of life in this world with a highly evolved and still-evolving vision of how the world *might be*. They could have declined participation on the grounds that they were not ready, not good enough. But life doesn't require that

we be "ready" or be something other than what we are: only that we
be available.

Aurobindo—the great Indian independence figure just before
Gandhi and then spiritual explorer, philosopher, poet—awakened to
the situation of his people in his native India. He knew something had
to change. And he turned to the profound depths of his native Hindu
religious tradition and community, in a searing *I-Thou* encounter which,
in turn, sent him directly to his own inner resources, which are one
with the Great Energy that is the life of all this Universe.

He found at the core of him an inner silence, and came to love it,
and out of it his words and his deeds came.

It won't come automatically just because you're around other people
who understand this and value it, but it sure helps to live within a community that aspires to this kind of consciousness, and supports it when
it shows up.

And so there was Aurobindo facing impossible odds, the weight of
overwhelming oppression. He himself was in constant danger. And just
then he wrote of a heart released from grief, and of experience "beyond
belief," and

> A Peace stupendous, featureless, still,
>   Replaces all . . .
> A silent unnamed emptiness content
>   Either to fade in the Unknowable
>   Or thrill with the luminous seas of the Infinite.

How is it that a person who decides there's more purpose to his life than
just living his own life in peace, who has instead thrown himself into
the epic struggle, can speak of a *heart released from grief*? Can speak of
a *peace stupendous*, of a *thrill* about his day-to-day existence? What an
odd place to find peace, release from grief, the thrill of life. But it seems
that *that is where we will find it*, in the midst of the struggle, buoyed up
by a Spirit, carried along by purposes greater than our own, something
worth living for and even dying for. So we face adversity today.

What is required is a fundamental intent about the meaning and
purpose of our lives. Not "being ready," not perfection.

To quote Aurobindo, "Every one has in him something divine,

something his own, a chance of perfection and strength in however small a sphere which [Life] offers him to take or refuse. The task is to find it, develop it and use it."

We are what we are. A greater purpose calls us just as we are, to enlist our best energies in its service. That intent, and not perfection, is what's required. Each of us must be able to say: *I am good for what I am good for, and this is my work and gift.* The communities we must create will make room for that gift and engage it. I am hardly the life of the party. I am absent-minded and rather intense. Sometimes I can barely remember my *own* name and I don't have all the social graces in the world. Whaddaya want?!

I know that the responsibility of the ministry with which I am charged does not always allow me to say popular things or easy things. But I must be faithful to the inner voice. I must speak from my own inner depths and not superficially. In authentic spiritual community, we learn from each other, are challenged by each other, are held to high purposes by each other. And what is valued is the unfolding of the authentic self, and the clear intent to pursue this journey, unfold truth, and carry on this work not for ourselves alone but for the sake of the world that might be.

But such a community isn't for everyone. Many liberal religious communities run aground here. You can't hold up an ensign that declares "We don't stand for anything in particular and we don't ask anything of you" and at the same time be a community of vision and profound purpose. We don't want anybody to be unhappy with us. And to the extent we care about offending or disappointing no one, we will excite nobody. As for our faith community, there will be no *there* there. I quote the historian Garry Wills: "The opposite of a bracing narrowness is flaccid inclusion." And commenting on the election to the United States Senate in Illinois in 1858 between Abraham Lincoln and Stephen Douglas:[3]

> [T]he genius of politics, as opposed to the mere practitioner—the Lincoln, not the Douglas—knows when compromise can go no

---

3 Garry Wills. *Certain Trumpets: The Nature of Leadership.* New York: Simon & Schuster, 1994, p. 50-52.

further without becoming incoherence. Douglas tried to hold together incompatible things . . . The worst nightmare of the congenital compromiser, who tries to please everyone, is to find that he has, in fact, angered everyone. . . . The believer in the system and nothing but the system is a pragmatist with no practical effect. Even fanatics accomplish more.

A congregation or community of people won't likely resemble an individual, only bigger, with a singular *I* at the core! That would be what Whitehead called a *dominant monad*. Instead it will be a collective of individuals with free minds, free wills, and choice. The choice to join a community of purpose and vision must therefore be a serious matter. Such a community has a right to ask that one's subsequent participation be of a higher quality than the *obstructionary*, in which the participant engages for no particular reason other than to enjoy the delicious feeling that one is able to obstruct. Nor is any single member of such a community entitled to veto its evolution and change, for better or worse. I don't think you get there without a seriously shared spiritual practice, and a real expectation that it matters. So a bit about the nature of spiritual community.

IT CAN BE SAID OF MANY congregations, certainly of our own Unitarian Universalist ones, that one could be forgiven for thinking "there's no *there* there." Diversity and the free mind are high values that we should prize. But is there nothing but diversity that we share?

Of course, there is. Lots. But we sometimes fear to state it.

To have any more than the thinnest film of compelling purpose, such a community has to be united and powered by a common vision. It must define itself. We cannot stand for there to be no *there* there. But our definition must remain fluid and open to the Beyond. Remaining fluid and open doesn't mean having no "there" there.

So I want to propose a conception of congregational life suggested to me by a member of First Unitarian Church in Orlando, where I served for a year as interim minister. Previously, he had participated in the nondenominational Church of the Savior in Washington, D.C., which understood itself in this way. Imagine, in the old churchy language, the

Nave and the Narthex.

Think: deeply committed core, or Nave (the central worship space). Think of it surrounded by the Narthex (literally "porch"), populated by those whose commitment is not so clear, at least not yet. They are hanging back "on the porch," contemplating, weighing, considering.

You can't hurry them. Some have inhabited the "porch" for years. Some turn up only for their favorite program and have little or no commitment to the mission of the whole. You want a well-populated porch. This is part of the "evangelism" of the committed core. These folks are still in relationship and may get around to joining the "company of the committed."

The Nave-dwellers owe it to those out on the Narthex to bear witness faithfully, to set the bar high, to be examplars, to inspire and guide. It may offend some odd reading of "equality" and "diversity," but failure to recognize any difference in commitment, in depth of experience, dilutes the potentialities of membership in a spiritual community. It doesn't really speak very compellingly to the newcomers and hangers-on. Andrew Cohen has called the distinction a "natural hierarchy"—as distinguished from a coercive or entitlement-based hierarchy.

We lose the distinction at the peril not of our own comfort or status, but of the highest future human possibility.

WHEN COMMUNITIES OF VISION gather—much is at stake. The crisis never really goes away: Aurobindo says, so very truly in his poem "Savitri," at the front of the book: "All we have done is ever still to do."

What must we do? First, recognize where we are, what is this moment in which we live. To do so is to begin to understand the meaning of our individual lives, and of the communities we create.

What it will take is more than just an individual transformation. What's required now is an *intersubjective* revolution, in communities of people guided by a different vision, living by different terms and conditions, supporting and rewarding different values. That is the indispensable reason for spiritual communities.

A community that makes room for this central quest, makes it part of the equation—will be electric.

It will free the creativity inherent in us.

It will open in us our best passions and energies.

It will stay focussed on its mission and do so with great imagination. It will not waste time and energy on trivia, spend long meetings to make one inconsequential decision. It will think bold thoughts; it will attempt significant things.

It will radiate respect, trust, and mutual regard.

It will be bound together by a meaningful intersubjective—and behavioral—covenant that makes clear what members are promising each other, that they cannot violate and remain members. This is still freedom. The door works both ways.

It will be a place where human lives are transformed from within, by the force of the power within them—and it will cherish the transformation.

It will take risks. It will give you space to make mistakes and learn and keep at it until you get it right.

It will work, really work, at finding the gifts and capacities of each of its members, and make a place for them. It will be a force and a factor and a healing presence in this world. This is no time for retrenchment, but a time to dare.

In 1990, VAÇLAV HAVEL STOOD before the United States Congress. This is what he said:

> Without a global revolution in the sphere of human consciousness, . . . the catastrophe toward which the world is headed—ecological, social, demographic, or general breakdown of civilization—will be unavoidable.

A revolution in the sphere of consciousness. A different, more evolved kind of human.

Yeh, we know: If we don't want to be the last gasping century of human life on Earth, something essential will have to change, in a very short time. A widening gulf of inequality renders a culture sick, we know. When we contemplate an economy in which the top one percent earn more than the bottom fifty percent and in 2010, CEO pay went up twenty-seven percent while worker pay (for those still working) went up two percent and while big corporations are paying no taxes but getting rebates—can we imagine a culture that would refuse to live with such inequity?

What kind of faith, and what kind of faith-community,—can mobilize us to do that, move us to do it and support us in doing it?

COMMUNITY, BECAUSE YOU'RE NOT going to be able to do it on your own. In 1994, Robert Wright published a tremendously hopeful book titled *Non-Zero*, in which he talks about cultural evolution—the great advances in human achievement—which he describes as virtually *pouring* from human societies that were *big* enough, *concentrated* enough, so that they could function like a many-celled brain, with all of its members sharing in a creative interaction. And he shows how other societies—too small, too sparse and isolated—remained stagnant or died out. No stimulation, no creativity. It's true of just about everything—even bacteria. Even congregations. Bacteria and congregations *both* solve problems by interacting, forming a kind of collective mind smart enough, stimulated enough, to grow to the next stage.

Brian Eno and Kevin Kelly carry the idea farther with Eno's concept of *scenius:* the creative energies and genius of a "scene," like the Beats, or the Transcendentalists, or the Bloomsbury Group, or the core figures in the Enlightenment. Kelly lists four characteristics: mutual appreciation, rapid exchange of ideas and techniques within a sphere of shared sensibility, a group rather than individual sense of achievement, and toleration of "maverick" novelty.

We cannot do what must be done in these times *in isolation.* We only come into our highest potentialities in communion with others who share our vision. While we face a crisis truly like none humanity has ever faced—human communities, including congregations, *are* the context for our being and our becoming—for good or for ill.

FOR VERY LONG AGES, HUMAN CULTURE was defined by authoritarian rules and myths and belief systems. And then human consciousness advanced, though of course not everywhere. The Unitarian Universalist movement represented a new kind of culture, incorporating the values of scientific, rational, free inquiry from the 18th-century Enlightenment, and then, in another advance beyond that, the values of pluralism, diversity, and respect—a wave that emerged in, like, the 1960s, and nothing so embodies its values as Unitarian Universalism. This most recent, real transformation—has been characterized by Ken Wilber and others as the postmodern "sensitive self," but it's time for *another* advance. Because *that* breakthrough brought a kind of inherent narcissism that cultivates the attitude that *"it's all about me."* So way too often, congregations look a little too much like clubs (existing for the pleasure of an entitled inner circle) or a store (where I expect to get what I want because, dammit, the customer is always right!).

What would it be like to engage with others in a place beyond the boundaries of our personal egos and dramas? What would it be like to be somewhere where you could communicate from a part of your self that is absolutely free from self-consciousness, that is fearless, uncorrupted, and passionately interested in the truth?

Maybe you've known something like that at least in brief moments. I have a very fresh and vivid memory of a gathering in Cambridge, Massachusetts, a conversation of such breadth and depth and reach and potency that when it ended, naturally, as if we were an orchestra at the end of a great score, we could only sit in silence.

Maybe you have experienced what I'm talking about. Maybe you yearn for it.

When it happens—a congregation can be a field for enlightenment and for the unfolding of human possibility. In that *context* each member's individual life-work can become clear and can find support and collaboration. In that context a truly compelling vision can come into being and be shared.

And there, human beings can begin to reach their finest potentials—literally creating a new edge of the possible. Something bigger than an interaction of egos is going on, and when the conversation falls into stale opinions or personal obsessions and agendas or theoretical abstractions, something about this new context that you have created together refocuses, returns to the inspired passion, the focused intensity, the evolutionary tension. You feel a kind of clarity that embraces all the best and highest in you with a breadth and depth and scope that's breathtaking.

You can sense the presence of a higher consciousness that can be revolutionary in its potential. Something ignites between you, and among you, and through you, that could never happen in the most brilliant of minds alone. That's where we find out how to create the future. That's where we finally see that we *can*.

When it happens, we will know with an assurance we've never known before that the world we dream is actually possible, and that our lives can take on the quality and force of that dream.

XIII

AFRAID OF THE JOURNEY

Walt Whitman
excerpted from "Song of the Open Road"

Afoot and light-hearted I take to the open road,
Healthy, free, the world before me,
The long brown path before me leading wherever I
*   choose.*

Henceforth I ask not good-fortune, I myself am good-
*   fortune,*
Henceforth I whimper no more, postpone no more, need
*   nothing,*
Done with indoor complaints, libraries, querulous criti-
*   cisms,*
Strong and content I travel the open road.

The earth, that is sufficient,
I do not want the constellations any nearer,
I know they are very well where they are,
I know they suffice for those who belong to them. . . .

You road I enter upon and look around,
I believe you are not all that is here,
I believe that much unseen is also here. . . .

You air that serves me with breath to speak!
You objects that call from diffusion my meanings and

give them shape!
You light that wraps me and all things in delicate
equable showers!
You paths worn in the irregular hollows by the roadsides!
I believe you are latent with unseen existences, you are so
dear to me. . . .

O highway I travel, do you say to me, Do not leave me?
Do you say Venture not—if you leave me you are lost?
Do you say, I am already prepared, I am well-beaten
and undenied, adhere to me?

O public road, I say back I am not afraid to leave you,
yet I love you,
You express me better than I can express myself,
You shall be more to me than my poem.

I think heroic deeds were all conceiv'd in the open air,
and all free poems also,
I think I could stop here myself and do miracles . . .

From this hour I ordain myself loos'd of limits and
imaginary lines,
Going where I list, my own master total and absolute,
Listening to others, considering well what they say,
Pausing, searching, receiving, contemplating,
Gently, but with undeniable will, divesting myself of the
holds that would hold me.

I inhale great draughts of space,
The east and the west are mine, and the north and the
south are mine.

I am larger, better than I thought,
I did not know I held so much goodness. . . .

Allons! to that which is endless, as it was beginningless,
To undergo much, tramps of days, rests of nights,
To merge all in the travel they tend to, and the days and
nights they tend to,
Again to merge them in the start of superior journeys,
To see nothing anywhere but what you may reach it and
pass it,
To conceive no time, however distant, but what you may
reach it and pass it,
To look up or down no road but it stretches and waits for
you, however long but it stretches and waits for
you . . . .
To know the universe itself as a road—as many roads—
as roads for traveling souls.

HOWEVER EAGERLY YOU MAY anticipate travelling, there's a particular kind of anxiety to a journey. I have a particular love for the UK. I like it fine when I get there, Scottish mountains and seaports, Kew Gardens, all my favorite British haunts. But first I have to get there.

That means airports and getting to them, and airport security and microscopic seats. And the anxiety. Which puts me of a mind to wonder why I'd ever leave home.

There's hardly a more fundamental image in the dreams of people, or in our mythology and scriptures, than this image of a journey. The story of a pilgrim people is the human story.

And the journey itself is frequently quite challenging. There are lots of images in humanity's body of mythology and literature to illustrate the point. There's Brendan of J.R.R. Tolkien's poem "The Death of St. Brendan," the Irish monk who sets out on the western seas and finds utopian lands, who scans gray waves for something out there, who journeys unknown roads and finds a great mountain rising out of the sea and wreathed in fire, yet rows on, not yet satisfied; like Moses climbing that mountain and seeing the rocky path before him vanishing in flame which he himself will enter. Or there's the twelfth-century Sufi story *The Conference of the Birds* about the soul's journey from ego to nondual union with the Divine, told in the form of an invitation to all the birds of the world to join an expedition home to the King's realm of love and fulfillment. All are invited and welcomed; nearly all are afraid, skeptical, preoccupied, attached to lesser values, self-absorbed. They go, but find the journey is long. Yet those who persist meet with a thousand suns and stars and moons, their radiance waxing brighter as they advance, and at the end is revelation and renewal. There is more than bother to this journey.

THIS BOOK IS ABOUT A RELIGIOUS VISION—an evolutionary, integral spirituality—that perceives this roaring Universe of Life as unfolding. You have not heard from *me* about a standing-still universe that doesn't change, or a changeless forever understanding of Truth, or changeless gods or a once-and-for-all Revelation. Our lives are a journey, and Life is a journey.

But we ache, we get tired, on this long human journey. And we are afraid. We know how much can go wrong. And so we dream, sometimes quite unrealistically, of where we started, a glorious golden magical past.

In 1841, Unitarianism in America represented a pretty young religious revolution. Yet already, as we saw in the Introduction, the luminous progenitor of Unitarianism here, William Ellery Channing, wrote to the British Unitarian spiritual giant James Martineau: that "old Unitarianism" would have to evolve. Despite its singular history marked by a courageous progress against "mental slavery" it had ossified, "gradually grown stationary," become a new orthodoxy. And he mused (here it is again),

> Perhaps this is not to be wondered at or deplored, for all reforming bodies seemed doomed to stop, in order to keep the ground, much or little, which they have gained. They become conservative, and out of them must spring new reformers, to be persecuted gener-

ally by the old.[1]

Which brings to mind those journeyers in the ancient Exodus story. They had set out on a journey and now they are wondering what they ever did *that* for.

They're following Moses and kvetching at him, yeh, but really that's not it. It's something inside them, some seed of destiny that makes them journey. So even though they complain, they walk on. There's nothing else you can do.

They were slaves, but they knew they were more than that. Something inside them told them they were more.

It's the same something that spoke in the Indian seer Sri Aurobindo, who died in 1950. He said that the appearance of humans in a material and animal world was

> the first glint of some coming divine Light, the first far-off promise of a godhead to be born out of Matter[2]

and he compared this human unfolding—from the most primitive state to the most sublime—to the difference between a "chained slave" and the "emerging . . . disk of a secret sun."

> Man is himself a little more than an ambitious nothing. He is a littleness that reaches to a wideness and a grandeur that are beyond him . . . This cannot be the end of the mysterious upward surge of Nature. There is something beyond, something that [human] kind shall be; it is seen now only in broken glimpses through rifts in the great wall of limitations. . . .[3]

What he is talking about is nothing more or less than the continued evolution of human consciousness. There has probably never been a more precarious moment in human history, a time of more peril—or more promise. At the moment, one percent of Americans control 40 percent of the wealth and take 23 percent of the income (it was 8 per-

---

1 *Memoir of William Ellery Channing, With Extracts from His Correspondence and Manuscripts, in Three Volumes.* London: John Chapman, 1843, vol. II, p. 409. (First published in Boston in 1842, year of his death; republished in 1874 by the American Unitarian Association.)

2 From *Man in Evolution*, excerpted in Robert McDermott, ed., *The Essential Aurobindo.* Great Barrington, Mass.: Lindisfarne Books, 1987, 2001, p. 64.

3 *Man in Evolution*, in *The Essential Aurobindo*, p. 65.

cent in 1980), and four hundred people clutch more of the wealth than 150 million fellow Americans. That's bad. This is far worse: the very physical balance of the air above us and the seas around us and the earth beneath us has been thrown into irrecoverable havoc, and an entire political part has taken its stand against science, and a national leader chosen for his compelling vision can see his way only to capitulation to the clamorous obdurate madness. And the question is, will we dare to continue this journey?— because we are now responsible for the continuing work of evolution.

BUT WHAT IF WE *DON'T* continue the journey? Suppose we opt out from this journey into territory where no one has yet been?

What if, instead, everything unravels?

Some, I know, actually hang their hope on that very calamity.

Let this corrupt civilization collapse. Maybe then we'll be forced back into a simpler, humbler, purer quality of life. If the big banks collapse, we can barter for pure organic homegrown food. There will be no Pentagon to think up new wars. And environmental collapse will teach the remaining society to live in harmony with nature.

I don't think so. I think what happens in the event of collapse is reversion, and barbarism, and armed camps, and desperate refugees, and disease, and hunger, and misery. I think we lose the magnificent achievements of human society and culture. And I don't think the loss of the achievements of human science and learning will seem like such a swell outcome.

No, we have to walk on. Except that now there isn't time for a walk. We have to move as fast as we can into a more highly-evolved way of being in the world.

Understand: evolution now cannot anymore mean simply *more*, *bigger, faster*. It can't mean that the future we dream is to be achieved by conquering somebody. That's *old* territory, the habits of a past that will not work anymore. It's not about mere *growth*, or even growth at all.

What happens when civilizations and cultures collapse? We might consult Jared Diamond, whose important 2005 book *Collapse: How Societies Choose to Fail or Succeed*, completes his documentation of the drama of catastrophic self-destruction as societies fail (or refuse) to discern what is happening and the consequences of the choices they make, like this:

> Like Easter Island chiefs erecting ever larger statues, eventually crowned by pukao, and like Anasazi elite treating themselves to necklaces of 2,000 turquoise beads, Maya kings sought to outdo each other with more and more impressive temples, covered with thicker and thicker plaster—reminiscent in turn of the extravagant conspicuous consumption by modern American CEOs. The passivity of Easter chiefs and Maya kings in the face of the real big threats to their societies completes our list of disquieting parallels.[4]

The consequences are suggested by the title of Bill McKibben's 2010 *Eaarth:*[5] Looks a lot like the planet we'd got used to, but it's a different planet; and it will not behave in the predictable, stable way we came to expect the friendlier Earth reliably to do. We are confronted by a new reality.

IT IS A JOURNEY, BUT NOT DOWN SOME well-trodden roads. We haven't been here before. Ken Wilber compares the enterprise to a train that has to lay the tracks as it rolls forward. Others can follow; we'll have to chart the way, sometimes with our heart in our throat. So watch out for the romantic primitivism of which we're perfectly capable.

Those Transcendentalist pioneers had a good deal in common with the European Romantics, and enjoyed significant contact with them; but their respective visions parted company in a dramatically consequential way. Consider Jean-Jacques Rousseau: "Everything degenerates in the hands of men," he lamented. In England, Wordsworth watched the French Revolution hopefully, then with horror when it degenerated into blood and terror. From then, he seemed overtaken by a profound

---

4 Jared Diamond, *Collapse: How Societies Choose to Fail or Succeed.* New York: Viking/Penguin Group, 2005, p. 177.

5 Bill McKibben, *Eaarth: Making a Life on a Tough New Planet.* New York: Times Books/Henry Holt, 2010.

despair about human possibility. But his American Transcendentalist friend Emerson looked at the possible future differently, through a nearly ecstatic optimism that was utopian and evolutionary. Why? A fundamental primitivism pervades Romanticism; the Transcendental vision (and more importantly here, the vision I'm proposing) has left primitivism and its cultural pessimism behind. It's evolutionary and even, yes, utopian.

The jeremiads are full of truth, and I've issued my share of them. There's plenty wrong; the call to turn from the wrong (*t'shuv;* repent) hasn't lost its applicability. But anything that deserves to be dignified by the descriptor *prophetic* has to arise from something more than lamentation and wrath. It has to come from an elevated vision of the possible. The judgment comes in the space defining the contradiction between the vision of the possible and things-as-they-are now. The turning must also be a turning *to* that highest possibility.

An example. This world of life faces a monumental ecological crisis. We will have to prevent the avoidable and adapt to the unavoidable, but how? Temperatures are rising, rainforests are shrinking and burning, vast swaths of soil are depleted and ruined, and there are soon to be ten billion people on this planet having to eat, requiring water, having to find ways to live less destructively with the ecology. We could: Develop new, safe nuclear technology that doesn't generate deadly masses of spent fuel. Combine organic, soil-nurturing agriculture with smart genetic engineering, developing plants that don't need chemical fertilizers and pesticides, that can survive the coming brutalities of climate and flooding and drought, waste less water, and reduce greenhouse gas output. For instance.

Primitivism says No, that's interfering with Nature, playing God. An evolutionary spiritual vision disagrees. It recognizes that *we are Nature*, in some important ways its highest achievement and smartest player. Our powers are godlike. It joins Stewart Brand in his declaration "We are as gods and HAVE to get good at it." No use talking about Somebody-Up-There who has the whole darn world and its future in His hands. It isn't like that.

Still, I say this in the context of a call for a spiritual revolution. Our surface-level egos, with the wants and fears and pretenses and defenses, don't do well in that god-role (he says, in a mild understatement). This demands a far bigger perspective, a kosmic quality of consciousness, an identification with a far bigger Self, an access to what J. Krishnamurti liked to call the Immensity Beyond Silence. Or the Ground of Being. Not out-there anymore. It is who and what we are—if we can back off far enough to grasp the Kosmic scope of all this, because face to face with that, the ego must bow to the god, and serve higher purposes. We are drawn into this realm of creative action in ways that will surprise us, by purposes beyond our imagining.

THOSE EXODUS TRIBES, TOO, seemed to forget the nature of their journey. Of course they never really knew *where* they were going, because they hadn't seen it yet. But they forgot the call, they forgot the promise, they forgot the necessity. They remembered only where they had been.

Why do we forget and lose our way?

Because, like the Exodus tribes, we recognize ourselves simply and solely as our past. And the answer to the question of our identity, or "Who am I?", becomes most often for us nothing more than an abstraction from memory, since what I know of myself is mostly always what I *was.*

But an identity based only on memory is only tracks and echoes from which the great energies of life have vanished.

And we forget—forget what calls us forward, forget this place to which we're going, which we've never seen but only dreamed, the world we must make—because we're afraid of the journey.

You may have noticed that we *make up our memories* as we go. So we remember where we came from somewhat differently than the way it really was.

In the place they came from, they had all the bread and water they could eat! They were provided with activities to do. They could make bricks. It was orderly. You could depend on it.

SO WE GLORIFY THE PAST. It shows up in the romantic way people look at their children.

There is an old Romantic notion about children—that they start life in some blissful state of union with the Divine Ground of Being and then eventually the child's *self* differentiates itself and this wonderful spiritual union is lost. As if we had fallen from some better state. And then later, perhaps, in adulthood, the self can "get spirituality" by making a spiritual U-turn in development, back to that original magical state of union with the Universe.[6]

But that's not what it is to be an infant or a child—some blissful state of divine union! Don't you remember? (No, you don't.)

The infant self is relatively peaceful, not because it's living in heaven, but because it isn't yet aware that there's also some hell out there.

An infant is really already immersed in samsara, as the Buddhists call it—it just doesn't know it yet. To become enlightened is far different from returning to an infant state.

Gradually that infant self will be introduced to the first Noble Truth of the Buddha, that there is suffering in this life, and desire that cannot be quenched. Maybe he or she will spend their entire life in this desperate quest for anything that will numb the raw and ragged feelings, blur the despair. And to the extent we lost track of some Essence about ourselves during those young years and replaced it with a false persona to help us get by, we are false to ourselves, we haven't begun the journey home.[7]

BUT SOMETHING ELSE can happen. Maybe you pursue the spiritual quest, the real object of this journey. Your life-journey leads you beyond the isolation of a separate-self.

That's the day you see the mountain wreathed in fire. It simply shows up one day along the journey and

---

6   See Ken Wilbur, *The Eye of Spirit*. Boston: Shambhala, 1997, pp. 53ff.

7   A point made with particular lucidity by A.H. Almaas in his *Brilliancy: The Essence of Intelligence*. Boston: Shambhala, 2006; and his *Diamond Heart, Book One: Elements of the Real in Man*. Shambhala, 1987, esp. "The Theory of Holes," 15-30.

now flares forth in consciousness in a brilliant burst of illumination and a shock of the unspeakably ordinary: it realizes its Supreme Identity with Spirit itself, announced, perhaps, in nothing more than the cool breeze of a bright spring day, this outrageously obvious affair.[8]

There is a blaze of enlightened comprehension: Everything that is—is always, already one with the Ground of all Being, which is every inch of your journey! You cannot sever or lose your oneness with the Life of all this Universe. It takes consciousness, a finer, higher consciousness, to sense it and know it.

IN THE DEVELOPMENT OF A NEW human life even still in the womb, it is as though the entire sweep of human evolution is represented in every child's growth.

A few billion years of evolution is played out in fast-forward in the development of every one of us. There is more to come. There is more truth, and a higher consciousness, to come.

SO THEN. WHY DO WE LOOK to the past as better, more brilliant and wise and pure?

Here is one reason. We have a problem believing that this human journey is heading anywhere good. We aren't so sure about the ascent toward Spirit that the great spiritual traditions proclaim. At first glance we cannot put it together: how can we account for Auschwitz and pointless wars and greed and ecocide and George W. Bush and Glenn Beck?

But the ugliest human impulses are not new; they're not modern inventions. They're a holdover from a more primitive time. It's just that now they're powered by new human capacities and powers. You cannot wipe out a continent and destroy whole cities with bows and arrows. But the *ugly impulses* are not new. Let us not glorify a barbaric past whose "glories" rested on the enslaved and tortured backs of millions of people. This world of life has more unfolding to do and so do we. We are not here to perpetuate what Ken Wilber calls the "preposterous groveling

---

8 Wilber, *The Eye of Spirit*, 54.

at any doctrine whose only authority comes from the fact that it was uttered by a really really ancient sage, centuries or preferably millennia ago." [9]

PLEASE DON'T SING "GIVE ME that old time religion" to me. It simply ISN'T good enough for us, or for our world.

Yes, there *is* an ancient perennial wisdom that is timeless, space-less, formless Truth, not bound to any time or place. But it, too, must unfold. It, too, is a journey. And it isn't the proprietary possession of any ecclesiastical institution or bishop or mullah or televangelist.

And what we are—must be more than a has-been identity consisting only of our past. We must believe in our own becoming; in each others' becoming. We must trust the evolutionary impulse at the heart of us. Here's the trouble with looking back. Time doesn't flow forward from a creator who *made* the world; it flows forward—it must flow forward TOWARD a power that *makes* the world. And that power is the evolution-ary impulse at the heart of us; it has no other hands than ours.

We are a part of that power, and its expressions.

I don't need that old-time religion, the fundamentalist "domin-ion-theology" that for far too long has wielded so much influence in Washington—

bound to the presumptive authority of an outmoded religious tradition that cannot be questioned —

freeze-dried religion:

just add water and stir

and it's all there, just the way it used to be.

But it can never be.

We are greater than our past *but that scares us.*

Yet something authentic and immediate and fresh is ready to unfold in us just as soon as we see through the layers of false persona and beliefs and patterns we think we need to navigate our way through this world.

_____

9 Wilbur, *The Eye of Spirit*, 66.

AND HERE WE ARE—OUR lives the result of the material given, what we have been and what we have done, mixed with the passions and dreams and force of character that drive us—and the journey calls us on, and evokes all that in us, and it draws from the hidden dreams and undiscovered powers within us—to become the people this new world requires. In this journey—this dust, these egoic selves that have navigated difficult passages and survived—have also developed vast powers and capacities. And we, this amalgam of god and dust—we will have to ensure that it is the *dust* that bows down to the *god*—that deepest, highest essence of ourselves that is the very evolutionary impulse at the heart of everything. All this unique package of qualities and capacities that we are must now be driven not by the ego's limitations: its fears and desires, its defenses and pretenses, its neuroses and narcissism. With our human capacity of choice, we must, again and again, decide for the god. Then, as Chapter Eight concluded, the god will fill the dust with glory. These lives of ours, in the service of a Kosmic purpose, made incandescent—even as we learn to live with the uncertainty of a journey.

THERE IS PLENTY THAT can go wrong.

In that mythic story in the Book of Exodus, the journeyers found out that you cannot get to the promised land without passing through some wilderness. There are wilderness periods in human history and there are wilderness patches in our lives. There are times of struggle between what was and can be no more, and what is to be but is not yet, and there you are, and it hurts.

You cannot get from the small stifling past to the wide radiant future without going through the wilderness, that place of nothingness and void and darkness where the accustomed things from the past where you have come from—are forgotten because they are no more, but the new life, the bold future, doesn't yet appear. All giving-birth takes place in such places.

It takes imagination—visionary moral imagination—to see around the corner, to envision a future. All those mythic journeyers could think of was where they had been. They got stuck in that wilderness in between. It doesn't take forty years to get across that wilderness, but that is how long they wandered there. They wandered until all those who remembered the past and couldn't let go of it—died and were gone, before they could move on.

FINALLY THEY TRUSTED THE JOURNEY itself and let it lead them home. They came to trust the energies and powers at work in their experience. Wherever they went was new. Nothing could ever be quite the same again. Not that they didn't *try* to make it the same! They were tired and afraid. The old and familiar was easy to remember.

And eventually we can come to trust what it is that moves us inwardly and calls us onward.

I have often said that, in its essence, true religion, the spiritual vision we need now, lies *not in turning again and again to ancient dreams* dreamed by those who inhabited a time and place far remote from us. The spiritual vision we need, —lies not in the return to ancient dreams, *but in the dreaming.*

WE ARE CARRIED FORWARD BY an inward necessity. There is, at the heart of things, an evolutionary impulse. We are meant to feel it.

For long years I was convinced, on the authority of St. Paul, that my particular gay humanity was an abomination in the eyes of God, the most loathsome perversion in God's universe. So the Bible and church seemed to say. It's probably a very good thing that many Christians now seek to reinterpret the ancient texts. But don't kid yourself: if St. Paul were to rematerialize this afternoon and find himself in the company of a modern-day group of those he'd condemned in *Romans* Chapter 1, he wouldn't approve of them—*unless, of course, during the intervening two thousand years, he'd learned something!* Which, had he taken his vitamins and lasted that long, alert and aware, I venture to say he would have done.

We have a journey to make, out of whatever captivities we know, beyond our own limitations, out of the expectations of a society that cannot see past its long-repeated habits, blind spots, defenses, pretenses, and limitations. We have a journey to make, too, beyond religious institutions that took fright to the journey long ago and got lost in the wilderness and wandered back to the old kingdom and dispensation because they're afraid of the journey and desperately clutch the past.

Let the witness of our lives ring as an invitation to many others to join this journey. Minds and hearts can change. I know: mine did.

We stand at a crossroads of human history. No, not even that: the road from here has yet to be laid and it's for us to lay it.

Ken Wilber writes that

> we are part and parcel of a single and all-encompassing evolutionary current that is itself Spirit-in-action, . . . and thus is always going beyond what went before—. . . dying and being reborn with each new quantum lurch, and often stumbling and bruising its metaphysical knees, yet always getting right back up and jumping yet again.[10]

We will trip and fall and fall back into habitual patterns, yeh. That is what happens when you're making new, previously untrod, pathways. And you won't be shocked and surprised that it happens that way. You have seen, you have clearly sensed, what it is that you are doing, the context of newness and experiment, of daring. So, quite unsurprised that you've tripped, you get up and journey on. You pay attention to the entire field, which includes yourself. You see it all clearly, including your own participation. You see and perceive, and learn.

But really what I'm talking about is not an individual endeavor. It's a shared enterprise. The journey gives us great gifts, and among these is ourselves, and each other.

There is an art-form to this. It involves seeing together, sensing together, thinking together, dreaming and creating together, as described particularly well by MIT's Otto Scharmer, in *Theory U: Leading from the Future as It Emerges*.[11] Communities of Spirit joined in the work of creative the future consciously, out of the deepest and highest essence of what we are, beyond ego, will want to be familiar with Scharmer's

---

10 Wilbur, *The Eye of Spirit*, 79.
11 San Francisco: Berrett-Koehler, 2009.

work. The task before us is more fundamental and more radical than the tools and tricks and technologies we typically grab onto.

Something is coming into being. But what will it be? Will it rise and live with all the energy of that evolutionary impulse whose fourteen billion years of work surrounds us, *is* us, *is* these minds and souls and hearts that we are? Will it in some way be the fulfillment and realization of what we are—our highest future possibility? Or will it merely manifest the limitations, the exhausted resources, of a dying era, of time past? (There are, after all, those whose vision of future possibility is bound within a fantasy of past glory, whether seen as the gun-toting wild west, as conquering bronze-age Israelites, or as concocted fundamentalist American founders. There is no imagination there; only fear, resentment, and a sense of loss.)

Creators of the possible future will have to lead, as Scharmer has it, *from* the future as it emerges. They will have to ignite the public imagination, blow it wide open. They will have to stand, humbly, with all their warts, as manifestations, nonetheless, of the upward surge of an evolving universe. However intense the struggle, the human presence is, so far as we know, the principle expression of the evolutionary impulse itself. Whoever and wherever you are—that presence is becoming conscious of its inescapable purpose as a roaring engine of creativity.

INDEX

For more information about Jay Deacon's work,
for audios and writings, and for
Jay's speaking engagements,
you're invited to visit
jaydeacon.net/

CPSIA information can be obtained at www.ICGtesting.com
Printed in the USA
BVOW11s0403240714

360300BV00006B/14/P